Japanese Moratorium on the Death Penalty

Mika Obara-Minnitt

Japanese Moratorium on the Death Penalty

palgrave
macmillan

Mika Obara-Minnitt
International Christian University
The Institute of Asian Cultural Studies
Tokyo, Japan

ISBN 978-1-137-56530-3 ISBN 978-1-137-55822-0 (eBook)
DOI 10.1057/978-1-137-55822-0

Library of Congress Control Number: 2016951226

Printed on acid-free paper

This Palgrave Macmillan imprint is published by Springer Nature
The registered company is Nature America Inc.
The registered company address is: 1 New York Plaza, New York, NY 10004, U.S.A.

Preface

On 4 October 2015, it was reported that Okunishi Masaru had passed away in a medical prison. Okunishi, aged 89, was then the longest-serving inmate in a Japanese prison, having been detained for 43 years since his death penalty was announced in 1972. He had been on death row on a charge of wine poisoning in Mie prefecture on 28 March 1961. He consistently stated that he was forced to make his confession, and it was during his ninth retrial petition that he died.

There are still unsolved cases in the process of pleading for retrials, some going back decades. By investigating the institutional and cultural dynamic behind such cases, this book seeks to illuminate the elite-driven nature of the death penalty policy in Japan, where miscarriages of justice can occur. I hope that this volume will help readers better understand why and how Japan retains capital punishment against the international trend, and inspire some of them to conduct further research on this issue or to join the abolitionist movement.

Mika Obara-Minnitt
Bletchley, England
April 2016

Acknowledgements

This book is the result of research that started in 2008 as a post-doctoral project at Loughborough University. My gratitude goes first and foremost to my supervisors, Dr Taku Tamaki and Dr Robert Dover. My PhD thesis could not have been completed without their critical insights and encouragement. I will be eternally grateful to them for inspiring me to pursue further academic research. I am also thankful to David T. Johnson who inspired me to discover my life's work, to my editors at Palgrave Macmillan USA for their interest and support, and to anonymous reviewers who helped me improve the earlier draft of the manuscript.

I am also indebted to all the 25 anonymous interviewees in Japan who gave me a tremendous amount of valuable first-hand information, despite the sensitive issue of capital punishment. NGO workers, attorneys, academics and others expressed their own views freely, and emotionally at times. Their passion appeared to result from very personal experiences, such as their religious views or the media coverage of capital punishment, including miscarriage of justice cases or serious murder cases. Most of their remarks were independent of the 'public opinion' that can be observed in media reports. Discovering this was very beneficial since it is evidence for my hypothesis that it is the Japanese government that supports capital punishment, and that 'public opinion' can vary greatly, depending on how people are asked questions on the issue and how much they understand of the system.

In particular, despite the nature of my research into events, some of which took place approximately 20 years ago, witnesses to or participants in those events were very co-operative during interviews: they included a former death row inmate, a former Minister of Justice and senior members of human rights NGOs. With regard to the former death row inmate, Menda Sakae,[1] his first-hand information on life in detention, including his dialogues with prison guards, helped illuminate the elite-driven nature of the capital punishment system. Postal correspondence with Sato Megumu, who was one of the Ministers of Justice during the *de facto* moratorium period between 1989 and 1993, provided an excellent opportunity to contrast his official statement on capital punishment, which can be found in parliamentary proceedings, with what he can currently say freely in his own words. Those who were not necessarily witnesses to or participants in the *de facto* moratorium, but have been engaged in current anti-death-penalty activities, or are keenly involved in the issue of capital punishment in general, were also interviewed. They include a representative of a victims' group; senior writers at newspaper agencies; a senior staff member at the Delegation of the European Union to Japan; and academics in law, sociology and EU–Japan studies. I believe that my interviews in Japan helped me test the considerable amount of secondary source analysis I have completed and added tremendous value to my research.

I owe a particularly strong debt to the Minnitt family. My wonderful husband, Sam Minnitt, supported me throughout this journey from the completion of my PhD project to the book manuscript. Special thanks also go to Diz Minnitt, who read the whole manuscript multiple times, and Helen Minnitt, who provided me with so much support and encouragement.

Last, but not least, I would like to thank my beautiful mother, Reiko Obara, for her everlasting love and support. This book is dedicated to her.

Note

1. Although it was difficult to approach Menda for interviews initially, the contact was achieved through the help of senior NGO staff: Shimaya Naoko, a core member of Forum 90; Tagusari Maiko, the Secretary General at the Center for Prisoners' Rights; and Yamazaki Hiroyuki, a representative of *Tanpopo no Kai*, a local anti-death-penalty NGO in Fukuoka Prefecture. In particular, Shimaya has currently been acting on behalf of Menda, and postal and email correspondence with Menda was achieved through her help.

Contents

List of Figures

List of Tables

CHAPTER 1

Introduction

The number of states that retain capital punishment is declining, with more than two-thirds having abolished it in law or practice.[1] International society has created a series of benchmarks for modern democracies regarding the abolition of capital punishment. These are represented by relevant covenants of the United Nations,[2] and the *acquis communautaire* that states must conform to before they can be admitted into the European Union (EU). Given that states tend to adhere to international norms in order to be recognised as legitimate members of international society,[3] it may appear that it is in states' interests to comply with the anti-death-penalty norm. Nonetheless, two industrialised democracies retain capital punishment against the international trend: the USA and Japan.

In the case of Japan, the government has consistently justified the retention and use of the death penalty on the basis of national law. However, the country has recently experienced a number of *de facto* moratorium periods on executions, for approximately one year from July 2009 to July 2010, one year and eight months from July 2010 to March 2012, and three years and four months from 1989 to 1993 (see Appendix A). This book addresses how the Ministry of Justice in Japan has justified capital punishment policy during these *de facto* moratorium periods. Examining the years before and after these periods, it seeks to examine the rhetoric and practice of the Ministry of Justice in its justification of capital punishment policy. The primary goal of this volume is to provide a better understanding of the elite-driven nature of the capital punishment system in Japan. It is concerned with three research questions: (1) Who are the real

M. Obara-Minnitt, *Japanese Moratorium on the Death Penalty*,
DOI 10.1057/978-1-137-55822-0_1

actors who get involved in capital punishment policy? (2) To what extent are domestic and cultural factors reflected in this process?; and (3) How was this policy justified by the Ministry of Justice during the execution-free periods?

1.1 Governmental Justification of Capital Punishment

The Ministry of Justice often cites five intertwined domestic factors in its official statements that justify the capital punishment system: (1) maintenance of legal order; (2) deterrent effect; (3) Japanese culture; (4) public opinion; and (5) victim satisfaction.[4] However, in-depth investigation of each claim provides alternative views. The government claims that capital punishment should take place as laid down in legal provisions in order to keep Japan *hōchi kokka* (a law-abiding country); capital punishment and the execution method used were declared constitutional by the Supreme Court on 12 March 1948; and hanging is stipulated by Article 11 of the Penal Code. However, the constitutionality and legality of the system are still controversial today. Whilst Article 31 of the Constitution of Japan stipulates that 'No person shall be deprived of life or liberty, nor shall any other criminal penalty be imposed, except according to procedure established by law', Article 36 of the Constitution provides that '[t]he infliction of torture by any public officer and cruel punishments are absolutely forbidden'. Moreover, whilst the responsibility of Ministers of Justice regarding the authorisation of execution orders is stipulated by Article 475 of the Code of Criminal Procedure, the legality and propriety of this provision have been debated amongst legal scholars.

Although governmental opinion polls indicate wide public support for the retention of capital punishment, based on a belief in its deterrent effect, the methodological defects of the survey questions have been pointed out by various scholars.[5] The government tends to proclaim that the capital punishment system has been retained in order to respect the feelings of the victims' bereaved families and a social norm that treats death as a price worth paying for serious crimes.[6] Nonetheless, opposing opinions by the anti-death-penalty victim lobby have often not been reflected. Rather, it appears that it is (1) government officials' recurring use of language, referencing Japanese culture, and (2) the media's excessive focus on the pro-death-penalty victim lobby that have made the public believe that the capital punishment system is deeply embedded in Japanese culture and can deter crimes. By unpacking the real key actors involved in this policy, and by examining how they try to construct a dominant discourse on capital punishment that refers to domestic and cultural factors, this book will clarify the real motive of the Ministry of Justice in justifying retention of the capital punishment system even during execution-free periods.

1.2 Research Background

Although studies on capital punishment in Japan have been conducted by scholars from different disciplines and from varied perspectives,[7] very few works have primarily focused on these periods, for two main reasons.[8] Firstly, capital punishment policy is characterised by confidentiality and secrecy,[9] which has made it challenging for activist groups or researchers to conduct empirical studies through access to pro-death-penalty actors, such as bureaucrats in the Ministry of Justice, or death row inmates. According to Kaga Otohiko, a former technical official at the Tokyo Detention Centre, 'postwar democracy was valid in the 1950s': researchers could interview death row inmates in person and publish their works freely.[10] Indeed, the issue of capital punishment was actively discussed within the Ministry of Justice. For example, the *Keibatsu to Shakai Kairyō no Kai* (Criminal Punishment and Social Reform Association) was founded in 1955 by staff at the Ministry of Justice, such as Masaki Ryo and Yoshikawa Eiji; and prison guards and detention centre custody officers also debated capital punishment passionately.[11] They wrote to the newspaper stressing the importance of abolishing the system, and presented such ideas in the Diet as well.[12]

However, after a *tsūtatsu* (circular) imposing restrictions on death row inmates' communication was issued on 15 March 1963,[13] a secretive policy was employed regarding capital punishment policy and interviews with death row inmates also became impossible, with a few exceptions.[14] When Kaga published the book *Shikeishū no Kioku* (Memory of Death Row Inmates) in 1980, the Ministry of Justice accused him of disclosing some significant information that he would not have known if he did not work in the Ministry; and public prosecutors also denounced his action as against the Public Service Act.[15] Therefore, when the International Federation for Human Rights carried out its first investigation in 2001, delegates could only meet senior civil servants from the Ministry of Justice, and their requests for interviews with death row inmates were denied.[16] The Ministry of Justice was still not eager to engage with the issue when I approached them for an interview in 2011.

It is also important to note that the Japanese government does not conceive the *de facto* moratorium periods as political events to be examined academically, and the Ministry of Justice refuses any research-related investigation into these eras. In my interviews, two Ministry of Foreign Affairs (MOFA) officials, one of whom was previously in the Ministry of Justice, were reluctant to discuss these periods with a presumption that there existed '*de facto* moratorium periods'.[17] They stated that although there were execution-free periods, it was inappropriate to consider them as politically stable periods when bureaucrats refrained from authorising executions.[18]

It is also worth mentioning that MOFA appeared to have another reason for not being eager to discuss the issue with a third party. According to a MOFA minister, MOFA is not in a position to express any independent opinion on capital punishment, and it only reproduces the policy of the particular Ministry that is in charge—the Ministry of Justice in this case—as a dominant voice of the Japanese government.[19] This supports the argument of Glenn D. Hook et al. that although MOFA is responsible for the day-to-day running of Japanese diplomatic policy and functions as Japan's window upon the world, 'its ability to direct and manipulate Japanese foreign policy is constrained by its own internal organizational limitations'.[20]

Questioning the existence of the *de facto* moratorium periods can be crucial to understand capital punishment policy in Japan. The Japanese government justifies capital punishment consistently on domestic, cultural and legal grounds. Executions tend to take place annually. However, since executions are sometimes postponed for years, some scholars and anti-death-penalty lobbyists tend to describe these periods as *de facto* moratorium periods. This volume will therefore investigate: (1) what the nature of the moratorium period is; (2) who tends to or tends not to call the execution-free period a *de facto* moratorium period; and (3) what factors tend to make an execution-free period look like a moratorium period.

1.3 Research Methodology

This book adopts a level-of-analysis approach that focuses on two main levels: the government and civil society. This is to capture the rich diversity and fluidity of institutional and social relationships amongst the actors. The main actors who will be examined at each level are: (1) officials and ministers in the Ministry of Justice and the Public Prosecutor's Office, and Diet members; and (2) public opinion, and anti- and pro-death-penalty non-governmental organisations (NGOs)/advocates. What merits some attention is that the capital punishment system has been the province of a narrow elite in the Ministry of Justice and the Public Prosecutor's Office, and the role that actors at civil society level can play in the context of these tightly knit institutional dynamics is limited. However, re-investigation of public opinion and the way in which the Japanese government strategically cites domestic factors for the justification of capital punishment can help illuminate the elite-driven nature of this policy. Similarly, although anti-death-penalty NGOs do not possess official status to get involved in capital punishment policy-making, it is beneficial to contrast their approach to capital punishment from human rights perspectives with the government's approach that is based on the issue of law and order.

Focusing on these actors at two levels, most of the initial research was conducted through an analysis of official documents from the Japanese government, such as parliamentary proceedings, public opinion surveys conducted by the Prime Minister's Office and the Supreme Court, and periodical reports by both international and domestic human rights NGOs. In handling these documents, discourse analysis was conducted. This was to assess what 'language' the Japanese governmental officials used surrounding the *de facto* moratorium periods, in order to construct a dominant discourse on capital punishment as legitimate, to gain public support to back up this policy and to avoid complying with the international norm.

Besides such documental analysis, in-depth interviews were conducted from April to June 2011 in Japan with 25 people, including government ministers, NGO staff, pro- and anti-death-penalty advocates, and scholars.[21] The primary aim of this research was to investigate the social and political background of the period 1980–2015 and in particular during the *de facto* moratorium periods, through the case study of the years 1989–1993, 2009–2010 and 2010–2012. This was to gain a better understanding of how the Ministry of Justice justified the capital punishment system, citing domestic factors. My interviews sought to avoid simplistic 'for or against' questions on the issue. Whilst capital punishment tends to divide people into two extremes—retentionists and abolitionists—much agreement may be observed at a more fundamental level, and disagreement can be observed even within each lobby. By customising questions depending on interviewees, the interviews sought to capture various opinions about the capital punishment system. This helped highlight the variety of views about capital punishment that exist in civil society, even whilst the Japanese government proclaims wide public support as justification for its continuation.

1.4 Outline

This section summarises the content of the volume and the main arguments discussed in each chapter. Chapter 2 presents an analytical framework by which Japan's capital punishment policy may be understood. The previous research poses various hypotheses about Japan's retention of capital punishment, considering historical, external and internal factors. This chapter examines the bureaucratic decision-making mechanism in Japan and clarifies the elite-driven nature of the capital punishment policy. It also examines the divergence between the Japanese government and anti-death-penalty bodies in approaching the issue of capital punishment.

The first part of Chap. 3 critically examines the validity of governmental justification for capital punishment on cultural grounds. Through reconsidering what kind of cultural features have been claimed to be associated with the capital punishment system in Japan, it clarifies how policy elites' recurring use of language that makes reference to culture influences the public and scholars in their belief that capital punishment policy is domestically and culturally determined. The second part proposes a better approach for investigating the *de facto* moratorium periods. Whilst some scholars and activists treat the execution-free periods as a politically significant phenomenon, as if they were not in line with government policy, this book clarifies that executions are not suspended because of any political initiatives. It contends that appropriate investigation of these periods can provide a better understanding of the elite-driven capital punishment policy in Japan.

Chapters 4, 5, 6 and 7 empirically examine how the Ministry of Justice justified the capital punishment system from 1980 to 2012. Chapter 4 focuses on the period from 1980 to 1989, when the government was legitimising the system despite the emergence of criminal justice issues, including the disclosure of successive miscarriages of justice. Chapter 5 examines the *de facto* moratorium period from 1989 to 1993. It investigates how the Japanese government consistently justified the system even when executions were put on hold for more than three years. Chapter 6 focuses on the period from 1993 to 2009. It examines how the government tried to maintain the dominant discourse on crime and punishment for the justification of capital punishment after executions were resumed. Chapter 7 focuses on the period from 2009 to 2012, including the two *de facto* moratorium periods. It examines the governmental discourse on the death penalty by both anti- and pro-death-penalty Ministers of Justice and the extent to which the introduction of the *saiban-in seido* (quasi jury system) influenced the governmental justification of capital punishment. Finally, the Conclusions summarise the main findings of the book and set out implications for the international and domestic anti-death-penalty advocates regarding their campaigns in Japan.

With regard to the writing style, I present Japanese names in Japanese order, with the family name first; and Japanese terms are written in italicised *romaji* (English transliteration of Japanese) throughout.

Notes

1. Amnesty International (2014) 'Abolish the Death Penalty'. Available at: http://www.amnesty.org/en/death-penalty [Accessed 17 March 2016]
2. For example, Article 3 of the Universal Declaration of Human Rights stipulates that 'Everyone has the right to life, liberty and security of person'; and Article 5 stresses that 'No one shall be subjected to torture or to cruel, inhuman or degrading treatment or punishment'. Moreover, the Second Optional Protocol to the International Covenant on Civil and Political Rights clearly aims at the abolition of capital punishment.
3. Axelrod, R. (1986) 'An Evolutionary Approach to Norms', *The American Political Science Review*, 80(4), pp. 1095–1111, p. 1105. Available at: http://www-personal.umich.edu/~axe/Axelrod%20Norms%20APSR%201986%20%282%29.pdf.; Finnemore, M. & Sikkink, K. (1998) 'International Norm Dynamics and Political Change', *International Organization*, 52(04), pp. 887–917, p. 895.
4. Ministers of Justice who proclaim these factors include: Okuno, S. (1980) *The 93th Legal Affairs Committee of the House of Councillors*, 16 October 1980, p. 8; Sakata, M. (1982) *The 96th Legal Affairs Committee of the House of Councillors*, 23 March 1982, p. 20; Sumi, E. (1984) *The 101st Legal Affairs Committee of the House of Councillors*, 27 March 1984, p. 8; Gotoda, M. (1993) *The 126th Legal Affairs Committee of the House of Councillors*, 29 March 1993, p. 3, and Moriyama, M. quoted in *Japan Times* (2002) 'Diet Group against Death Penalty to Make its Move, 4 October 2002'. Available at: http://www.japantimes.co.jp/text/nn20021004b1.html [Accessed 17 March 2016]

5. Sato, M. (2008) 'Public Opinion and the Death Penalty in Japan', Centre for Capital Punishment Studies, 4, pp. 1–39; *op.cit.* and Sato, M. (2009) 'Deliberative Survey on the Japanese Death Penalty System', *Institute for Contemporary Asian Studies*, Temple University. Available at: http://www.tuj.ac.jp/icas/pdf/icjs_090616.pdf [Accessed 17 March 2016]
6. Moriyama *Ibid.*
7. See Johnson, D.T. (2002) *The Japanese Way of Justice: Prosecuting Crime in Japan*, Oxford University Press, USA; Johnson, D.T. (2006) 'Japan's Secretive Death Penalty Policy: Contours, Origins, Justifications, and Meanings', *Asia-Pacific Law & Policy Journal*, 7, pp. 62–124; Schmidt, P. (2002) *Capital Punishment in Japan*, Brill Academic Publishers; Sato, M. (2008) *Ibid*; Johnson, D.T. & Zimring, F.E. (2009) *The Next Frontier: National Development, Political Change, and the Death Penalty in Asia*, Oxford University Press, USA; and Fuse, Y. (2009) 'Publicity and Secrecy Concerning Execution: Contrast between the U.S. and Japan' in Annual Meeting of the American Society of Criminology, Marriott Downtown, Philadelphia, 4 November 2009.
8. The literature which touches upon the *de facto* moratorium periods includes: Schmidt (2002) *Ibid*; Johnson (2006) *Ibid*; and Ambler, L. (2008) 'The People Decide: The Effect of the Introduction of the Quasi-Jury System (Saiban-In Seido) on the Death Penalty in Japan, Northwestern Journal of International Human Rights, Article 1, Volume 6, Issue 1, pp. 1–23.
9. Johnson, D.T. (2005) 'The Death Penalty in Japan: Secrecy, Silence, and Salience' in A. Sarat & C. Boulanger (eds) *The Cultural Lives of Capital Punishment: Comparative Perspectives.* Stanford University Press, pp. 251–73; and Johnson (2006) *Ibid.*
10. Kaga, O. & Yasuda, Y. (2008) '*Taidan: Shikei wa Shaki wo Yaban ni suru* (Dialogue: Capital Punishment Makes the Society Uncivilised)', *Sekai*, p. 127.
11. Kaga, O. & Yasuda, Y. (2008) *op. cit.* p. 129.
12. *Ibid.*
13. See Chap. 2 for the details of detention conditions.
14. For example, a writer, Saito Michinori, has been corresponding with a death row inmate, Odajima Tetsuo, both in person and by post, periodically since July 2006.
15. Kaga, O. & Yasuda, Y. (2008) *op. cit.* p. 127.

16. The International Federation for Human Rights (2008) 'The Death Penalty in Japan: The Law of Silence – Going against the International Trend', October 2008, pp. 1–68, pp. 3–4. Available at: http://www.fidh.org/IMG/pdf/japon505a2008.pdf. [Accessed 17 March 2016]
17. Interview with two MOFA officials, Tokyo, 17 June 2011.
18. *Ibid.*
19. Interview with a MOFA minister, Tokyo, 9 May 2011.
20. Hook, G.D., Gilson, J., Hughes, C.W., & Dobson, H. (2001) *Japan's International Relations: Politics, Economics and Security*, London: Routledge, p. 45.
21. In order to encourage cooperation, I agreed in my initial contacts with interviewees that they would remain anonymous in my publication. For this reason, unless otherwise stated, interviewees' real names are not mentioned.

CHAPTER 2

The Two-Sided Triangle: Capital Punishment Policy Decision-Making—A Framework for Analysis

2.1 Introduction

The existing research poses various hypotheses on Japan's retention and justification of the capital punishment system. In particular, David T. Johnson demonstrates nine hypotheses from three perspectives: historical, external and internal.[1] The aim of this chapter is to fill the gap in this area of knowledge and to provide an appropriate analytical framework to understand Japan's capital punishment policy. In order to do this, it examines the Japanese decision-making mechanism and investigates the extent to which it accounts for the power dynamics surrounding capital punishment policy.

The first section of this chapter reviews the current academic approach to considering the Japanese government's retention of capital punishment. It uses the same nine sub-headings as Johnson's work. In order to assess the validity of each claim, the second section introduces the Japanese decision-making model called the Iron Triangle, which is composed of: (1) bureaucrats of the economic ministries and agencies, (2) politicians of the ruling party and (3) leaders of the business community.[2]

The third section of the chapter applies this decision-making mechanism to capital punishment policy and re-defines the power relationships between the actors. The first two actors can be: (1) bureaucrats in the Ministry of Justice and the Public Prosecutor's Office and (2) Ministers of Justice and politicians of the Liberal Democratic Party (LDP) (1955–2009; 2012 to date) and the Democratic Party of Japan (DPJ) (2009–2012). However, since important decisions tend to be made by

M. Obara-Minnitt, *Japanese Moratorium on the Death Penalty*,
DOI 10.1057/978-1-137-55822-0_2

the former actors, often irrespective of the latter, this section of the chapter explains why bureaucrats exert tremendous power over capital punishment policy. Furthermore, it is argued that the third actor, which replaces the business community, has not been systematically established in the literature. Although pressure groups which support the government's pro-death-penalty policy may be suggested, capital punishment is primarily a bureaucrat-led policy, and locating pressure groups in the triad as actors of equal influence or power to the other two is dubious. Unpacking the key actors in the institutional framework within which policy elites operate, this part of the chapter clarifies the applicability of the Iron Triangle model to capital punishment policy.

Having illuminated the elite-driven nature of capital punishment policy, the second section of this chapter examines the governmental approach to capital punishment. The ineffectiveness of the anti-death-penalty lobby in getting involved in capital punishment policy can be partly explained by its limited role in the bureaucrat-led decision-making process. However, it also appears to stem from a divergence between the Japanese government and anti-death-penalty advocates on their approach to the issue of capital punishment. Through investigating detention conditions and the execution procedure in detail, this section highlights the fact that the Japanese government has been treating capital punishment policy as an issue of law and order, not as an issue of human rights.

2.2 Existing Hypotheses on the Government's Retention of Capital Punishment

2.2.1 Historical Factors

Johnson poses the following three factors as the historical explanation of Japan's retention of capital punishment: (1) the US occupation; (2) the characteristics of Japanese political parties; and (3) Japan's geographical position and its stability as a democratic country.[3] Firstly, the US occupation was intended to disarm the military, eradicate imperialist thinking and firmly root democracy in Japan. The aims included 'the downsizing of the emperor from "god" to mere "symbol of the State and of the unity of the people", the renunciation of war, the creation of due process rights, and the establishment of the principle of equality of the sexes, of the Diet as the highest organ of state power, of the power of judicial review, of land redistribution, and so on'.[4] However, since capital punishment remained a part of Japanese criminal justice, Johnson introduces the hypothesis that the USA may have left the system intentionally in order to execute seven war criminals in the Tokyo War Crime Trial in 1948.[5] In other words, his assumption is that Japan would have abolished capital punishment in the post-war period if that had been included in US policy at that time.[6]

Secondly, Johnson mentions the characteristics of Japanese political parties and their resistance to political changes, including the abolition of capital punishment. The Japanese government was ruled by a pro-death-penalty LDP for approximately 54 years from its foundation in 1955 to when the Democratic Party of Japan defeated it in 2009; and the LDP regained power in 2012. In Johnson's hypothesis, the government's retention of capital punishment stems from the LDP's policy on the issue and its perpetual dominance.[7] Thirdly, Johnson points out Japan's geographical position and its stability as a democratic country. For example, since Japan is geographically distant from Europe, the EU's anti-death-penalty norm may not appeal to the Japanese government.[8] Another hypothesis he suggests is that since Japan is in a geographically important area and has already established its status as a democratic country, international society does not want to appear to be punishing Japan for failing to comply with international norms.[9]

2.2.2 External Factors

With regard to external factors, Johnson mentions Japan's relationship with two states and one region: the USA, South Korea and Asia. Given that the USA and Japan are the two remaining industrialised democracies that retain capital punishment against the international trend, it is often put forward by scholars that if all the 50 states in the USA abolish capital punishment, Japan will follow suit.[10] South Korea is also being mooted as a possible key country that could influence Japan's policy-making. The last execution in South Korea took place on 30 December 1997 and since then its government has been implementing a *de facto* moratorium. Therefore, Johnson's hypothesis is that Japan would mirror South Korea's policy if that country abolished capital punishment in law, as he believes that Japan wants to protect its self-image as a leader in Asia and does not want to allow South Korea to stand out in any policy area.[11] Johnson also suggests a link between Japan's retention of capital punishment and a lack of regional organisations in Asia, such as an East Asian Community. His claim is that no Asian organisations exist that can make the abandonment of capital punishment a criterion to which Japan must conform before being admitted as a member, as is the case with the EU.[12]

2.2.3 *Internal Factors*

Finally, Johnson raises three internal factors: (1) strong public support for capital punishment; (2) a unique Japanese view on sin and human rights; and (3) a 'punitive' way of thinking from the perspective of victims' bereaved families. Public opinion is one of the primary reasons for the Japanese government's retention of capital punishment. Governmental opinion poll results have revealed that the vast majority of Japanese citizens, 80.3 per cent in 2014 and 85.6 per cent in 2009, support the system (see Appendix B). It is often said amongst government officials that it is a unique Japanese mentality on life and death that has been contributing to Japan's retention of capital punishment.[13] According to this argument, the Japanese public believes that execution through capital punishment is the only way for some offenders to atone for their crimes and that it functions as social justice for the victims' bereaved families. Thus, Johnson suggests that domestic factors have been playing a significant role.

Whilst existing hypotheses cover a wide range of domestic and international factors, the actual decision-making tends to be conducted by selected bureaucrats in a closed institutional framework, irrespective of cultural features or external pressures. In order to evaluate each hypothesis, the following section clarifies who is involved in capital punishment policy-making.

2.3 Japanese Decision-Making: The Iron Triangle Model

It is important to clarify how the Constitution of Japan lays down where power resides in Japanese decision-making. According to Article 1, sovereignty resides with the people; and Article 65 stipulates that executive power is vested in the Cabinet. The Cabinet is composed of (1) the Prime Minister, who is elected by members of the Diet, and (2) other Ministers of the State (Article 66). Regarding the selection of Ministers of State, the Prime Minister appoints them, a majority of them being chosen from amongst the members of the Diet (Article 68) in order 'to insure a government accountable to the electorate'.[14] As Nathaniel B. Thayer states:

> After the prime minister has decided what sort of a cabinet he intends to choose, he will call for recommendations of lower house members from the faction leaders and of upper house members from party leaders in the House of Councillors. Factional balance and the selection of able men will be the two principles which guide the prime minister in the selection of his new cabinet. Particular attention will be paid to the economic posts. After the prime minister has selected his new officers, they will be attested to by the emperor, a proclamation of the new cabinet will be issued, and the cabinet will formally be set in motion.[15]

During this process, 'the staff rarely proposes candidates on its own initiatives, but restricts itself to commenting on the proposed cabinet lineup given it by the prime minister'.[16] In the meantime, cabinet changes stem from the following two factors. Firstly, Article 69 stipulates that 'If the House of Representatives passes a non-confidence resolution, or rejects a confidence resolution, the Cabinet shall resign en masse'. Secondly, 'The Prime Minister may remove the Ministers of State as he chooses' (Article 68) considering the fact 'that the present cabinet is not working well, that the present government policies are not going smoothly, or that the public is tired of the same old faces and the same old voices'.[17]

Thus, the constitutional provisions portray Japan as a parliamentary democracy (Articles 65, 66, 68), with the Prime Minister exerting a key role in forming a cabinet. However, research has shown that Japan is in reality a 'bureaucratic authoritarian' country.[18] In other words, it is a cluster of bureaucrats, or higher civil servants, who play significant roles in the government. In fact, cabinet reshuffles carried out approximately every year do not allow cabinet members to exercise executive power, and the Prime Minister has practically 'no explicit legal authority enabling him to insist on policy innovation outside his Office, force a Cabinet colleague to take a particular course of action or even divulge a particular piece of information'.[19]

A discrepancy between theory and practice can be observed in the power dynamics within the Japanese government. A model that has been widely used to account for these power dynamics in the decision-making process is the Iron Triangle, which consists of bureaucrats, party politicians and the business community, which is represented by the *Keidanren*, the Japan Business Federation.[20] Of the three, bureaucrats play a significant role in both policy-making and policy implementation in Japan. Approximately 80 per cent of all legislation passed is drafted by bureaucrats, and Diet members merely rubber-stamp the documents.[21]

As Karel van Wolfren argues, '[t]he law-making process is usually over by the time a bill is submitted to the Diet'.[22] This may appear at first sight a simple result of the bureaucrats' long tenure of office in contrast to party politicians. Whilst bureaucrats are usually employed for life, 'LDP cabinet ministers rotate their jobs on average about once a year, and are rarely in post long enough to stamp their ideas on a particular ministry, even if they were minded to do so'.[23] However, the bureaucrat-led decision-making system has also been strengthened by other intertwined factors: (1) the fluidity of bureaucrats within the triad; (2) their power relations with the business community; (3) the standardised educational background of bureaucrats; (4) the Japanese decision-making process, which prefers 'group consensus'; and (5) the continuous domination of the LDP. Through examining these aspects, this section will clarify why bureaucrats tend to play a pivotal role within the Iron Triangle.

Bureaucrats tend to occupy important posts in the business community and the ruling party through a system of *amakudari*, or 'descent from heaven'. *Amakudari* is a custom of outplacement by which senior high-profile bureaucrats from governmental agencies such as the Ministry of International Trade and Industry move to the private and public sectors such as the Bank of Japan, commercial banks, trade and industry associations, and the boardrooms of private enterprise.[24] Moreover, about 25 per cent of the LDP Diet members are ex-bureaucrats under a similar system,[25] and they try 'to represent the interests of their former ministry [...so that] their [...] personal connections with their former colleagues would [not] fade'.[26]

Whilst the business community provides the government with funding, bureaucrats tend to influence their activities through a practice of *gyōsei shidō*, or administrative guidance. According to Ellis S. Krauss:

> Administrative guidance is a general term that encompasses formal and informal methods of implementing policy, from the issuing of formal administrative ordinances that have the force of law, to informal communication that attempt to persuade social groups to go along voluntarily with a policy.[27]

Although this practice is not legally binding, the business community tends to abide by it. This is because:

> Governmental officials are responsible for approval of applications for almost every conceivable business activity. If they do not like an applicant, for whatever reason, they can hold off a decision on that person's applications.[28]

Therefore, although *gyōsei shidō* only requires 'voluntary co-operation' from the business community in theory, it is almost compulsory in practice.[29]

What characterises bureaucratic decision-making is that the bureaucrats tend to act on precedents (*senrei shugi*),[30] and make conservative decisions without inviting new ideas from other people with different backgrounds or experiences. What makes this possible is that they make up a standardised elite group. Bureaucrats tend to be recruited disproportionately from Japan's most prestigious universities through competitive examination,[31] the prime example being the Law Faculty of Tokyo University. As John C. Campbell contends, 'attracting the best students from the best universities makes the Japanese bureaucracy more effective in terms of sheer talent, and public respect encourages self-confident leadership'.[32] This not only helps them agree to follow precedents but also helps to smooth consensual decision-making when a new proposal is made. Since 'new graduates can readily plug into the established alumni network',[33] it is easy for them to build human connections, which is useful for this process.

Indeed, what also symbolises the Japanese decision-making process is that bureaucrats maximise the use of available measures in order to reach consensus in advance. What creates an 'illusion of consensus' in particular is the *ringi* system, with the use of *nemawashi*.[34] Under the *ringi* system, a proposal is passed around the ministry to gain approval from superior officials.[35] Stamps indicate approval, and those who disapprove do not put a stamp on the proposal; while those who want to give conditional approval put it either sideways or upside down.[36] However, what deserves attention is that this system: (1) does not expect open objection during; and (2) the top authority dealing with the issue usually approves the proposal, considering the long process that must have taken place. The practice of *nemawashi*, or 'binding the roots of a plant before pulling it out',[37] often takes place in order to help reach a 'group consensus'. As van Wolferen argues:

> *Nemawashi* involves talking with the concerned parties so as to prepare them to 'accept' a plan, as one prepares the ground for planting something. Such spadework does not invite 'democratic' objection (with the option of rejection), as a similar process would in the West.[38]

Moreover, '[w]hether or not a *ringi* proposal is approved by the [...head] is primarily determined by who has approved it by the time it gets to him'.[39] Considering the long process, which could take a month until it reaches the top authority, he usually approves the proposal.[40] In addition, what characterises the bureaucrat-led decision-making system is that the *ringi* system is not always used for the aforementioned purpose with regard to less important matters but 'serves to circulate information about decisions already made'.[41]

Finally, what has made the triad highly interdependent is the perpetual domination of the LDP,[42] from 1955 to 2009 (with 1993 as an exception) and from 2012 to today. As Duncan McCargo argues, '[t]o a large extent, studying the politics of Japan means studying the politics of one leading party, the Liberal Democratic Party (LDP)';[43] and post-war economic reconstruction could never have been achieved without this mechanism.[44]

This section has introduced the Iron Triangle model—discussing bureaucrats' significant role in this triad, in which they make the most of their personal networks within the ruling party and the business community—together with the Japanese decision-making tradition and the stability of the ruling party. Having examined the elite-driven decision-making mechanism, the subsequent section evaluates the extent to which the Iron Triangle model fits into the decision-making mechanism regarding capital punishment policy.

2.4 Application of the Iron Triangle Model to Capital Punishment Policy

In order to investigate the applicability of the Iron Triangle model to capital punishment policy, it is important to examine which people in which governmental agencies (1) underpin the legal legitimacy of the system, (2) get involved in the actual running of the system, and (3) represent and justify the policy on legal, domestic and cultural grounds both internally and externally.

Firstly, the role that the Supreme Court plays in the government's justification of capital punishment will be clarified. Although the constitutionality and legality of the capital punishment system and the execution method used have been controversial in Japan, the Supreme Court consistently declares that they do not conflict with any legal provisions. Examining the people who serve as judges at the Supreme Court, this section clarifies why they tend to make decisions in favour of the government. Secondly, it highlights the role that the Public Prosecutor's

Office plays in the system. Even though it is the Ministry of Justice that is responsible for capital punishment policy, in practice the public prosecutors get involved in the crucial part of the policy. This section explores how the Public Prosecutor's Office, which is a subordinate institution of the Ministry of Justice, runs the capital punishment system in reality.

Related to this, the third part will examine the limited power of Ministers of Justice in capital punishment policy. Given that non-authorisation by Ministers of Justice can delay executions, at first sight their personal convictions may appear to be a crucial factor. However, the short tenure of Ministers of Justice being one reason, this section clarifies that it is employed-for-life bureaucrats in the Ministry of Justice who are involved in the actual decision-making process. Finally, the section critically investigates whether or not pressure groups can fit into the triad regarding capital punishment policy. Although the pro-death-penalty lobby's claims may appear to have been reflected in governmental decision-making, this is not the case in practice. This section argues that capital punishment policy is primarily elite-driven, and important decisions are made irrespective of the voice of pro-death-penalty NGOs or the victim lobby.

2.4.1 The Supreme Court

It is the Supreme Court that consistently proclaims the constitutionality and legality of the capital punishment system, and makes the final judicial decisions regarding death sentences. Given that Article 76 of the Constitution of Japan stipulates that judicial power is vested in the Supreme Court,[45] and Article 77 also provides that 'Public prosecutors shall be subject to the rule-making power of the Supreme Court', the Supreme Court is theoretically independent from bureaucratic control. Having said that, there exist certain customs regarding the appointment of Supreme Court judges which can lead the Supreme Court to make decisions favouring the positions of the Public Prosecutor's Office on capital punishment. In fact the Supreme Court has overturned decisions on capital cases or the constitutionality of the capital punishment system made in lower-level courts.[46] Keeping the bureaucratic control by the Public Prosecutor's Office in mind, this section examines how the Supreme Court has been resisting domestic debate on the constitutional and legal issue of the capital punishment system; and why legal ambiguity is observed regarding the death sentences imposed by the Supreme Court.

2.4.1.1 Bureaucratic Control in the Appointment of Supreme Court Judges

According to Matsui Shigenori, 'The Supreme Court consists of the Chief Justice, who is to be designated by the Cabinet and appointed by the Emperor, and 14 Associate Justices to be appointed by the Cabinet (Article 79, Section 1)'.[47] Supreme Court judges thus appear to be appointed at the discretion of the Cabinet, but there exist several customs regarding this process. The 15 Supreme Court judges are usually composed of 'six judges, four private attorneys, and five others, including two prosecutors, two government bureaucrats and one academic', and it is customary for the Chief Justice of the Supreme Court to recommend a candidate for the category of judges to the Prime Minister.[48] What merits some attention in this recommendation process is that the average age of candidates tends to be 64 or 65, and they share the perspectives of former prosecutors on criminal justice issues:

> Since the lower court judges must retire at the age of 65, this means that the position of the Supreme Court Justice has become the final honorary position for judges after retirement. Most of the Justices who are appointed from among the ranks of judges have had experience as chief judges of a major High Court such as the Tokyo High Court or the Osaka High Court. This pattern is also evident with respect to other appointees. For instance, Justices who are appointed from attorneys are generally former presidents of major Bar associations. Justices who are former prosecutors are likely also to be high-ranking prosecutors in the Prosecutors' Office.[49]

As Matsui rightly points out, 'As a result, eight out of 15 judges are always appointed from among former judges or former prosecutors, thus ensuring they constitute the majority'.[50] This makes it easier and effective for Supreme Court judges to act on precedents (*senrei shugi*) or *nemawashi* to reach a group consensus and to overturn decisions on capital cases made in lower-level courts, leaving legal ambiguity. Keeping this bureaucratic decision-making system within the Supreme Court in mind, the next section examines the constitutionality and legality of the capital punishment system.

2.4.1.2 Constitutionality of the Capital Punishment System

As briefly discussed in the Introduction, capital punishment was declared constitutional by the Supreme Court on 12 March 1948, and so was the execution method, which is specified as hanging in Article 11 of the Penal Code.[51] However, domestic debate on the constitutionality and legality of this system is still open-ended. For example, whilst Article 31 of the Constitution of Japan stipulates that 'No person shall be deprived of life or liberty, nor shall any other criminal penalty be imposed, except according to procedure established by law', Article 36 of the Constitution provides that '[t]he infliction of torture by any public officer and cruel punishments are absolutely forbidden'. The key point regarding this debate appears to be that the Japanese government has not solved or does not intend to solve a 'legitimacy problem' regarding the cruelty of hanging. As Austin Sarat argues:

> To be legitimate at all, state killing must appear to be different from the violence to which it is opposed and to which it is seen as a response. A crucial part of this difference is in the way law deals with those accused of capital crimes and those who are sentenced to death.[52]

In order to justify state killing, or to distinguish it from homicide which states criminalise, most states of the USA, the other remaining industrialised democracy which retains capital punishment, have been employing lethal injection, since it is meant to kill death row inmates 'more softly and humanely' without unnecessary pain.[53] On the other hand, the Japanese government has been sticking to the claim that 'state killing is state business',[54] on the basis of Article 31 of the Constitution of Japan and Article 11 of the Penal Code. This is because the Japanese government treats capital punishment policy as an issue of criminal justice and believes that it has the right to choose its own criminal justice system without interference from international society.[55]

However, the constitutionality and legality of the capital punishment system are not only a concern amongst legal experts but also for death row inmates, and the latter have fought against the Supreme Court. For example, Matsushita Kesatoshi, a death row inmate in the Tokyo Detention Centre at the time, in 1958 claimed that hanging is in conflict with Article 36 of the Constitution of Japan. However, the Supreme Court rejected this case in 1960, referring to its previous decision in 1955. In a more recent case, a claim by attorneys for Takami Sunao was turned down on 31 October 2011;[56] and Wada Makoto, presiding judge at the Osaka District Court, declared that hanging was constitutional.[57] The Supreme Court, which includes former public prosecutors, appears to simply represent government positions on this issue, and to proclaim the constitutionality and legality of the capital punishment system.

2.4.1.3 Criteria for Capital Punishment

With regard to death sentences, it is also the Supreme Court that makes the final decisions based on the Penal Code. However, in reality there does not appear to exist a clear and consistently applied set of sentencing criteria that delineates the boundary between capital punishment and life imprisonment,[58] and public prosecutors tend to influence the judicial decision-making. First of all, capital punishment is applied to the following crimes in Japan, all specified in the Penal Code:

(1) insurrection (Article 77(1));
(2) instigation of foreign aggression (Article 81);
(3) assistance to the enemy (Article 82);
(4) arson of inhabited buildings (Article 108);
(5) detonating explosives (Article 117);
(6) damage to inhabited buildings by flood (Article 119);
(7) overturning of trains (Article 126(3));
(8) endangering traffic by overturning of a train (Article 127);
(9) pollution of water supplies with poisonous materials and causing death (Article 146);
(10) homicide (Article 199);
(11) robbery causing death or injury (Article 240);
(12) rape at the scene of a robbery causing death thereby (Article 241),

Besides these, the following crimes are also deemed to merit capital punishment:

(1) organised homicide (Article 3 of the Act on the Partial Revision of the Act on the Punishment of Organized Crime, Control of Crime Proceeds and Other Matters; and Article 199 of the Penal Code);
(2) hostage murder (Article 4 of the Act on Punishment of Compulsion and Other Related Acts Committed by Those Having Taken Hostages);
(3) aircraft hijacking (Article 2 of the Act on *Punishment* of Unlawful Seizure of Aircraft);

(4) acts of piracy (Article 4 of the *Law* on Punishment of and Measures against Acts *of* Piracy);
(5) illegal use of explosive substance (Article 1 of the Criminal Regulations to Control Explosives)

Currently, the vast majority of death row inmates have been charged for the crime of robbery causing death or injury;[59] and the 'Nagayama Criteria' have been used as a standard for the Supreme Court to impose capital punishment on offenders since 1983. Between October 1968 and April 1969, 19-year-old Nagayama Norio stole a gun from a US military base, and shot two security guards and two taxi drivers with a handgun in Tokyo, Kyoto, Hakodate and Nagoya.[60] The Juvenile Law stipulates that those younger than 19 cannot be punished with death, and Nagayama was 19 and ten months at the time of the crime. In accordance with the Juvenile Law, Nagayama was sentenced to death in 1979.

This case led to a debate amongst the legal experts on whether or not there should be a clear distinction when sentencing those aged between 18 and 19, and whether those aged over 18 should be punished harder.[61] Nagayama also tried to defend himself by linking the motivation for the murder and robbery to his poverty and ignorance, and published a best-selling book, *Muchi no Namida* (Tears of Ignorance), with over 270,000 copies having been printed by 1990. His claim was considered in his trial, and the Tokyo High Court overturned the sentence of capital punishment and sentenced Nagayama to life imprisonment in 1981. The decision was based on the following claim: 'The government should have saved the accused from his poor surroundings, it would be unfair to ignore the lack of proper welfare policies and lay all the responsibility to him'.[62]

However, the Supreme Court reversed the High Court's decision, and on 8 July 1983 issued the Nagayama Criteria with nine main factors to be taken into account in imposing capital punishment.[63] According to *Saikō Saiban sho Hanrei* (the Supreme Court Criminal Report) Vol. 37, No. 6, 'The death penalty can be applied only when the criminal's culpability is extremely grave and the ultimate punishment is unavoidable from the viewpoint of balance between the crime and the punishment as well as that of crime prevention effects, taking into account' the following nine factors:

(1) the nature of the homicide in question;
(2) the motivation behind it;
(3) the method employed in the killing;

(4) the number of people killed;
(5) the feelings of the bereaved family toward the culprit;
(6) the magnitude of the social implications of the case;
(7) the age of the defendant;
(8) whether the defendant has a prior criminal record; and
(9) whether the defendant has demonstrated any remorse for what he or she has done[64]

On the basis of these newly established criteria, Nagayama's death sentence was finally upheld in 1990, and he was executed at the age of 47 on 1 August 1997. According to Sonobe Itsuo, one of the four judges in the Nagayama case, not all the factors have equal weight in the death sentence: high importance is attached in particular to the method of killing and the number of those killed.[65] Therefore, after the Nagayama Criteria were issued, there emerged a general understanding that the number of the victims in murder cases is the crucial factor in handing down capital punishment.

2.4.1.4 Legal Ambiguities Regarding Death Sentences

In the meantime, it deserves some attention that the Supreme Court has been imposing capital punishment in a few cases which involved a sole victim, reflecting the sixth criterion—the magnitude of the social implications of the case. The first case is that of a 36-year-old male, Kobayashi Kaoru, who kidnapped, sexually assaulted and murdered a seven-year-old girl in Nara prefecture on 17 November 2004. Considering the nature of this crime,[66] Kobayashi was sentenced to death on 26 September 2006 and executed on 21 February 2013. In a second case three men, who had met through an Internet site, kidnapped, robbed and murdered a 31-year-old woman in Aichi prefecture on 24 August 2007. The misuse of the Internet was highlighted in the rulings,[67] and the death sentence of one of the men was finally upheld in 2009, whilst the others were sentenced to life imprisonment in 2011 and 2012 respectively.

A third case is that of an 18-year-old male who broke into a house in Hikari city in Yamaguchi prefecture on 14 April 1999, and strangled a woman and her baby; this case is discussed in detail in Chap. 3. He was initially sentenced to life imprisonment in consideration of his age and the possibility that he could be rehabilitated. However, the Supreme Court rejected an appeal by the defendant, and the death sentence was finally upheld on 20 February 2012.

The legal ambiguities regarding death sentences may suggest at first sight that the Supreme Court reflects domestic crime and public sentiment sensitively. In a case study of England and Wales, Michael Hough, Helen Lewis and Nigel Walker proclaim the influence of public opinion in the judiciary process: 'In theory the severity and proportionality of tariffs are determined by legislatures and judiciaries; but in practice both have an eye on the audience [...who is] the man in the street'.[68] Having said that, as Julian V. Roberts cautions, it is not necessarily right to overestimate such social factors in the Supreme Court rulings.[69] Rather, more attention needs to be paid to: (1) how public sentiment on crimes tends to be shaped and measured; and (2) how Supreme Court decisions are made independently from these factors in Japan in reality.

According to the results of *Shakai Ishiki ni Kansuru Yoron Chōsa* (Opinion Poll on the Public Image of Japanese Society), the proportion of the Japanese public who thought crime was worsening was 17.5 per cent in 2015. However, results on the same issue from other years show that those who believed crime was worsening increased from 10 per cent in 1990 to 32.4 per cent in 1995; and stayed over 30 per cent from 2002 to 2009, reaching 47.9 per cent in 2005.[70] Scholars argue that the increase in public fear of crime mainly stemmed from an increase in reported crimes during this period; and that the rapid increase in reported crimes was itself a result of a change in the police policy of counting crimes after the Okegawa Stalking Murder Case in 1999.[71] Since this murder incident could have been avoided if the police had dealt with the victim's claim more carefully, relatively trivial crimes, which would have previously been ignored, started to be formally reported.[72] This generated a sudden and drastic increase in overall recorded crime and decrease in clear up rate in the statistics.[73] The media only highlighted these statistics, and public anxiety about the state of society appeared to have surged, thereby influencing the opinion poll results.[74]

Furthermore, regarding the weight of public opinion about Supreme Court decisions it is important to acknowledge the elite-driven nature of capital punishment policy. As Hamai Koichi and Thomas Ellis argue, 'If public prosecutors recommend the death sentence in court, which they do increasingly frequently [...], it has recently become more certain that this will be the sentence of the court'.[75] It may still appear that public prosecutors reflect the criminal situations at the time and public response to them. However, 'the Japanese prosecutors [a]re much more independent from political pressure and the public opinions than their American counterparts',[76] since they pay no electoral price for being non-responsive. Therefore, whilst public outcry about criminality may appear to be reflected in Supreme Court rulings on capital cases, it is important to acknowledge the mechanism by which public fear is generated, and who uses such expressions of fear in order to recommend the death sentence in court.

The following section further investigates how the Public Prosecutor's Office exerts tremendous power in capital punishment policy.

2.4.2 The Public Prosecutor's Office

As already mentioned, both the Ministry of Justice and the Ministry of Foreign Affairs (MOFA) have maintained that capital punishment comes under the aegis of the Criminal Affairs Bureau in the Ministry of Justice,[77] and the Public Prosecutor's Office is merely a subordinate institution within the Ministry of Justice. However, in practice public prosecutors possess the greatest power in judicial issues.[78] This section highlights the fact that public prosecutors become involved in the crucial part of capital punishment policy through: (1) generating confessions from offenders in order to result in sentences of capital punishment; (2) hindering measures by which death row inmates could be proved innocent; and (3) taking initiatives regarding executions, such as preparing documents that notify the Minister of Justice about who is to be executed next.

2.4.2.1 Interrogations to Generate Confessions

Drawing on the existing work on the 'exceptional efficiency' of the Japanese criminal justice system,[79] where public prosecutors obtain confessions from suspects at a rate of over 90 per cent,[80] Johnson has compiled an empirical study detailing how Japan's 2,000 prosecutors exercise their formidable powers. He calls Japan a 'paradise for prosecutors' because:

> prosecutors have virtually unlimited discretion in deciding whether or not to prosecute. [...] [W]hatever they decide, they are free to go by their own rules, or those of their superiors, regardless of the evidence in hand or their personal belief regarding the suspect's guilt.[81]

Despite the fact that Article 38 of the Constitution of Japan specifies that forced confession cannot be used as evidence,[82] it lies at the heart of the Japanese criminal justice system:

> In Japan confessions are the king of evidence, and prosecutors are given wide legal latitude to compose them in their own words and to use them as evidence at trial [...] [T]he law gives investigators many tools to *extract* confessions: time, the single most effective instrument in their arsenal; a convenient place (police detention cells); control over meetings between suspects and defense counsel; and so on.[83]

Suspects are detained in *daiyō kangoku* (police detention cells) for up to 23 days for interrogation, and there are no rules governing human rights standards for treatment of suspects. For example, prosecutors are not required to tape or video-record interrogations.[84] According to the interviews conducted by *Jiji Press* with interrogators, this is *to respect the wills of offenders*: some offenders demand to be interrogated only in private with a single investigator, so that matters revealed will remain in the interrogation room.[85] In other words, they may not tell the truth to the investigators if the whole interrogation is to be videotaped, since the real motive is usually something private or embarrassing, which they do not want to be known to members of their families or to the general public when they are released from prison.[86]

Scholars challenge such a claim, and argue that interrogations are not videotaped because what often takes place in *daiyō kangoku* is torture with the aim of generating confessions.[87] However, although the Fukawa case recently highlighted the necessity for a visual record of interrogation in *daiyō kangoku*, the Public Prosecutor's Office has not tackled this issue. The Fukawa case concerns a murder-robbery incident in Ibaraki prefecture on 30 August 1967, when Sakurai Shoji and Sugiyama Takao, aged 20 and 21 respectively at the time of the crime, were suspected of the murder of a 62-year-old carpenter.[88] Despite the fact that neither their fingerprints nor their hair were found at the murder scene, they were forced to make confessions after a series of long interrogation sessions, and were sentenced to life imprisonment on 3 July 1978.[89] After being released on parole in November 1996, they repeatedly submitted petitions for retrials, and their petition was finally accepted in September 2005. Tape recordings of their 'confessions' were found to have been edited in 13 places, and a new DNA test confirmed the innocence of the two men in June 2011, some 44 years after the initial guilty verdict.[90] The then Minister of Justice, Eda Satsuki (January to September 2011), demanded that, in light of this case, tape and video-recording of interrogations should be mandatory.[91] The Parliamentary League to Realise the Visualisation of

Interrogations within the Democratic Party of Japan also supported his initiative. However, no progress has been made.

As Van Wolferen points out, 'The prosecutor's activities are not directed by the principle of *in dubio pro reo* ('when in doubt, favour the accused')'.[92] Rather, the degree to which suspects make a display of remorse is an important factor for public prosecutors in recommending sentences,[93] and interrogations are carried out for days and nights during this period until confessions are extracted. Furthermore, since prosecutors are evaluated in terms of their efficiency in solving cases,[94] 'once he has decided to prosecute, he will not accept being shown in the wrong'.[95] Therefore, public prosecutors even resort to using the right to submit immediate appeals against retrials in order not to lose face, which results in miscarriages of justice.[96]

In fact, besides the four major retrials in the 1980s,[97] there are still unsolved cases in the process of pleading for retrials, some going back decades. The Okunishi case is one of them. Okunishi was the longest-serving inmate in Japan until 4 October 2015, when he passed away at the age of 89 in a medical prison. He had been detained for 43 years since his death penalty was finalised in 1972, for the charge of wine poisoning at a community meeting in Nabari in Mie prefecture on 28 March 1961. This incident led to five deaths, including his wife and lover, and a further 12 women became sick. Okunishi was 35 at the time, and although he initially confessed that he put pesticide into the wine to end the love triangle, he retracted his statement straight away.[98] It is very likely that he was forced to confess during the long interrogation. Despite the fact that the First Court in 1964 ruled that he was innocent owing to a lack of evidence, the Public Prosecutor's Office filed an objection and Okunishi was sentenced to death in 1969. He petitioned for a retrial multiple times and the Nagoya High Court ordered a retrial in 2005, which was again objected to by the Public Prosecutor's Office. The defence team raised the issue that the pesticide detected in the wine appeared to have been different from what Okunishi had confessed to have used, but this was not considered in the court to be 'new evidence'.[99] Okunishi's defence team also demanded that the Public Prosecutor's Office disclose all evidence, including a photograph from the crime scene, which could have become an important piece of evidence to prove Okunishi's innocence, but this did not happen either.[100] As a lawyer, Kaido Yuichi, argues, 'There is a problem with the system in that prosecutors are allowed to file complaints. Retrials should be part of a system that saves victims who have been wrongly convicted.'[101] Okunishi had been in a medical prison since 2012 when he developed pneumonia, and he died during his ninth retrial petition. Although his retrial petition was due to be cancelled with his death, his family is planning to plea for a new retrial petition on his behalf.

Another recent case which grabbed media attention is the Hakamada case. On 27 March 2014, Hakamada Iwao, a former boxer aged 78 at the time, was released from death row having been there for 46 years since 1968. According to the presiding judge, Murayama Hiroaki, 'the possibility of his innocence has become clear to a respectable degree, and it is unbearably unjust to prolong the defendant's detention any further'.[102] Using the Hakamada case as an example, the next section explores how exactly the Public Prosecutor's Office generates confessions from the innocent and hinders measures by which death row inmates could be proved innocent.

2.4.2.2 Public Prosecutors and Miscarriage of Justice Cases: the Hakamada Case

On 30 June 1966, a family of four—a miso paste company executive, his wife, their son and daughter—was murdered in Shizuoka prefecture.[103] The house had been burgled and set on fire. Hakamada, who was working at the company's factory, was suspected and arrested in August 1966. He was questioned for 240 hours over 20 days, being beaten with sticks and not allowed to sleep.[104] The sleep deprivation and beatings took their toll and he felt forced to 'confess' in September that year.

What the Public Prosecutor's Office needed to prove Hakamada guilty was 'evidence' besides his confession. Before the first trial, more than a year after the crime, five bloodstained items of clothing were discovered in a tank of miso paste in the factory.[105] Prosecutors insisted that they belonged to Hakamada, and this became crucial 'evidence'. However, what merits some attention is the timing, their being found just in time for Hakamada's first trial, and the size of the clothing. According to a worker at the factory at the time, the tank was regularly checked to ensure it was empty, as it was used to contain faulty miso paste returned from customers.[106] If clothing had been placed in the tank at the time of the crime, the worker's testimony suggests that someone would have noticed it. It is very likely that someone put the clothes in the tank so that they were available as evidence to support the charge.

A pair of trousers found in the tank was too small for Hakamada. However, prosecutors insisted that the tag of the trousers said size B, which was the correct size. The manufacturers of the trousers made a statement afterwards, clarifying that the B on the tag was a colour code, not a size code.[107] This could have been a very important statement, but prosecutors did not disclose it and insisted that they belonged to him, and that he wore them at the time of the crime.

Hakamada's death sentence was upheld by a Tokyo High Court in 1976 and by the Supreme Court in 1980, which made him eligible to be executed at any time. It is worth noting that whilst a number of NGO groups supported Hakamada,[108] Kumamoto Norimichi, one of the judges who handed down the death sentence in 1980, also fought for Hakamada afterwards.[109] Kumamoto, 30 at the time, doubted that Hakamada was guilty, given that only one out of 45 written confessions presented by prosecutors seemed valid.[110] Others were not coherent in their motive for the crime or how the crime was committed. However, Kumamoto was overruled by two other senior judges and had to write a death sentence. According to Kumamoto, two other judges insisted that Hakamada was guilty, presumably because overturning the previous rulings by the Tokyo High Court would harm their future promotion. Feeling the qualms of conscience, Kumamoto resigned several months after the ruling had been made.[111] As the *New York Times* reported, '[a]lthough Hakamada's defense team filed its first plea for a retrial the next year, it took almost three more decades to make its way through the courts, only to be rejected in 2008'.[112]

Hakamada consistently stated that he was forced to confess to the murder case in 1966. However, he had exhibited signs of mental illness since his death sentence was finalised by the Supreme Court in 1980.[113] This was believed to have been due to long imprisonment in solitary confinement in constant fear of execution—as the execution schedule is only notified to the condemned person on the morning of execution. He was not deemed in a fit condition to meet his family or attorney to discuss a retrial. His letters to his sister became gibberish over time,[114] and he refused to acknowledge her existence by 2000. In 2003, when Setagaya Ward Mayer, Hosaka Nobuto, visited Hakamada, he appears to have been suffering from delusions, stating that he was an omnipotent god.[115] It was not until the Tokyo Family Court ruling in 2008 that Hakamada was certified as suffering from psychological illness due to long imprisonment.[116] Article 479 (1) of the Code of Criminal Procedure stipulates that 'If a person condemned to death is in a state of insanity, the execution shall be stayed by order of the Minister of Justice'. However, no action was taken immediately by the Tokyo Detention House or the Ministry of Justice.

Because of Hakamada's mental condition, it was not until 3 February 2012 that an official meeting was finally able to be held at the Shizuoka District Court as part of the process applying for a retrial. The main focus of the discussion was to re-conduct DNA analysis to examine five pieces of clothing which were stained with the victims' blood. Nonetheless, the Public Prosecutor's Office protested against the proposal, claiming that if the DNA examiner came to the detention centre to take some samples from Hakamada it would result in 'confidentiality issues'. The Public Prosecutor's Office stated that it had to be staff of the National Research Institute of Police Science who undertook such work.[117] This response by the Public Prosecutor's Office to Hakamada's defence team in 2012 implied that avoiding the potential that information regarding detention conditions would leak out into the public arena overrides proving the guilt or innocence of a man who has been on death row for more than four decades. However, in the ruling on 27 March 2014, it was finally clarified that analysis revealed that Hakamada's DNA did not match any of the samples found on the clothes which had been used as evidence of his involvement in the crime.[118] Following this, the Shizuoka District Court ordered a retrial, claiming that fabricated evidence had been used by prosecutors.[119]

Hakamada's sister, Hideko, visited Tokyo Detention House on the same day to tell him about the District Court's decision to reopen the case. However, Hakamada responded, '*Sonna koto wa uso da. Jiken wa mō owatta. Kaere.*' ('That's a lie. The Hakamada case is over. Go home because this does not involve any of you').[120] As mentioned earlier, Hakamada has been suffering from mental health issues due to his long imprisonment and had refused even to see his sister or attorney—it was the first meeting between them in three and a half years.[121] According to one of Hakamada's lawyers, 'He appears to be unable to fully understand that he was released. [...] We will tell him of that at some point in the future, considering his condition.'[122]

The media currently use *moto shikeishū* (former death row inmate) to describe Hakamada, but his status as a death row inmate has not been changed legally. This is because the Shizuoka District Public Prosecutor's Office filed an immediate appeal against the retrial order on 31 March 2014. The Public Prosecutor's Office asked for 'the Tokyo High Court to reanalyze the DNA collected from the clothing, meaning it could take more than a year for the court to decide whether the case should be retried'.[123] According to Article 448 (1) of the Code of Criminal Procedure, 'When there are grounds for a request for a retrial, a ruling shall be rendered to commence a retrial.' Furthermore, Article 448 (2) stipulates that 'When a ruling to commence a retrial has been rendered, a ruling may be rendered to suspend execution of the sentence.' However, it does not specify any rules about freeing inmates if such situation comes about. Hakamada was freed exceptionally by *tsūjō kōkoku* (ordinary appeal) following the presiding judge Maruyama's statement that 'it is unbearably unjust to prolong the defendant's detention any further'.[124]

In the Legal Affairs Committee on 24 April 2014, a Diet member, Nihi Sohei, asked Tanigaki Sadakazu, Minister of Justice at the time, his opinion of the fact that one innocent man had been detained on death row for 46 years. However, Tanigaki only replied that he would refrain from commenting on an individual death row inmate.[125] Nihi then asked whether or not Hakamada would be receiving any financial support from the government now that he had been freed from death row. However, the Director-General of the Criminal Affairs Bureau, Hayashi Makoto, denied this, stating: 'Given that the Shizuoka District Public Prosecutors Office filed an immediate appeal and it has been debated whether or not Hakamada would be allowed to have a retrial, the Ministry of Justice has not considered granting him the life security benefits.'[126]

In summary, the response of the Public Prosecutor's Office to Hakamada's defence team in 2011 implied that securing confidentiality can override proving the guilt or innocence of a man who has been on death row for more than four decades after a miscarriage of justice.[127] As already discussed, public prosecutors endeavour to gain confessions in order to solve cases 'efficiently', and recommend sentences to the court. However, when their decision is about to be challenged by the defence team, they appear to try to hinder this in order not to lose face. This case indicates that the priority of the Public Prosecutor's Office is 'solving' cases efficiently in order to maintain a high conviction rate, and capital punishment policy does not appear to have been dealt with as an issue concerning human life.

2.4.2.3 Public Prosecutors' Initiatives on Executions

Finally, it must be made clear that prosecutors are also responsible for the preparation of documents that notify the Minister of Justice who is to be executed next and when. This is based on Article 472 of the Code of

Criminal Procedure, which provides that execution is carried out on the initiative of the head of the Public Prosecutor's Office. It appears inappropriate for public prosecutors to be in charge of this task, especially given the fact that it is prison guards in the Correction Bureau under the Ministry of Justice who deal with death row inmates on a daily basis and are intimately aware of their health and mental condition. However, it is important to note again that prosecutors have a near monopoly on important posts in the Ministry of Justice. The positions of Director-General of the Criminal Affairs Bureau and the Correction Bureau in the Ministry of Justice are regularly filled by former prosecutors, not by senior prison officers; and in many cases, the latter post tends to be given to someone with no practical experience in correction. Since they are prime candidates, within a few years, for promotion to Chief Public Prosecutor, they merely try to ensure that offenders cause no trouble during their periods in office.[128]

In the meantime, the highest position given to those with practical experience in correction is head of the Regional Correction Headquarters.[129] Since holders of this post will be transferred to another prison after several years, naturally they also place emphasis on avoidance of trouble or incidents during their term. Thus, the Correction Bureau does not tend to have an environment that welcomes new ideas or opinions from prison officers that might improve the current situation. It is considered best to follow what has been the rule for decades, their prime objectives being (1) to discourage offenders from seeking redress, initiating a lawsuit or disclosing information about prison life; and (2) to keep death row inmates in good health and mental condition *so execution will be carried out smoothly*.[130] Consequently, whilst capital punishment policy has been dealt with under the aegis of the Criminal Affairs Bureau in the Ministry of Justice, the Public Prosecutor's Office plays a prominent role in the running of this policy, from generating confessions from suspects to taking initiatives regarding executions.

2.4.3 *The Ministry of Justice*

Having examined the way in which the Public Prosecutor's Office gets involved in the crucial part of capital punishment policy, this section examines the limited role that Ministers of Justice can play, in contrast to the bureaucrats in the Ministry of Justice and the Public Prosecutor's Office. The first part examines the legal responsibility and rights of Ministers of

Justice regarding this policy. More precisely, through examining Article 475 of the Code of Criminal Procedure, which specifies the responsibility of Ministers of Justice regarding authorisation of executions, it discusses the legality and propriety of some Ministers' refusal to authorise executions because of their personal beliefs. The second part divides past Ministers into three types according to their interpretations of Article 475, and their attitudes towards capital punishment in general. Highlighting a divergence amongst Ministers of Justice in their views on capital punishment on legal, moral, and cultural grounds, the third part clarifies why personal convictions of Ministers of Justice cannot have a significant influence on capital punishment policy.

2.4.3.1 Legal Responsibility of Ministers of Justice Reconsidered

Pro-death-penalty advocates claim that non-authorisation by Ministers of Justice is a neglect of their official duty, and is against the legal provision in Article 475 and 476 of the Code of Criminal Procedure. According to Article 475 (1), 'Execution of the death penalty shall be ordered by the Minister of Justice'. Article 475 (2) provides more details and requires the Minister to do this 'within six months from the date when the judgment becomes final and binding', although this excludes the period during which applications or requests for a retrial or pardon are made. In other words, Article 475 (2) 'grants the Minister broad discretion to extend this period almost indefinitely depending on various factors, such as requests for a retrial or pardon'.[131] Furthermore, Article 476 provides that executions shall be conducted within five days upon the order by the Minister of Justice.

Based on these legal provisions, bureaucrats in the Ministry of Justice tend to argue that non-authorisation can create 'unfairness' amongst death row inmates and their families, and amongst the bereaved families of the victims, especially when a pro-death-penalty Minister takes over from one who is opposed to the death penalty.[132] On the other hand, it should be noted that some scholars who study law and the Constitution of Japan contend that Ministers of Justice are not necessarily bound by the provisions of Article 475. Mizutani Norio, professor of law at Osaka University, notes that Article 32 of the Act on *Keiji Shūyō Shisetsu oyobi Hishūyōsha no Shogū ni Kansuru Hōritsu* (Penal Detention Facilities and Treatment of Inmates and Detainees) stipulates:[133]

> (1) Upon treatment of an inmate sentenced to death, attention shall be paid to help him/her maintain peace of mind. (2) Measures such as counseling or lectures which may contribute to helping the inmate sentenced to death to maintain peace of mind shall be taken by obtaining cooperation from nongovernmental volunteers.[134]

Therefore, Mizutani argues that Ministers of Justice do not have to authorise executions until a death row inmate's peace of mind is secured.[135] Secondly, he suggests it is reasonable that Ministers of Justice do not authorise executions when debates on capital punishment are taking place both inside and outside the country.[136] Internationally, there is a broad and growing consensus against the death penalty, represented by various covenants of the UN and the *acquis communautaire* established by the EU. Domestically, it should be noted that Japan introduced *saiban-in seido* (quasi-jury system) on 21 May 2009. Under this newly introduced system,[137] panels usually composed of three judges and six lay assessors,[138] who are chosen from the electoral register, determine both guilt (or innocence) and the sentence to be imposed.[139] Since the inclusion of the public as lay assessors, the majority of whom have little in-depth knowledge of law or criminology, and their involvement in imposing death sentences, this new legal system has raised public consciousness of capital punishment policy (see Chap. 7).

Similarly, in interviews with a professor of law and a researcher into the Japanese constitution, both scholars defended the legality of decisions by Ministers of Justice not to comply with Article 475, since it is a mere *kunji kitei* (advisory provision).[140] Article 13 of the Constitution of Japan provides that 'All of the people shall be respected as individuals. Their right to life, liberty, and the pursuit of happiness shall, to the extent that it does not interfere with the public welfare, be the supreme consideration in legislation and in other governmental affairs.' Article 99 of the Constitution of Japan stipulates that 'The Emperor or the Regent as well as Ministers of State, members of the Diet, judges, and all other public officials have the obligation to respect and uphold this Constitution'. Therefore, according to the constitutional scholar, it is not necessarily illegal for Ministers of Justice to refrain from authorising executions, even though it may seem to be against the Code of Criminal Procedure; but rather it is mandatory for Ministers of Justice to be extraordinarily careful with decisions that relate to matters of life or death, as stipulated in Article 13 of the

Constitution.[141] It is also their responsibility to encourage debate in the Diet or amongst the public in order to amend the law if necessary.[142]

Thus the 'responsibility' of Ministers of Justice provided in Article 475 of the Code of Criminal Procedure has been interpreted in various ways by scholars in reference to the relevant articles in the Act on Penal Detention Facilities and Treatment of Inmates and Detainees, and the Constitution of Japan. Similarly, whilst most Ministers of Justice appear to construe this provision as an official duty, others stress its 'advisory' nature. The next section illuminates a divergence amongst Ministers of Justice regarding their views on Article 475 of the Code of Criminal Procedure and the issue of capital punishment in general.

2.4.3.2 Ministers of Justice: Different Views on Capital Punishment

According to Petra Schmidt, there are roughly three types of Ministers of Justice: the doves, the hawks and the in-betweens. More precisely, they are: (1) those who are opposed to the death penalty and refuse to authorise executions because of their personal convictions or religious beliefs; (2) those who are in favour of the death penalty and authorise the executions; and (3) those who are opposed to the death penalty but dutifully authorise the execution of one or two inmates annually (see Table 2.1).[143]

The prime examples of doves are Eda Satsuki (14 January 2011 to 2 September 2011) and Hiraoka Hideo (2 September 2011 to 13 January 2012). Eda was outspoken on the issue of capital punishment and showed his anti-death-penalty sentiment clearly throughout his term of office. In his first press conference on 15 January 2011, he described capital punishment as a *kekkan no aru* (defective) penalty, raising the possibility of wrongful executions.[144] Although he was criticised for this remark and promptly retracted it, he only rephrased the term *kekkan no aru* to *nayami ga ōi, nayamashi* (troublesome),[145] in the Legal Affairs Committee on 9 August 2011, and proclaimed his opinion.

In the Legal Affairs Committees on 9 March and 9 August 2011, Eda posed a fundamental question over the responsibility of Ministers of Justice regarding authorisation of executions: why must the death penalty be authorised by the Minister of Justice whilst other criminal affairs are dealt with by administrative officers through administrative procedures? Eda suggested that the reason for final decisions regarding executions being left to Ministers of Justice was presumably that they had in their position to consider domestic and international trends comprehensively; and it was not right for them to authorise executions mechanically.[146] Moreover, like

Table 2.1 Three Types of Ministers of Justice

Name	*Sex*	*Year*	*Length of Appointment*	*Numbers of Executions*	*Party*
The Doves					
Eda Satsuki	Male	14 Jan. 2011 to 2 Sep. 2011	8 months	0	Democratic Party of Japan (DPJ)
Hiraoka Hideo	Male	2 Sep. 2011 to 13 Jan. 2012	4 months	0	DPJ
Tanaka Keishu	Male	1 Oct. 2012 to 23 Oct. 2012	23 days	0	DPJ
The Hawks					
Hatoyama Kunio	Male	27 Aug. 2007 to 2 Aug. 2008	1 year	13	Liberal Democratic Party (LDP)
Yasuoka Okiharu	Male	2 Aug. 2008 to 24 Sep. 2008	2 months	3	LDP
Mori Eisuke	Male	24 Sep. 2008 to 16 Sep. 2009	1 year	9	LDP
Yanagida Minoru	Male	17 Sep. 2010 to 22 Nov. 2010	2 months	0	DPJ
Ogawa Toshio	Male	13 Jan. 2012 to 4 Jun. 2012	5 months	3	DPJ
Taki Minoru	Male	4 Jun. 2012 to 1 Oct. 2012	4 months	4	DPJ
Taniguchi Sadakazu	Male	26 Dec. 2012 to 3 Sep. 2014	1 year and 8 months	11	DPJ
Matsushima Midori	Female	3 Sep. 2014 to 20 Oct. 2014	1 month	0	DPJ
The In-between					
Chiba Keiko	Female	16 Sep. 2009 to 17 Sep. 2010	1 year	2	DPJ

*Full data from 1980 to 2015 can be found in Appendix C.

the constitutional scholars, Eda claimed that Article 475 of the Code of Criminal Procedure was a mere advisory provision, and argued that there was no legal problem in not authorising execution orders.[147]

The next Minister, Hiraoka Hideo, showed a similarly critical attitude towards the issue of capital punishment in Diet meetings. In the Legal Affairs Committee on 25 October 2011, he stressed that it was important for Ministers of Justice to consider various factors regarding capital punishment, and that they should not therefore simply authorise execution orders dutifully.[148] He spoke of the international trends that the Japanese government should bear in mind: (1) only three out of 34 Organisation for Economic Co-operation and Development (OECD) countries retain capital punishment; (2) one of those three, South Korea, has abolished the system in practice; and (3) 16 [now 19],[149] out of 50, US states have abolished the system.[150] Regarding the interpretation of Article 475 of the Code of Criminal Procedure, Hiraoka expressed the same view as Eda, and implied that ministers' non-compliance with this provision would not necessarily generate legal problems such as apparent neglect of an official governmental duty.[151]

Examples of those categorised as hawks include: (1) Gotoda Masaharu, (2) Mikazuki Akira, (3) Hatoyama Yukio, (4) Ogawa Toshio and (5) Taki Minoru. Gotoda Masaharu (12 December 1992–9 August 1993) showed a consistent pro-death-penalty attitude, and resumed the authorisation of executions in March 1993 for the first time in three years and four months. He insisted that once a judge sentenced a convicted criminal to capital punishment, the Minister of Justice should authorise the execution as specified in the law: this was to maintain legal order in Japan, and those unhappy with the responsibility should resign immediately.[152] This approach was also followed by his successor, Mikazuki Akira (9 August 1993–28 April 1994), who authorised executions for four death row inmates, believing in the deterrent effect of capital punishment.

Hatoyama Kunio (27 August 2007–26 September 2008) ordered executions of 13 detainees in less than a year. Since this was the largest number of executions since Gotoda resumed them in March 1993, *Asahi*, a major Japanese newspaper which is committed to opposing the death penalty, condemned his behaviour by calling him *Shinigami*, or the Grim Reaper, on 20 June 2008. Although the number of executions began to invite foreign criticism, especially from human rights groups such as Amnesty International, Hatoyama stressed that capital punishment was a strictly domestic issue. He defended it not only on utilitarian grounds, saying that it was necessary to achieve social justice, but also on cultural grounds, declaring that capital punishment was an indigenous system deeply rooted in Japan's own history and culture:[153] Hence, he said, outside parties should have no say.

In a more recent case, in his inauguration speech as Minister of Justice on 13 January 2012, Ogawa Toshio (13 January 2012–4 June 2012) expressed a similar attitude and said it was the legal responsibility of the Minister of Justice to authorise execution orders. With the number of death row inmates in Japan reaching about 130, the largest number since the end of the Second World War, Ogawa stated: 'It's a very hard duty, but I want to take job responsibility. [...] It isn't in line with the spirit of the law for the number of death row inmates to continue increasing without executions.'[154] In the Legal Affairs Committee on 16 March 2012, he also indicated his pro-death-penalty attitude:

> Non-authorisation within six months of the final verdict has been a kind of a trend since the end of the war, and I do not intend to authorise executions of all of them at once. However, I have not changed my mind to fulfill my official duty to authorise executions.[155]

During his term, Ogawa authorised three executions in total. Finally, Taki Minoru (4 June 2012–1 October 2012; 24 October 2012–26 December 2012) took a similar approach to Ogawa's, and tried to justify capital punishment on legal grounds. He stressed in the Legal Affairs Committee on 15 June 2012 that capital punishment was a fair system equipped with an opportunity to open retrials, and a reprieve could also be granted when appropriate.[156] Then, on 28 August 2012, he emphasised the legal responsibility of Ministers of Justice regarding executions as follows:

> It is not in line with the legal provisions that Ministers of Justice neglect the duty of authorising executions due to personal convictions. Once the Supreme Court handed down a death sentence after going through the agony of judging whether a person should live or die, the Ministry of Justice should respect the decision.[157]

Although Taki stayed in office for only about four months in his first term, he authorised executions of four inmates—two each on 3 August and 27 September 2012.

Chiba Keiko (16 September 2009–17 September 2010) is an example of an 'in-between' Minister of Justice. Chiba had a long history as an outspoken anti-death-penalty advocate and member of the Parliamentary League for the Abolition of the Death Penalty. Although she resigned from the Parliamentary League when she was given the appointment, for nearly a year she managed to avoid authorising executions. Members of several NGOs opposing the death penalty looked forward to celebrating one year free of executions.[158] However, on 28 July 2010 two death row inmates were executed without prior notice, much to the chagrin of anti-death-penalty activists. Newspaper and television coverage shed light on positive aspects of the event. Chiba became the very first Minister of Justice to witness a hanging, and in press conferences she stressed the need for a fundamental debate on capital punishment:

> It is not that I changed my mind [...] I attended the executions as I believe it is my duty to see them through. [...] Witnessing [them] with my own eyes made me think deeply about the death penalty, and I once again strongly felt that there is a need for a fundamental discussion.[159]

She showed her enthusiasm by setting up a study group on the issue within the Ministry of Justice, and allowed the media access to the execution sites in order to spur domestic debate.[160] Based on testimony from prosecutors who witnessed the hangings, details of how death row inmates are brought to the venue and exactly how they are executed were disclosed officially on television for the first time, though most of these details had been available in existing literature compiled by NGOs. Nonetheless, anti-death-penalty NGOs were disappointed with her political decision. They saw this as nothing but a performance by the Ministry of Justice to show that a *de facto* moratorium would not occur even under a Minister who opposed the death penalty.[161] They complained that Chiba's achievements (setting up a study group, allowing media access to the execution chamber and disclosing execution details) could have been made without authorising even one execution.

From examination of the three different types of Ministers of Justice, it may appear at first sight that personal convictions of Ministers of Justice can influence capital punishment policy: pro-death-penalty Ministers tend to authorise executions in a businesslike manner; and anti-death-penalty Ministers tend to postpone this decision in reference to the 'advisory nature' of Article 475 of the Code of Criminal Procedure. Having said that, in reality Ministers of Justice cannot influence capital punishment policy in the long run, and it is bureaucrats in the Ministry of Justice, most of whom are former prosecutors with a substantial personal network within the Ministry, who exert decisive influence.

As McCargo argues, cabinets are shuffled almost yearly, and Ministers do not stay in office long enough to root new ideas within the Ministry.[162] This holds true in the Ministry of Justice, and even if Ministers of Justice are minded to bring conscious changes to the Ministry with the aim of abolishing capital punishment, they cannot do so within their short term, which only lasts for one year on average (see Appendix C).

For example, Chiba initiated a study group on the issue of capital punishment within the Ministry of Justice; allowed media access to the execution chamber; and disclosed execution details to the public officially. However, she appears to have failed to set either short-term goals, such as placing a moratorium period, or long-term goals, such as the introduction of alternative penalties or the abolition of capital punishment. Indeed, a later Minister of Justice, Ogawa, sought to reframe Chiba's actions, claiming that the original purpose of the internal study group within the Ministry of Justice must have been to simply discuss the abolition and retention of capital punishment or to recognise the current situation, and not necessarily to create an alternative system.[163] Although study group meetings have taken place on ten occasions since 6 August 2010, none has been held since 19 December 2011.[164]

Similarly, former Ministers such as Eda denounced the capital punishment system as 'defective';[165] and Hiraoka introduced the subject of the international trend of abolishing capital punishment in the Legal Affairs Committee.[166] However, neither of them appeared to have succeeded in promoting abolitionism within the Ministry of Justice, because of their short tenure of office. As a result, most of the Ministers naturally tend to focus on following precedents during their terms. In other words, they tend to proclaim the retention of capital punishment on legal, domestic and cultural grounds, and complete their official 'duty' or authorise executions in a business-like manner before the end of the calendar year.

Consequently, even if the personal characteristics of Ministers of Justice may appear to determine the future course of capital punishment policy, it is important to acknowledge that they can only play a limited role, being constrained within the institutional framework where the bureaucrats operate with a substantial network over a long period. After an examination of the elite-driven decision making system governing capital punishment policy in Japan, the next section will investigate which actors can or cannot replace the business community in the Iron Triangle model when it is applied to capital punishment policy.

2.4.4 *Pressure Groups*

Given that Ministers of Justice including Moriyama tend to justify the capital punishment system on the grounds of respecting the feelings of bereaved families,[167] pro-death-penalty pressure groups such as the victim lobby may appear to fit into a position to complete the triad. However, the decision-making takes place within tightly knit institutional dynamics, where selected elites in the Ministry of Justice and the Public Prosecutor's Office have a near monopoly, and there are problems in locating pressure groups in the triad as actors of equal influence or power. This section examines where exactly NGOs can be situated regarding capital punishment policy.

Firstly, through examining the legal standing of Japanese NGOs compared with those in the rest of the world, the limited role that pro-death-penalty pressure groups can play in governmental decision-making dynamics in Japan is clarified. Secondly, the lack of partnership between the Japanese government, the business community and anti-death-penalty NGOs is investigated. In order to avoid or solve miscarriage of justice cases in practice, it would be helpful to the government if campaigners outside the judiciary could 'intervene' in capital punishment policy. However, this section clarifies why the bureaucratic decision-making mechanism does not allow anti-death-penalty NGOs to gain official standing in this area. Finally, this section notes the difference between Japanese and international anti-death-penalty NGOs in the way they see themselves and the possible outcomes of their campaigns within Japanese governmental power dynamics.

2.4.4.1 Standing of NGOs in the International Scene

According to Claude E. Welch Jr, NGOs have now stepped into the domain traditionally reserved for governments and have been bypassing the nation-state system.[168] For example, NGOs can 'deal[…] with problems that grow slowly and effect society through the cumulative effect on individuals—the "soft" threat of environmental degradation, denial of human rights, population growth, and lack of development'.[169] Moreover, they can function as 'checks and balances' or watchdogs for the government. This holds true for selected NGOs in Japan to some extent: NGOs in the area of international development and humanitarian relief have been working in tandem with the Japanese government.[170]

However, this does not imply that the standing of NGOs has significantly increased in Japan, or that they have started to get involved in the governmental decision-making mechanism. In reality, these NGOs are in the hands of the bureaucrats and the business community: senior high-profile bureaucrats tend to occupy the important posts in NGOs under the practice of *amakudari*, and the business community tends to support these NGOs since they can obtain tax exemption from the government.[171] Although NGOs may appear to have been providing mutual benefit within the Iron Triangle, they are particular groups that the government can use to add legitimacy to their policy through cooperation.[172] Therefore, even if anti-death-penalty NGOs can 'check' Japan's human rights records or function as watchdogs, they have not been allowed to contribute to efforts to 'balance' official policy. In order to further investigate this issue, the following part clarifies (1) why Japanese NGOs in particular fields have been working closely with the Japanese government and the business community; (2) why anti-death-penalty NGOs have not gained a higher status in Japan; and (3) the extent to which domestic and international anti-death-penalty NGOs are aware of this closed power dynamic.

2.4.4.2 Legal Standing of NGOs in Japan

It is important to acknowledge the striking difference between the legal status of NGOs in Japan and in the rest of the world by referring to the provisions of the Constitution and the Civil Code of Japan. As Sook-Jong Lee and Celeste Arrington argue, NGOs in Japan and those in the rest of the world 'tend to operate at different levels of politics, employ distinctive strategies and organizational structures, and adopt different stances toward their governments'.[173] For example, whilst Northern counterparts in particular are usually described in Western literature as large, well funded and prestigious, with either professional or semi-professional staff, Japanese NGOs tend to be smaller and scattered across the nation, lacking sustainable and managerial capability.[174]

It may appear at first sight that this stems from a difference between Asian and Western countries. However, variation can also be observed within Asian countries. In the mid-1990s, South Korean presidents sought to involve NGOs in governmental decision-making in order to legitimise their democratic reform agendas: as a result, South Korean NGOs have been working on political issues nationwide.[175] By contrast, the Japanese government inhibited the formation of civic professional groups, which contributed to the formation of small, localised and volunteer-based NGOs.[176]

Indeed, the inability of Japanese NGOs to function like those in other states stems from the regulations set out in the Constitution and the Civil Code of Japan. As Frank J. Schwartz claims, 'Japan may be the strictest of all advanced industrial democracies in regulating the incorporations of nongovernmental organizations'.[177] Although freedom of association is guaranteed in Article 21 of the Constitution of Japan, Article 34 of the Civil Code of Japan sets some restrictions on giving NGOs legal status.[178] Therefore, out of two categories of NGOs—incorporated associations (*hōjin*), or unincorporated associations (*nin-i dantai*)/ civic groups—the majority are in the latter category, not registered with the state. The low standing of NGOs in Japan has contributed to a lack of professional staff as well. Whilst NGOs in developing countries such as Cambodia, Indonesia, Egypt and Palestine offer NGO staff salaries and prestige equivalent to those of governmental posts, and Western NGOs also offer competitive salaries to highly skilled personnel, Japanese NGOs offer low salaries and less prestige.[179] This has led qualified personnel to seek job opportunities not in NGOs but in international organisations, such as the UN.[180]

Impartiality is an issue, as the Japanese government tends to influence the goals of particular NGOs by filling their important posts under a practice of *amakudari*, or by supporting them financially. With regard to unincorporated associations, although Article 89 of the Constitution of Japan imposes some financial restrictions,[181] Article 25 specifies that 'the State shall use its endeavors for the promotion and extension of social welfare and security, and of public health'. Therefore, Article 89 has been re-interpreted to oblige the state to provide support for private organisations.[182]

However, in return, financial dependency on the government can create a patron–client relationship, which can make NGOs quasi-governmental organisations or sub-contractors.[183] Whilst most NGOs in the world tend to be financially independent of governments, since their revenue is largely from individual donations, membership fees and sales of publications, development and humanitarian relief NGOs in Japan tend to accept funding from the government, even though they face direct supervision.[184] For example, the Japan Platform, which aims to provide humanitarian assistance to crisis areas, gets funding not only from the government but also from the business community: the government can impact the goals of the

Japan Platform, and the business community can obtain tax exemption.[185] Thus, it is only NGOs in particular issue areas that can work in tandem with the government and the business community, since they can help to bring mutual benefits within the Iron Triangle.

After a domestic movement to give civic groups incorporated status surged in the 1990s, the Non-Profit Organisation (NPO) law was passed on 25 March 1998, making the application process for associations easier. Moreover, although conservative leaders in the LDP, in particular, used to perceive NGOs as adversarial towards the government, party politicians appear to have started to show some recognition of them as important partners of the government.[186] Domoto Akiko, of the Social Democratic Party of Japan, criticised the bureaucratic decision-making system and called for the inclusion of NGOs at a meeting of the House of Representatives Committee on Finance on 18 November 1994.[187] Similarly, Hatoyama Yukio, one of the core founders of the Democratic Party of Japan, stressed the importance of shifting Japanese society from being state-centred to being citizen-centred.[188] Kato Koichi in the LDP stressed in the House of Representatives Budget Committee on 27 January 1995 that over the previous few years LDP leaders had started to acknowledge the utility of NGOs.[189] With the introduction of the NPO law, and following changes in governmental officials' attitude towards these entities, NGOs and NPOs have received far more recognition in Japan.

In the meantime, what needs to be noted again is that those considered as crucial partners in Japanese decision-making are still mostly NGOs in the area of international development or humanitarian relief. Human rights NGOs in general and anti-death-penalty NGOs do not enjoy similar prestige when it comes to participating in Japanese human rights policy, and the Japanese government tends to resist their pressures. The following section further investigates why partnership between anti-death-penalty NGOs and the Japanese government or the business community cannot take place.

2.4.4.3 Lack of Cooperation Between Anti-Death-Penalty NGOs and the Government

Whilst the government is keen on incorporating international development NGOs into its Official Development and Welfare Policies, in order to add legitimacy, a similar attitude cannot be observed concerning human rights NGOs and capital punishment policy. This appears to be because (1) building partnership with NGOs which do not favour governmental policy does not lead to mutual benefits within the Iron Triangle; and (2) the Japanese government considers it appropriate to leave this issue of law and order to bureaucrats in the Ministry of Justice and the Public Prosecutor's Office, without inviting criticisms from campaigners outside the judiciary.

In fact, human rights NGOs do not have official consultation status when it comes to the drafting of official reports on the human rights record in Japan. For example, regarding the submission of periodical reports to the UN Human Rights Committee, human rights NGOs cannot participate in the drafting process. They only see the reports submitted by the government after they are published by the UN, and have to submit alternative reports separately.[190] This lack of communication with human rights NGOs regarding their recommendations implies that they are undervalued as a governmental partner. For instance, Amnesty International Japan works closely with domestic anti-death-penalty NGOs such as Forum 90 and the Centre for Prisoners' Rights, and protest statements are issued in joint names. However, the Japanese government does not make any formal comments on recommendations made by Amnesty International or other human rights NGOs in written form, except for direct communication at NGO-led seminars. Domestic anti-death-penalty NGOs, in particular, are often seen by the Japanese government as representing a tiny fraction of public opinion, since governmental opinion poll results indicate a wide public support for the capital punishment system.

Anti-death-penalty NGOs can contribute to avoiding or solving miscarriage of justice cases. This was particularly evident when anti-death-penalty NGOs started to act on behalf of innocent death row inmates in the 1980s. NGO bodies tried to step into the judicial decision-making process, believing that miscarriage of justice cases could not be left to the judiciary,[191] where Supreme Court decisions tend to be heavily influenced by the recommendations given by public prosecutors. However, the Japanese government tends to claim that the Japanese criminal justice system is equipped with a fair retrial system, which can prevent miscarriages of justice,[192] and hence anti-death-penalty NGOs do not have an official say.

Most NGO staff continue anti-death-penalty campaigns while fully aware that their voice cannot be heard by the government. In other words, domestic anti-death-penalty NGOs appear more objective about their own campaigns compared with international ones, since they acknowledge the fact that capital punishment policy is elite-driven and NGOs are outside the decision-making process. Whereas they continue their grassroots campaigns, such as collecting signatures from supporters and submitting them to Ministers of Justice as an alternative voice to the 'public opinion' found in the governmental opinion polls, they appear to be objective about the outcome. For example, regarding their possible impact on the execution-free period from 1989 to 1993, most of the NGO workers whom I interviewed denied that they had any impact, referring to the elite-driven nature of policy.[193] Therefore, whilst international anti-death-penalty bodies tend to try to urge the Japanese government to abolish capital punishment by applying pressure with reference to global trends, domestic anti-death-penalty NGOs tend to focus on influencing public opinion through grassroots activities.[194]

2.4.4.4 Lack of Cooperation Between Anti-Death-Penalty NGOs and the Business Community

With regard to the business community, it should be noted that there are some partnerships with human rights NGOs. According to a survey, '*Kigyō ni Okeru Jinken Sonchō no Torikumi no Genjō—70 Sha no Jirei Yori*' (Reality of the Enterprises' Efforts in Respecting Human Rights: Case Study of 70 Enterprises) in 2005,[195] which was conducted by the Buraku Liberation and Human Rights Research Institute (BLHRRI), 81.4 per cent (57 companies) of the companies include respect for human rights in their corporate ethical codes.[196] Issue areas that they engage in range from personal data protection to non-discrimination at the time of recruitment against people of *buraku* origin,[197] those with disabilities and women. The survey result shows that 52.9 per cent (37 companies) have partnerships with NGOs on the *buraku* issue; 20 per cent (14 companies) on issues relating to people with disabilities; and 11.4 per cent (eight companies) in issues concerning women.[198] Furthermore, whilst human rights that companies are required to protect were limited to domestic employees' working rights until the 1970s, various issues outside labour–management relations have now also been tackled comprehensively. They include issues of: (1) child labour and forced or bonded labour employed by suppliers abroad; (2) destruction of indigenous people's traditional way of life; and (3) indirectly taking part in human rights violation by building partnerships with companies accused of aiding apartheid in South Africa, or making business deals with the military government of Myanmar.[199]

In order to raise their profile in the international business scene, Japanese companies have also been keen to build partnerships with international organisations through complying with their human rights protection initiatives. The prime example is the idea of Corporate Social Responsibility (CSR),[200] which refers to embracing responsibility for further social good by adhering to ethical standards and international norms. CSR-related standards have also been set by international organisations and NGOs,[201] and it is worth noting that *Keidanren*, or the Japan Business Federation, also adopted the Charter for Good Corporate Behaviour in 1991,[202] corresponding to the international trend of supporting CSR.[203] Among the internationally recognised human rights initiatives, Global Impact, which was declared in 1999 by the UN, is based on the idea that 'open markets and human well-being can go hand in hand'.[204] Its prime objective is 'to align business operations and strategies everywhere with ten universally accepted principles in the areas of human rights, labour, environment and anti-corruption',[205] and out of approximately 21,350 in all, 447 Japanese firms and organisations currently support this initiative.[206]

Whilst there exist some partnerships between the business community and human rights NGOs, it is difficult to observe any in the area of capital punishment. This fact appears to be closely related to the question of whether proclaiming abolitionism in companies' corporate principles would help their business interests. In fact, partnership with anti-death-penalty NGOs would not bring any mutual benefits to the Iron Triangle. Provision of funding to anti-death-penalty NGOs, which are not in favour of governmental policy, would undermine companies' relations with the government. Given that capital punishment policy has been dealt with as an issue of law and order, it is natural that the business community would not show any interest in opposing that policy, unless it would provide them with the prestige that internationally recognised organisations can offer. Since governmental opinion polls show strong public support for capital punishment, it is natural for companies to assume that supporting abolitionism in their corporate principles would risk business opportunities. Consequently, whilst the business community shows some commitment to human rights issues both domestically and internationally, its motive appears to be heavily related to commercial interests.

2.4.5 *Is the Iron Triangle Model Applicable to Capital Punishment Policy?*

Having discerned the actors who (1) underpin the legal legitimacy of the system, (2) get involved in the actual running of the system and (3) represent and justify the policy on legal, domestic and cultural grounds both internally and externally, it is important to evaluate the extent to which the Iron Triangle model can account for capital punishment policy-making.

Firstly, bureaucrats play a tremendous role in capital punishment policy. Whilst Ministers of Justice are the top authority on this issue, and their personal characteristics may appear to influence policy-making in the short term, it is the bureaucrats in the Ministry of Justice who consistently justify the retention of the system on legal, domestic and cultural grounds, and ensure continuation of the policy. Given that the ruling party, the LDP, is pro-death-penalty in nature, LDP party politicians may also appear to possess a significant power in the other corner of the triad. However, important decisions regarding this policy are made by bureaucrats often irrespective of the views of party politicians. As Van Wolferen argues, approximately 80 per cent of all legislation passed is drafted by bureaucrats, and Diet members merely rubber-stamp the documents.[207] This holds true for capital punishment policy: LDP party politicians, who tend not to stay in office for more than one year because of the frequent cabinet reshuffles, cannot get involved in the actual policy-making process. The reason why the ruling party, the LDP in particular, appears to be holding power in the triad is that approximately 25 per cent of the LDP Diet members are ex-bureaucrats under the *amakudari* system; and the perpetual dominance of the LDP appears to have allowed bureaucrat-led policy-making.[208]

Secondly, it should be recalled that the Public Prosecutor's Office, a subordinate institution of the Ministry of Justice, is involved in the crucial part of capital punishment policy, from generating confessions by accused persons to taking initiatives regarding executions. In theory, the Supreme Court is independent of bureaucratic control and makes the final judicial decisions regarding death sentences. However, it tends to be heavily influenced by the recommendations of public prosecutors.[209] The majority of the Supreme Court judges are composed of former judges, prosecutors and bureaucrats who share similar views on criminal justice issues, and the traditional Japanese decision-making system helps them reach a group consensus.

Finally, with regard to what can take the place of the business community in the triad model, the pro-death-penalty victim lobby may appear to fit, given that the Japanese government often cites the feelings of the victims' bereaved families. However, NGOs cannot support a corner of the triad, since neither pro- nor anti-death-penalty NGOs have the official status to get involved in capital punishment policy. Only selected NGOs are allowed to contribute to Japanese decision-making for mutual benefit within the bureaucrats–politicians–business community triad, and anti-death-penalty NGOs, which are not in favour of governmental policy, have not been included in this dynamic.

Consequently, the application of the Iron Triangle model to capital punishment policy presents difficulties, given that this policy is primarily elite-driven, and important decisions are made irrespective of the views of party politicians or pressure groups. The following section examines the governmental approach to capital punishment policy in detail. It highlights that capital punishment policy has been merely treated as one of the governmental policies on which Ministry bureaucrats make sure precedents are followed.

2.5 Capital Punishment Policy as an Issue of Law and Order

As already discussed, it is important to note that capital punishment policy has been dealt with in the Ministry of Justice as an issue of law and order. There are two government agencies concerned with human rights protection in Japan: the Human Rights Bureau in the Ministry of Justice and the Human Rights and Humanitarian Affairs Division in MOFA. I approached both of these bodies to see if they would agree to an interview. In January 2011, the Human Rights Bureau declined my request, stating that it was not in charge of capital punishment. I was urged to contact the Criminal Affairs Bureau.

In the meantime, two senior officials in the MOFA division, one of whom was previously in the Ministry of Justice, agreed to be interviewed in June 2011 thanks to the help of another MOFA minister. Initially, the two former officials did not respond to my request. However, the minister, a vocal anti-death-penalty activist who belongs to the Parliamentary League against the Death Penalty, agreed to my interview cordially, and forwarded my letter to them again. Although the interview with two MOFA officials in the Human Rights and Humanitarian Affairs Division was thus achieved, they denied any responsibility for dealing with the issue of capital punishment, now or in the future. According to them, there is no issue on earth that is *not* related to human rights; however, it is impossible to deal with every single issue in the human rights divisions in governmental agencies, so they have to better prioritise major issues and tackle them efficiently.[210] Both groups thus maintained that capital punishment was an issue of legal punishment under the aegis of the Criminal Affairs Bureau in the Ministry of Justice.

2.5.1 *'Institutional Ambivalence' in Japan's Capital Punishment Policy*

Whilst capital punishment is thus justified on legal grounds and run by the Ministry of Justice, 'institutional ambivalence' can also be observed in Japan's capital punishment policy. According to David Garland:

> [t]he visible sign of this ambivalence are laws that go unenforced, sentences that go unexecuted, legal proceedings that create endless delays, and a great deal of discomfort on the part of the judges, government ministers, and penal officials charged with administering the punishment.[211]

This applies in the case of Japan: (1) there are no clear and consistently applied sentencing criteria to identify the boundary between capital punishment and life imprisonment cases; (2) time between sentences and executions varies; (3) a 'hesitant' attitude can be observed in the execution procedure; (4) the Ministry of Justice maintains a secretive policy on this system; and (5) the Ministry does not appear particularly enthusiastic about conducting a large number of executions per year (see Appendix A). Firstly, not all of the nine factors in the Nagayama Criteria have to be fulfilled for the death sentence to be imposed. As already discussed, death sentences can be imposed for cases which involve a sole victim.

Secondly, '[c]ondemned inmates are selected for execution on the basis not of longevity on death row but of other ill-defined criteria'.[212] Whilst the average time between sentence and execution is approximately a decade or longer, inmates from certain high-profile cases may have been strategically chosen in order to gain support from the public. For example, regarding the execution of Nagayama Norio on 1 August 1997, Johnson, Hara Yuji and Yasuda Yoshihiro all independently claim that the Ministry of Justice appeared to have justified his execution following a spate of similar juvenile murder cases.[213] As will be discussed in detail in Chap. 4, public interest in Nagayama's activities as a novelist through the 1980s to 1990s was prominent. Therefore, the Ministry of Justice appeared to have chosen the execution date carefully so that the public would not protest.[214] In fact, 1997 was a year in which successive violent juvenile crimes started to occur. Among them, the Sakakibara case attracted plenty of media attention and generated public outcry. After the offender was arrested on 28 June 1997, Nagayama was executed on 1 August 1997, which was within less than two months. Therefore, anti-death-penalty advocates considered that the Ministry had a political strategy to justify Nagayama's execution in line with the outbreak of similar crimes.

Thirdly, although the Japanese government consistently justifies the judicial right to deprive a person of life in order to maintain legal order in Japan, some efforts on behalf of prison guards who get involved in hanging show a hesitant attitude on the part of the Ministry of Justice regarding state killing. Article 472 of the Code of Criminal Procedure provides that execution is carried out on the instructions of the head of the Public Prosecutor's Office.[215] Prison guards cover the inmate's eyes with a white cloth and tie both arms behind with handcuffs and legs with strings.[216] Once a noose is placed around the prisoner's neck, three prison guards press buttons on the wall, each pressing one: only one of the three buttons really works, a device to relieve the psychological burdens of prison guards.[217] When the correct button is pressed, the 90 centimetre square plate that the inmate is standing on opens, and he falls down for around 4 metres; the rope becomes taut when he reaches about 15 centimetres from the ground.[218] It is worth noting that even if the door falls instantly, inmates do not die immediately; it takes 15–20 minutes, which violates the UN Convention against Torture. Prison guards who carry out the execution receive special payment worth ¥20,000 ($177.96),[219] and according to an in-depth interview by Hara, usually they spend the money on drinks to forget what happened at the execution venue, or donate it to the offertory box at the shrine, praying for the executed person to rest in peace.[220] Given that fake buttons have been equipped for hanging and special payment is provided to relieve psychological burdens, the Japanese government appears to have a legitimacy problem about state killing.

Finally, the Ministry of Justice maintains a secretive policy regarding this system and does not disclose information about death row inmates. As will be discussed in Chap. 3 in detail, it was only from November 1998 that the Ministry of Justice started to disclose when executions took place and of how many convicts, and only from November 2007 that the names of those executed started to be disclosed. Until then, it was anti-death-penalty NGOs that were reporting the names of the executed through their own investigations. What is more, in order to distract the public or hinder the abolitionist lobby from voicing dissent, Japan does not usually conduct executions during parliamentary sessions or on public and political holidays, with some exceptions.[221] The extreme secrecy surrounding this system may imply that the government is not confident about the legitimacy of this policy. Although numbers of annual executions reached 15 in 2008 (the largest numbers in decades), Japan is one of the world's least frequent users of capital punishment compared to other retentionist countries.[222] It has been discussed in the existing literature that the Ministry's retention of capital punishment relates to:[223] (1) securing annual funding by acting on precedents; and (2) the lack of legal status and rights of death row inmates as a result of the state's approach to the policy from the viewpoint of law and order. The following section examines the Ministry's secretive policy and assesses the existing hypotheses regarding the retention of the capital punishment system.

2.5.2 *The State's Approach to Human Rights of Death Row Inmates*

It is suggested in the existing literature that annual executions are linked to the Ministry's survival. In a parallel case, the Ministry of Land, Infrastructure and Transport conducts roadworks across the nation at the end of the year in order to use up the annual budget.[224] If the Ministry does not spend the same amount of the funds as in the previous year, a smaller fund could be allocated the following year. Likewise, bureaucrats in the Ministry of Justice appear to seek to execute certain numbers of death row inmates a year in order to keep the capital punishment system in use.[225] Of course, this does not necessarily mean that capital punishment would be abolished as a result of lack of funds. It might continue because of the conservative nature of the Japanese bureaucratic decision-making system. In other words, the Ministry of Justice has been treating this policy as an issue of law and order, and tends to act on precedents and conduct executions annually in order to leave a record that the system has been in use.

Relating to this point, another argument is that the Ministry's dutiful conduct appears to relate to death row inmates' lack of legal status or rights. According to Kakusho Toyokazu, these have not been officially established in Japan.[226] Since death row inmates do not fall into the category of 'prisoners' in the Japanese government's eyes, executions tend to be conducted as a 'duty' relating to law and order. Whilst prisoners in general are supposed to go back to society after correction and rehabilitation, that is not the case for death row inmates unless they are proved innocent in retrials or reprieved.[227] Referring to Article 484 of the Code of Criminal Procedure,[228] Kakusho argues that death row inmates are considered by the government as those who are merely waiting for execution.[229] More precisely, detention is *shikei no shikkō no ichibu shikkō* (a part of the execution procedure), and what prison guards have to make sure is that death row inmates are in good health so that executions will be conducted in an uneventful manner.[230] Indeed, once the inmates are executed, they are counted as those 'released from prison'. As Kawai Mikio analyses, this must be partly to maintain statistical coherence with regard to the numbers of inmates that come in and go out after correction and rehabilitation;[231] but partly because there is an idea in the Ministry of Justice that death row inmates can be 'released' only through execution.[232] Whilst other prisoners complete their sentence through rehabilitation, death row inmates appear to be expected to add to their death sentence by generating a feeling of remorse through being detained in a solitary cell with limited communication with others.[233] The Ministry of Justice does not allow them to atone for deaths they have caused in any other way, and makes prison guards ensure that this process is not disrupted by inmates' suicide.[234]

The Ministry of Justice's stance on death row inmates is evident in detention conditions and the execution procedure in Japan. Whilst death row inmates are detained isolated from their close families, they can maintain contact with chaplains.[235] This system might at first sight appear to have been prepared by the Ministry of Justice out of concern for death row inmates, but it needs to be noted that the chaplain system has been strategically run by the Ministry of Justice in order to conduct executions 'smoothly'. Approximately 70 per cent of chaplains are Buddhists, the remainder being Shintō and Christian. Their purpose is to help inmates develop a feeling of remorse and prepare them to be executed in a peaceful state of mind. However, Menda Sakae, a former death row inmate, is disturbed by the emphasis that Buddhist chaplains place on the teaching of karma: he contends that if inmates are encouraged to believe that they were already doomed by their previous life, they may resign themselves to the inevitable and refrain from fighting against what they know to be a miscarriage of justice.[236]

Limited correspondence between death row inmates and their families or friends, and lack of prior notification to them before executions, appear to be justified by the government on the theory that excessive communication can hinder death row inmates from 'concentrating on death'. However, as Johnson claims:

> If isolation helps the condemned to 'accept the inevitable' and 'prepare for death,' it does so by killing twice: first socially and then physically. If secrecy is designed to protect the 'honor and privacy' of the offender's family, it does so by sacrificing democratic values [...such as] transparency, accountability, and openness.[237]

2.5.3 *Japan's Retention of Capital Punishment on Legal Grounds*

Kakusho's argument about death row inmates' lack of legal status or rights can be supported by a recent statement of a judge in the Hiroshima District Court on 23 May 2012. A death row inmate, convicted in the Hikari murder case,[238] sued the author and publisher of a book, *Fukuda kun wo Koroshite Nani ni Naru?* (What's the Point of Killing Fukuda through Capital Punishment?),[239] over the violation of his right to privacy.[240] However, the judge at Hiroshima District Court, Ueya Shin-ichi, turned down his claim on 23 May 2012, clarifying that 'Death sentence has been sentenced to the plaintiff, and *there is no risk of great loss to him*'.[241] Ueya's remark highlighted the state's approach to capital punishment and its neglect to ensure the basic rights of death row inmates. More precisely, his remarks can be interpreted as suggesting that the violation of basic rights cannot be a major issue for death row inmates, since they are merely waiting for death.

In summary, capital punishment has been treated as an issue of law and order and has been justified upon the basis of:

(1) Article 31 of the Constitution of Japan, which allows a legal punishment to deprive a person of life or liberty exceptionally;
(2) the Penal Code and the Nagayama Criteria, which specify crimes that are punishable by death and set out nine main criteria;
(3) Articles 475 and 476 of the Code of Criminal Procedure, which stipulate the responsibility of Ministers of Justice regarding the timing of authorising and conducting executions;
(4) Article 11 of the Penal Code, which specifies the execution method as hanging;

(5) Article 472 of the Code of Criminal Procedure, which provides that execution is carried out on the instructions of the head of the Public Prosecutor's Office; and
(6) Article 98 (1) of the National Civil Service Law, which specifies that civil servants have to carry out duties set by senior staff.

Whether the Ministry of Justice officially holds executions, abolishes the capital punishment system or installs an alternative penalty such as life imprisonment without parole, it requires the Ministry to repeal or amend the existing legal provisions. Given that the Ministry of Justice tends to endeavour to act on precedents based upon law, it is unlikely that the Ministry will take such an initiative. However, it merits particular attention that whilst the Japanese government thus justifies capital punishment as a legal penalty, 'institutional ambivalence' is observed in the low number of annual executions compared to other retentionist countries, ill-defined criteria on the selection of death row inmates and mental and financial support for prison guards who are involved in the actual execution.

2.6 Conclusion

This chapter has presented an overview of the way in which capital punishment policy has been run within the tightly knit institutional framework, exploring the applicability of the Iron Triangle model; and has clarified the government's approach to this policy through examining detention conditions and execution procedure. After reviewing the current academic approach to Japan's retention of capital punishment, the first section introduced Japan's elite-driven policy-making within the bureaucrats–politicians–business community triad. Noting that the three actors are highly interdependent because of the perpetual dominance of the LDP, it examined the extent to which this model fits the decision-making process for capital punishment policy. Firstly, it highlighted bureaucratic control of this policy through examining the Supreme Court, key government agencies and pressure groups. This chapter contended that whilst the Supreme Court is theoretically independent of institutional power dynamics, it tends to make decisions reflecting the Public Prosecutor's Office's approach to capital punishment.[242] Although the Public Prosecutor's Office is a subordinate institution of the Ministry of Justice, in practice it is involved in a crucial part of this policy, from obtaining confessions from accused persons to taking initiatives regarding executions.

Secondly, presenting the divergence of personal beliefs amongst Ministers of Justice on the issue of capital punishment, this chapter argued that these cannot be a determining factor for retaining or abolishing the capital punishment system. Although the Minister of Justice is a top authority for this policy in theory, each Minister tends not to stay in office for more than a year because of cabinet reshuffles, and cannot influence the capital punishment question in the long run. This chapter argued that it is instead a cluster of employed-for-life bureaucrats in the Ministry of Justice and the Public Prosecutor's Office who exert tremendous power in the actual decision-making process.

Thirdly, the chapter critically examined the role that pressure groups can play in this policy. Although the Japanese government tends to justify capital punishment on grounds of respecting the feelings of victims' bereaved families, they do not possess a significant role in the triad in reality. Similarly, anti-death-penalty NGOs have not been included in the decision-making system even though they could function as a watchdog and help the judicial authority solve or avoid miscarriage of justice cases with their own investigations. Since capital punishment has been treated by the government as a criminal justice issue, anti-death-penalty NGOs have not been admitted as appropriate bodies to advise the government.

The applicability of the Iron Triangle model to capital punishment policy was then evaluated. It has been argued that capital punishment policy is primarily elite-driven, and that decision-making is conducted by the bureaucrats in the Ministry of Justice and the Public Prosecutor's Office independently of the views of party politicians or pressure groups. Although the ruling party may appear to play an equal role to bureaucrats, this is because of the fluidity of bureaucrats under the system of *amakudari*, and the long dominance of the LDP has helped bureaucrat-led decision-making to become institutionalised.[243] With regard to the pressure groups, they do not appear to hold the corner of the triad, since they have not been allowed to get involved in capital punishment policy making. Therefore, in the application of the Iron Triangle model to capital punishment policy, the triad is not a perfect triad, and decision-making is primarily bureaucrat-led. In other words, whilst bureaucrats exert tremendous power and the LDP supports that power with an array of intimate personal networks, actors in the third corner have been missing, which makes the triad incomplete.

The second section of the chapter further investigated the governmental approach to capital punishment policy. It showed that the Ministry of

Justice has been dealing with this policy as an issue of criminal justice on the basis of law, and not as an issue of human rights. Such a governmental approach can be observed in the detention conditions and execution procedure, which do not place much emphasis on the human rights of death row inmates, but rather on how to detain and execute them in an uneventful manner. Nonetheless, capital punishment policy leaves a legitimacy problem regarding state violence, as represented by: (1) the ambivalence in the borderline between capital punishment and life imprisonment and in the timeline between sentences and executions; (2) the special consideration shown to prison guards who are involved in the actual hanging; (3) extreme secrecy surrounding the policy; and (4) small-scale executions compared to other retentionist countries.

This policy has been consistently justified on the basis of law, and it is unlikely that the Ministry of Justice would repeal or amend these provisions to halt executions or abolish the system. However, it is important to question the validity of the Japanese government's position that the death penalty is merely a matter of law and order. Given that 'institutional ambivalence' demonstrates that the Japanese government is not fully confident about the legitimacy of the policy, international and domestic human rights NGOs could use this as a starting point to redefine the death penalty as illegitimate use of state power, and eventually as a human rights violation.

The following chapter examines how the Japanese government has justified capital punishment with reference to domestic and cultural factors, and investigates the validity of its arguments. It will also explore how the study of the *de facto* moratorium period can inform scholars and activists about the elite-driven nature of capital punishment policy.

Notes

1. Johnson, D.T. (2011) *Nihon ga Shikei wo Sonchi suru Riyū: Kokonotsu no Kasetsu* (Why Japan Retains Capital Punishment: Nine Hypotheses) in A. Fukurai (ed) *Shikei to Mukiau Saiban-in no Tame ni* (For Lay Judges who Handle Capital Punishment Sentencing), Tokyo: Gendai Jinbun Sha.
2. McCargo, D. (2004) *Contemporary Japan*, 2nd ed, New York: Palgrave Macmillan, p.110.
3. Johnson, D.T. (2011) *op. cit.* pp. 141–4.

4. Johnson, D.T. & Zimring, F.E. (2009) *The Next Frontier: National Development, Political Change, and the Death Penalty in Asia*, Oxford University Press, USA, pp.60–1.
5. *Ibid*; Johnson (2011) *op. cit.* p. 142.
6. Johnson (2011) *Ibid*
7. Johnson (2011) *op. cit.* p. 143.
8. Johnson (2011) *op. cit.* p. 144.
9. *Ibid.*
10. Johnson, D.T. (2005) 'The Death Penalty in Japan: Secrecy, Silence, and Salience' in A. Sarat & C. Boulanger (eds) *The Cultural Lives of Capital Punishment: Comparative Perspectives*, Stanford: Stanford University Press, pp. 251–73, p. 253; Johnson, D.T. (2011) *Ibid.*
11. Johnson (2011) *op. cit.* p.147; Johnson (2005) *op. cit.* p. 253, 266.
12. According to the two scholars (Bae, S. (2008) *When the State No Longer Kills: International Human Rights Norms and Abolition of Capital Punishment*, Albany: State University of New York Press, p. 79 and Johnson (2011) *op. cit.* p. 148), although there are already various organisations in this area, such as: (1) the Association of Southeast Asian Nations (ASEAN); (2) ASEAN+3 that include China, Japan, Korea; (3) the East Asia Summit (EAS); and (4) Asia-Pacific Economic Cooperation (APEC), their main focus is on the economy and security, not human rights.
13. Okuno S. (1980) *The 93th Legal Affairs Committee of the House of Councillors*, 18 December 1980, p. 8; Goto, M. (1989) *The 116th Legal Affairs Committee of the House of Councillors*, 5 December 1989, p. 3; Moriyama Mayumi quoted in *Japan Times* (2002) 'Diet group against Death Penalty to Make Its Move, 4 October 2002'. Available at: http://www.japantimes.co.jp/text/nn20021004b1.html [Accessed 4 February 2016]
14. Thayer, N.B. (1969) *How the Conservatives Rule Japan*, Princeton: Princeton University Press, p. 180.
15. Thayer (1969) *op. cit.* p. 183.
16. Thayer (1969) *op. cit.* p. 185.
17. Thayer (1969) *op. cit.* p. 182.
18. Van Wolferen, K. (1989) *The Enigma of Japanese Power: People and Politics in a Stateless Nation*, New York: Macmillan, p. 272.

19. Neary I. (2004) 'Parliamentary Democracy in Japan', *Parliamentary Affairs*, 57(3), pp.666–681, p. 675.
20. McCargo (2004) *Contemporary Japan*, 2nd ed, New York: Palgrave Macmillan, p. 110; *Keidanren* is 'a federation of leading industrial organisations such as the automobile manufacturers' association, the shipbuilders' association, the iron and steel federation, the petroleum association and the chemical industry association, together with trading companies, wholesale business, banks, insurance companies and securities companies', Van Wolferen (1989) *op. cit.* p. 34.
21. Van Wolferen (1989) *op. cit.* pp. 33, 145.
22. Van Wolferen (1989) *op. cit.* p. 145.
23. McCargo (2004) *op. cit.* p. 105.
24. Boyd, R. (1987) 'Government-Industry Relations in Japan: Access, Communication, and Competitive Collaboration', *Comparative Government-Industry Relations: Western Europe, the United States, and Japan*, pp. 61–90, p. 68.
25. Krauss, E.S. (1989) 'Politics and the Policymaking Process' in E. S. Krauss & T. Ishida (eds) *Democracy in Japan*, Pittsburgh: University of Pittsburgh Press, pp. 39–64, p. 53.
26. Van Wolferen (1989) *op. cit.* p. 143.
27. Krauss (1989) *op. cit.* p. 51.
28. Van Wolferen (1989) *op. cit.* p. 344.
29. Van Wolferen (1989) *op. cit.* pp. 344–5.
30. Mori, T. (2008) *Shikei: Hito wa Hito wo Koroseru, Demo Hito wa Hito wo Sukuitai tomo Omou* (Death Penalty: People Could Kill People, but People Also Feel Like Saving People), Tokyo: Asahi Shuppan Sha, p. 18.
31. Krauss *Ibid*; Campbell, J.C. (1989) 'Democracy and Bureaucracy in Japan', in E. S. Krauss & T. Ishida (eds) *Democracy in Japan*, Pittsburgh: University of Pittsburgh Press, pp. 113–137, p. 115; Ramseyer, J.M. and Rosenbluth, F.M. (1998) *The Politics of Oligarchy: Institutional Choice in Imperial Japan*, New York: Cambridge University Press, p. 60; Richardson, B. (1998) *Japanese Democracy: Power, Coordination, and Performance*, New Haven: Yale University Press, p. 109.
32. Campbell, J.C. (1989) 'Democracy and Bureaucracy in Japan', in E. S. Krauss & T. Ishida *op. cit.* p. 116.
33. Van Wolferen (1989) *op. cit.* p. 111.

34. Van Wolferen (1989) *op. cit.* p. 339.
35. Yamada, Y. (1985) *Ringi to Nemawashi* (*Ringi* and *Nemawashi*), Tokyo: Kōdansha Gendai, p. 102.
36. De Mente, B. (1975) *Japanese Manners and Ethics in Business*, Phoenix: Phoenix Books, p. 87; Ruch, W.V. (1984) *Corporate Communications: A Comparison of Japanese and American Practices*, Westport, Connecticut: Quorum Books, p. 71.
37. Vogel, E.F. (1975) *Modern Japanese Organization and Decision-making*, Berkeley: University of California Press, p. xxii.
38. Van Wolferen (1989) *op. cit.* p. 338.
39. De Mente (1975) *op. cit.* p. 88.
40. Ruch (1984) *op. cit.* p. 72.
41. *Ibid*
42. Krauss (1989) *op. cit.* pp. 39, 52.
43. McCargo (2004) *op. cit.* p. 114.
44. McCargo (2004) *op. cit.* pp. 106, 110.
45. According to Article 76, 'The whole judicial power is vested in a Supreme Court and in such inferior courts as are established by law. No extraordinary tribunal shall be established, nor shall any organ or agency of the Executive be given final judicial power. All judges shall be independent in the exercise of their conscience and shall be bound only by this Constitution and the laws.'
46. This also holds true of other government policies. For example, whilst lower-level courts sentenced major companies guilty of causing hazardous pollution in the 1960s, the Supreme Court overturned their decisions and 'helped precipitate new legislation and the setting up of an environmental agency' (McCargo *Ibid*).
47. Matsui, S. (2010) *The Constitution of Japan: A Contextual Analysis*, Oxford: Hart Publishing, p. 123.
48. *Ibid*
49. Matsui (2010) *op. cit.* p. 124.
50. Matsui (2010) *op. cit.* pp. 123–124.
51. Although the execution method in Japan varied from strangulation or decapitation, to *seppuku* or ritual disembowelment, after the Meiji Restoration in 1868 Japan made hanging the official execution method, importing the Western criminal system.

52. Sarat, A. (2002) *When the State Kills: Capital Punishment and the American Condition*, Princeton: Princeton University Press, p. 19.
53. Sarat (2002) *op. cit.* p. 60; Johnson (2005) *op. cit.* p. 259.
54. Johnson (2005) *op. cit.* p. 260.
55. Moriyama M. (2001) *The 153rd Legal Affairs Committee of the House of Representatives*, 19 October 2001, p. 8.
56. Takami, aged 41 at the time of the crime, set fire to a *pachinko* parlour in Osaka on 5 July 2009, killing five people and injuring ten. He was sentenced to death on 31 October 2011.
57. *Nikkei* (2011) '"*Kōshukei wa Gōken*": *Pachinko Ten Hōka de Shikei Hanketsu, Osaka Chisai*'(Hanging in Constitutional: Death Sentence for Setting Fire to the Pachinko Parlour, Osaka District Court), 31 October 2011.
58. Schmidt, P.(2002) *Capital Punishment in Japan*, Brill Academic Publishers, pp. 45, 55.
59. Supreme Court (2012) *Saiban-in Seido no Jisshi Jyōkyō ni Tsuite* (About Implementation Status of the Quasi-Jury System), p.1. Available at: http://www.saibanin.courts.go.jp/topics/pdf/saibanin_kekka.pdf [Accessed 4 February 2016]
60. Métraux, D.A. (2009) 'The Nagayama Criteria for Assessing the Death Penalty in Japan: Reflections of a Case Suspect', *Southeast Review of Asian Studies*, 31, pp. 282–289, pp. 283–284.
61. Hara, Y. (2001) *Naze Shikei wa Kakusareru noka* (Why Death Penalty is Hidden), Tokyo: Takarajimasha Shinsho, pp. 54–55, 65.
62. *Japan Times* (2007) '10 Years after Hanging, Killer Still Offers Lessons to be Learned', 1 August 2007.
63. Supreme Court (1983) *Saikō Saiban sho Hanrei* (*The Supreme Court Criminal Report*), 37, No. 6, 8 July 1983.
64. Supreme Court (1983) *op. cit.* p. 609 translated in Métraux (2009) *op. cit.* p. 6.
65. *Yomiuri* (2009) 'Unmasking Capital Punishment: "Nagayama Criteria" A Hot Issue 25 Years on'. 8 March 2009.
66. According to the *Japan Times* on 27 September 2006 ('"Wanted to be Executed Quickly": Pedophile to Hang for Killing Nara Girl' http://www.japantimes.co.jp/news/2006/09/27/national/pedophile-to-hang-for-killing-nara-girl/#.VYsoufl_Okp [Accessed 4 February 2016]), 'He took a photo of the dead girl

and sent it to her mother over the girl's mobile phone, and about a month later sent her a message threatening to target the girl's younger sister as well.' He had already spent three years in prison for his attempted killing of a five-year-old girl in October 1991, and had been paroled from 1996 (*Asahi* (2004) 'Nara Slaying/Caught', 31 December 2004. Available at: http://www.asahi.com/english/nation/TKY200412310078.html [Accessed 4 February 2016]).

67. *Japan Times* (2007) 'Three Men Who Met on Net Charged over Slaying', 27 August 2007. Available at: http://search.japantimes.co.jp/cgi-bin/nn20070827a1.html [Accessed 4 February 2016]
68. Hough, M., Lewis, H. & Walker, N. (1988) 'Factors Associated with "Punitiveness" in England and Wales', in Walker, N. and Hough, J.M. (eds) *Public Attitudes to Sentencing: Surveys from Five Countries*, Aldershot: Gower Publishing, pp. 203–217, p.1.
69. Roberts, J.V. (2002) 'Public Opinion and Sentencing Policy' in S. Rex and M. Tonry (eds) *Reform and Punishment: The Future of Sentencing*, Cullompton: Willan Publishing, pp. 18–39, p. 22.
70. Hamai, K. & Ellis, T. (2008) '*Genbatsuka*: Growing Penal Populism and the Changing Role of Public Prosecutors in Japan?', *Japanese Journal of Sociological Criminology*, 33, pp. 67–92, p. 67; Prime Minister's Office (1990, 1995, 2000, 2005, 2009 and 2015) *Shakai Ishiki ni Kansuru Yoron Chōsa* (*Opinion Poll on the Public Image of the Japanese Society*).
71. Hamai, K. & Ellis, T. (2006) 'Crime and Criminal Justice in Modern Japan: From Re-integrative Shaming to Popular Punitivism', *International Journal of the Sociology of Law*, 34(3), pp. 157–178, p. 162; On 26 October 1999, a 21-year-old woman was stabbed to death by a man hired by her former boyfriend and his brother, at Okegawa station in Saitama prefecture. Although the victim had filed complaints to the police that her former boyfriend was stalking her and defaming her and her family, they had been turned down by the police since this would cause extra paperwork for them (*Japan Times* (2005), 'Stalker-Killer's Life Term Upheld', 21 December 2005).
72. Hamai & Ellis (2006) *op. cit.* pp. 163–164.
73. Kawai, M. (2004) *Anzen Shinwa Hōkai no Paradox: Chian no Hōshakaigaku* (The Paradox of Destruction of Security Myth:

Sociology of Law in Security), Tokyo: Iwanami Shoten, p. 39; Hamai & Ellis (2006) *op. cit.* p. 166.

74. With regard to media coverage of crime and its impact on the public, see Chap. 6.
75. Hamai, K. & Ellis, T. (2008) *op. cit.* p. 73.
76. Johnson, D. T. (2002) *The Japanese Way of Justice: Prosecuting Crime in Japan*, New York: Oxford University Press cited in Hamai & Ellis (2008) *op. cit.* p. 83.
77. Interview with two MOFA officials, Tokyo, 17 June 2011
78. Van Wolferen (1989) *op. cit.* p. 222.
79. Consistent writers on this issue include: Johnson, C (1972) *Conspiracy at Matsukawa*, Berkeley and Los Angeles: University of California Press; Clifford, W (1976) *Crime Control in Japan*. Lenham: Lexington Books; Aoyagi, F. (1986) *Nihonjin no Hanzai Ishiki* (Japanese Consciousness on Crimes). Tokyo: Chūō Kōronsha; Foote, D.H (1992a) Benevolent Paternalism of Japanese Criminal Justice. *The California Law Review* 80: 317–390; Foote, D.H (1992b) From Japan's Death Row to Freedom. *Pacific Rim Law & Policy Association* 1: 11–103; Haley, J.O (1992) Criminal Justice in Japan. *Journal of Japanese Studies* 18(2): 553–556; Mukherjee, S. (1994) What is So Good about The Low Crime Rate in Japan. *Australian Rationalist* 37: 7–19.
80. Johnson (2002) *op. cit.* p. 243.
81. Van Wolferen (1989) *op. cit.* pp. 220–221.
82. According to Article 38 of the Constitution of Japan: 'No person shall be compelled to testify against himself. Confession made under compulsion, torture or threat, or after prolonged arrest or detention shall not be admitted in evidence. No person shall be convicted or punished in cases where the only proof against him is his own confession.'
83. Johnson (2002) *op. cit.* p. 39.
84. This is in contrast to the practice in states such as the UK, Canada, Australia and many states of the USA. For example, it became mandatory to video-record in the UK in 1986, in Alaska in 1985 and Minnesota in 1994 (Johnson (2002) *op. cit.* p. 273).
85. *Jiji Press* (2010) '*Jiji.com: Torishirabe Kashika no Yukue*' (Journey of Visualisation of Interrogation), 1 May 2010. Available at: http://www.jiji.com/jc/v?p=new-special-investigation0001 [Accessed 4 February 2016]

86. *Ibid.*
87. Johnson (2002) *op. cit.* p. 279.
88. *Mainichi* (2011) '*Fukawa Jiken: Saishin Muzai, Mukikakutei kara 33 Nen, Kensatsu Shuchō Shirizokeru*'(Fukawa Case: Proved Innocence after Retrial, 33 Years after Life Sentence was Confirmed, Rejecting Public Prosecutor's Office's Claim), 24 May 2011.
89. *Mainichi* (2008) 'High Court Upholds Lower Court Decision to Retry Two Men Convicted of 1967 Murder', 14 July 2008.
90. *Mainichi* (2011) *Ibid.*
91. *Jiji Press* (2011) '*Zenmen Kashika no Shikō Shiji, Tokusō Jiken de Kenji Sōchō ni: Eda Hōshō*'(Minister of Justice Eda Instructs the Public Prosecutor General Visualisation of Interrogation: Special Investigation Case), 8 April 2011.
92. Van Wolferen (1989) *op. cit.* p. 222.
93. Van Wolferen (1989) *op. cit.* p. 188.
94. Johnson (2002) *op. cit.* pp. 243–244.
95. Van Wolferen (1989) *op. cit.* p. 221.
96. According to Article 448 (1) of the Code of Criminal Procedure, 'When there are grounds for a request for a retrial, a ruling shall be rendered to commence a retrial', and Article 448 (2) also provides that 'When a ruling to commence a retrial has been rendered, a ruling may be rendered to suspend execution of the sentence'. However, public prosecutors can submit immediate appeals against this decision since Article 450 stipulates that 'An immediate appeal may be filed against a ruling as prescribed in Article 446, paragraph (1) of Article 447, paragraph (1) of Article 448, or paragraph (1) of the preceding Article.'
97. They are the Menda case, the Saitagawa case, the Shimada case and the Matsuyama case, which will be discussed further in Chap. 4.
98. *Japan Times* (2015a) 'Death of Condemned Inmate who Died while Claiming Innocence Raises Questions over Retrial System', 5 October 2015. Available: http://www.japantimes.co.jp/news/2015/10/05/national/social-issues/condemned-inmate-died-claiming-innocence-raises-questions-retrial-system/ [Accessed 4 February 2016]
99. *Japan Times* (2015b) 'Retrial System Needs Revamping', Opinion, 7 October 2015, Available: http://www.japantimes.

co.jp/opinion/2015/10/07/editorials/retrial-system-needs-revamping/ [Accessed 4 February 2016]

100. *Japan Times* (2015a) *Ibid.*
101. *Ibid.*
102. *New York Times* (2014) 'Soul-Searching as Japan Ends a Man's Decades on Death Row', 27 March 2014. Available at: http://www.nytimes.com/2014/03/28/world/asia/freed-after-decades-on-death-row-man-indicts-justice-in-japan.html?_r=0 [Accessed 4 February 2016].
103. *Asahi* (2014) '*Hakamada Jiken no Kettei Yōshi: Saishin Kaishi Seikyu*' (Summary of the Hakamada Case Rulings: Calling for Retrials), 28 March 2014. Available at: http://www.asahi.com/articles/DA3S11053243.html [Accessed 4 February 2016].
104. *New York Times* (2014) *Ibid.*
105. *Asahi* (2014) *Ibid.*
106. *Asahi* (2013) '"*Shōko wa Netsuzō" Aratamete Shuchō: Hakamada Jiken Saishin Seikyū no Ikensho*'("Evidence Had been Fabricated": Written Opinion on Calling for Hakamada Case Retrials). Available at: http://www.asahi.com/articles/TKY201312020071.html [Accessed 4 February 2016]
107. Fukushima, M. (2014) *The 186th Audit Committee of the House of Councillors*, 21 April 2014, p. 44.
108. A number of NGO groups who have supported Hakamada include: his sister, Hideko aged 81; a local boxing federation and Amnesty International.
109. *New York Times* (2014) *Ibid.*
110. *Asahi* (2014) *Ibid.*
111. *New York Times* (2014) *Ibid.*
112. *Ibid.*
113. *Asahi* (2014) 'Lawyers: Prosecutors' Appeal Exacerbates Hakamada's Suffering', 1 April 2014. Available at: http://ajw.asahi.com/article/behind_news/social_affairs/AJ201404010061 [Accessed 4 February 2016]
114. *New York Times* (2014) *Ibid.*
115. *Asahi* (2014) '*48 nen me no "Mujitsu" Hakamada Jiken Saishin Kettei: Chōki Kōsoku Kokoro Mushibamu Shikei Shikkō no Kyōfu*' ("Innocence" after 48years: Order of Commencement of Retrial for Hakamada Case, Heart Undermined by Long Imprisonment, Fear of Executions), 29 March 2014. Available at: http://www.

asahi.com/articles/DA3S11055388.html [Accessed 4 February 2016]

116. *Asahi* (2014) '48 nen' *Ibid.*
117. *Mainichi* (2012) '*Hakamada Jiken: Sansha Kyōgi, DNA Kantei no Jiki Mitei, Shikeishu no Ane "Hayaku Shite"*'(Hakamada Case: Three roundtable, Date of DNA Test Unscheduled, 'Hurry Up' Says His Sister), 4 February 2012.
118. *Asahi* (2014) 'Lawyers' *Ibid.*
119. *Mainichi* (2012) *Ibid.*
120. *Asahi* (2014) '48 nen' *Ibid.*
121. *Asahi* (2014) '*Hakamada*' *Ibid.*
122. *Asahi* (2014) 'Lawyers' *Ibid.*
123. *Ibid.*
124. *New York Times* (2014) *Ibid.*
125. Tanigaki, S. (2014) *The 186th Legal Affairs Committee of the House of Councillors*, 24 April 2014, p. 18.
126. Hayashi, M. (2014) *The 186th Legal Affairs Committee of the House of Councillors*, 24 April 2014, p. 18.
127. On 13 April 2012, a DNA analysis result revealed that Hakamada's DNA was not found on any of the clothes used as the evidence of the crime. Hakamada's defence lawyer has currently been preparing for retrials, which can be permitted on the submission of newly discovered evidence (*Chūnichi* (2012) '*Hakamada Jiken: Kensatsu gawa no "Fuicchi"*'(Hakamada Case: Mismatch on the Side of Public Prosecutors), 16 April 2012).
128. Kikuta, K. (2002) *Nihon no Keimusho* (Japanese Prison), Tokyo: Iwanami Shoten, p. 22.
129. *Ibid.*
130. *Ibid.* and Mori, T. (2008) *Shikei: Hito wa Hito wo Koroseru, Demo Hito wa Hito wo Sukuitai tomo Omou*, Tokyo: Asahi Shuppan Sha, p. 216.
131. Advocates for Human Rights (2012) 'JAPAN: Fourteenth Session of the Working Group on the Universal Periodic Review, Human Rights Council, 22 October – 5 November 2012', p. 7.
132. *Yomiuri* (2009) '*Shikei' Dōnaru, Haishi Ronja, Chiba Hōshō Shūnin de*'(Death Penalty, What Happens after the Appointment of Anti-Death-Penalty Minister of Justice, Chiba), 21 September 2009.

133. Mizutani, N. (2010) '*Saiban no Shikkō*' (Enforcement of Trials) in A. Goto and Yuji Shiratori (eds) *Shin Konmentar: Keiji Soshō hō* (New Konmentar: Code of Criminal Procedure), Tokyo: Nihon Hyoron Sha, p. 1092.
134. Ministry of Justice (2007) *Keiji Shūyō Shisetsu oyobi Hishūyōsha no Shogū ni Kansuru Hōritsu* (*Act on Penal Detention Facilities and Treatment of Inmates and Detainees*), 25 May 2007. Available at: http://www.japaneselawtranslation.go.jp/law/detail/?ft=1&re=01&dn=1&x=42&y=5&co=01&ky=act+on+penal+detention+facilities+and+treatment+of+inmates+detainees&page=2 [Accessed 4 February 2016]
135. Mizutani (2010) *Ibid.*
136. Mizutani (2010) *Ibid.*
137. In Japan, the jury system was used from 1928 to 1943. Under this system, jurors used to determine guilt or innocence, and the sentence to be imposed was determined by the judges.
138. According to Article 2 of *Saiban-in no Sanka suru Keiji Saiban ni Kansuru Hōritsu* (The Lay Assessor Act), panels are composed of one judge and four lay assessors for certain cases such as those where guilt seems beyond doubt.
139. Article 13 of *Saiban-in no Sanka suru Keiji Saiban ni Kansuru Hōritsu* (The Lay Assessor Act).
140. Interview with two constitutional scholars, Tokyo, 13 May 2011.
141. *Ibid.*
142. *Ibid.*
143. Schmidt (2002) *op. cit.* pp. 63–73.
144. *Financial Times* (2011) 'Japan to Consider Abolishing Death Penalty', 21 January 2011.
145. Eda. S. (2011) *The 177th Legal Affairs Committee of the House of Representatives*, 9 August 2011, p. 6.
146. *Ibid.*
147. Eda, S. (2011) *The 177th Legal Affairs Committee of the House of Representatives*, 9 March 2011, p. 5.
148. Hiraoka, H. (2011) *The 179th Legal Affairs Committee of the House of Representatives*, 25 October 2011, p. 13.
149. Currently 19 US states have abolished the death penalty: Alaska, Hawaii, Illinois, Iowa, Maine, Michigan, Minnesota, New Jersey, North Dakota, Rhode Island, Vermont, West Virginia,

Wisconsin, Massachusetts, Connecticut, New Mexico, New York, Maryland and Nebraska.

150. Hiraoka (2011) *Ibid.*
151. Hiraoka (2011) *Ibid.*
152. Gotoda. M. (1993) *The 126th Legal Affairs Committee of the House of Councillors*, 29 March 1993.
153. Hatoyama, K. (2008) *The 169th Legal Affairs Committee of the House of Representatives*, 11 April 2008, p. 25.
154. *Japan Times* (2012) 'New Minister Won't Shirk from Hangings Inmates on Death Row at Postwar High; Hirata Arrest to Spare Cultists', 15 January 2012.
155. Ogawa, T. (2012) *The 180th Legal Affairs Committee of the House of Representatives*, 16 March 2012, p. 11.
156. Taki, M. (2012) *The 180th Legal Affairs Committee of the House of Representatives*, 15 June 2012, p. 44.
157. Taki, M. (2012) *The 180th Legal Affairs Committee of the House of Councillors*, 28 August 2012, p. 5.
158. Interview with two NGO staff, Tokyo, 17 May 2011.
159. *Christian Science Monitor* (2010) 'Japan Announces Death Penalty Review after Hanging Two Men', p.1. Available at: http://www.csmonitor.com/World/Asia-Pacific/2010/0729/Japan-announces-death-penalty-review-after-hanging-two-men [Accessed 4 February 2016]
160. *Asahi* (2010) '*Shikei Shikkō ni Tachiai Chiba Hōshō: "Konpon kara no Giron ga Hitsuyō"*', 28 July 2010.
161. Centre for Prisoners' Rights (2010) '*Chiba Keiko Hōmu Daijin ni yoru Shikei Shikkō ni Kōgi Suru*' (We Protest against Executions Authorised by Minister of Justice Chiba Keiko), 28 July 2010. Available at: http://cpr.jca.apc.org/archive/statement#990 [Accessed 4 February 2016].
162. McCargo (2004) *op. cit.* p. 105.
163. Ogawa, T. (2012) *The 180th Legal Affairs Committee of the House of Representatives*, 16 March 2012, p. 32.
164. Ministry of Justice (2013) *Shikei no Arikata ni Tsuite no Benkyō Kai* (Study Group on What Death Penalty Should be). Available at: http://www.moj.go.jp/keiji1/keiji02_00005.html [Accessed 4 February 2016]
165. *Financial Times* (2011) *Ibid.*
166. Hiraoka (2011) *Ibid.*

167. *Japan Times* (2002) 'Diet group against Death Penalty to Make Its Move, 4 October 2002'. Available at: http://www.japantimes.co.jp/text/nn20021004b1.html [Accessed 4 February 2016]
168. Welch, C.E. (2001) 'Conclusion' in C. E. Welch (ed) *NGOs and Human Rights: Promise and Performance*, Philadelphia: University of Pennsylvania Press, pp. 261–280, p. 263.
169. Mathews, J.T. (1997) 'Power Shift', *Foreign Affairs*, 76(1), pp. 50–66, p. 63.
170. Hirata, K. (2002) *Civil Society in Japan: The Growing Role of NGOs in Tokyo's Aid and Development Policy*, New York: Palgrave Macmillan, p. 37.
171. Lee, S.J. & Arrington, C. (2008) 'The Politics of NGOs and Democratic Governance in South Korea and Japan', *Pacific Focus*, 23(1), pp. 75–96, p. 84.
172. Japanese NGOs in the field of international development have made important progress and gained official status to influence governmental foreign aid policy. Although Japan has been the top donor of foreign aid with Official Development Assistance (ODA), it was often criticised in the 1950s–70s for giving *himotsuki enjo* (tied aid), whereby Japanese grant and loan aid was tied to purchases from Japan. Faced with international criticism, the MOFA started to adopt untied loans, and its focus also shifted to software aid, which includes training local community health practitioners (Hirata 2002, *Ibid*). The number of Japanese international development NGOs increased following that change in aid policy, and they have become an integral part of ODA policy.
173. Lee and Arrington (2008) *op. cit.* p. 76.
174. Holmén, H. & Jirström, M. (2009) 'Look Who's Talking!: Second Thoughts about NGOs as Representing Civil Society', *Journal of Asian and African Studies*, 44(4), pp. 429–448, p.431; Welch (2001) *op. cit.* 268.
175. Lee and Arrington (2008) *op. cit.* p. 78.
176. Lee and Arrington (2008) *op. cit.* p. 77.
177. Schwartz, F. (2002) 'Civil Society in Japan Reconsidered', *Japanese Journal of Political Science*, 3(02), pp. 195–215, p. 195.
178. According to Article 34 of the Civil Code, 'Any association or foundation relating to any academic activities, art, charity, wor-

ship, religion, or other public interest which is not for profit may be established as a juridical person with the permission of the competent government agency.'

179. Hirata (2002) *op. cit.* p. 40.
180. *Ibid.*
181. Article 89 of the Constitution of Japan specifies that 'No public money or other property shall be expended or appropriated for the use, benefit or maintenance of any religious institution or association, or for any charitable, educational or benevolent enterprises not under the control of public authority.'
182. Schwartz (2002) *op. cit.* p. 203.
183. Schwartz (2002) *op. cit.* p. 203–204; Yamamoto, T. (1998) *The Nonprofit Sector in Japan*, New York: Manchester University Press, p. 127.
184. Lee and Arrington (2008) *op. cit.* p. 90.
185. Lee and Arrington (2008) *op. cit.* p. 84.
186. Kato, K. (1995) *The 132nd Budget Committee of the House of Representatives*, 27th January 1995, p. 28.
187. Domoto, A. (1994) *The 131st Committee on Finance of the House of Councillors*, 18th November in 1994, p. 25.
188. Hatoyama, Y. (1996) '*Minshutō, Watashi no Seiken Kōsō*', *Bungei Shunjū, November*, pp.112–130, p. 122.
189. Kato (1995) *Ibid.*
190. Neary, I. (2002) *Human Rights in Japan, South Korea and Taiwan*, London: Psychology Press, p. 66; (2002) *The State and Politics in Japan*, Oxford: Polity Press, p. 202.
191. Van Wolferen (1989) *op. cit.* p. 226.
192. Hatano, A. (1983) *The 99th Legal Affairs Committee of the House of Representatives*, 10 August 1983, p. 23; Hayashi, H. (1984) *The 101st Legal Affairs Committee of the House of Representatives*, 2 March 1984, p. 38; Taki, M. (2012) *The 180th Legal Affairs Committee of the House of Representatives*, 15 June 2012, p. 44.
193. Postal correspondence with an NGO worker, 28 February 2011; and interview with an NGO worker, Tokyo, 12 April 2011.
194. Interview with two NGO members, Tokyo, 17 May 2011.
195. 90 per cent of companies that answered the survey are large companies of capital scale with more than ¥500 million ($4.4 million).

196. Buraku Liberation and Human Rights Research Institute (BLHRRI) (2005) '*Kigyō ni Okeru Jinken Sonchō no Torikumi no Genjyō: 70sha no Jirei Yori*'(Reality of the Enterprises' Efforts in Respecting Human Rights: Case Study of 70 Enterprises), pp. i–26, pp. 26–28. Available at: http://blhrri.org/kenkyu/bukai/jinken/kigyo/kigyo_survey_r/kigyo_survey_r.pdf [Accessed 4 February 2016]
197. According to BLHRRI ((2012) 'What is Buraku Discrimination?', p. 1. Available at: http://blhrri.org/blhrri_e/blhrri/buraku.htm [Accessed 4 February 2016]), *Buraku* people are: 'the largest discriminated-against population in Japan. They are not a racial or a national minority, but a caste-like minority among the ethnic Japanese. They are generally recognized as descendants of outcaste populations in the feudal days. Outcastes were assigned such social functions as slaughtering animals and executing criminals, and the general public perceived these functions as "polluting acts" under Buddhist and Shintoist beliefs.'
198. BLHRRI (2005) *op. cit.* p. iv. Other companies also have links with NGOs of several other issue areas such as *zainichi*, or ethnic Korean residents born and brought up in Japan; international human rights; and human rights education, although the breakdown is not disclosed in the survey result.
199. Tanimoto, K. (2004) '*Kigyō no Shakaiteki Sekinin (CSR) to Jinken*' (Corporate Social Responsibility and Human Rights), *Buraku Liberation and Human Rights Research Institute*, 158, pp. 10–21, pp. 11–12, 15. Available at: http://blhrri.org/info/book_guide/kiyou/ronbun/kiyou_0158-02.pdf [Accessed 4 February 2016]
200. According to McWilliams, A. et al. (McWilliams, A., Siegel, D.S. & Wright, P.M. (2006) 'Corporate Social Responsibility: Strategic Implications', *Journal of Management Studies*, 43(1), pp. 1–18, pp. 1–2.), examples of CSR are (1) to commit to prevent global warming by manufacturing aerosol products with no fluorocarbons, and to reduce emissions and pollution abatement by promoting recycling; (2) to promote employee empowerment by non-discrimination of women and minorities; and (3) to work closely with community organisations.
201. They include: the Global Compact by the UN; the OECD Guidelines for Multinational Enterprises; the ILO Declaration

on Fundamental Principles and Rights at Work; Sustainability Reporting Guidelines by the Global Reporting Initiative; and Social Accountability 8000 by Social Accountability International.

202. The charter was renamed 'the Charter of Corporate Behaviour' in 1996.
203. Keidanren (2004) 'Charter of Corporate Behavior: Nippon Keidanren'. Available at:http://www.csr-weltweit.de/uploads/tx_jpdownloads/csr_japan01_charter.pdf [Accessed 4 February 2016]
204. United Nations (2002) 'Cambridge, Massachusetts, 11 October 2002 – Secretary-General's address at event marking the 50th Anniversary of the MIT Sloan School of Management', 11 October 2002, p. 3. Available at: http://www.un.org/sg/statements/index.asp?nid=105 [Accessed 4 February 2016]
205. United Nations (2008) *United Nations Global Compact: Corporate Citizenship in the World Economy*, p. 2. Available at: http://www.unglobalcompact.org/docs/news_events/8.1/GC_brochure_FINAL.pdf [Accessed 4 February 2016]
206. United Nations (2015) 'Our Participants'. Available at: https://www.unglobalcompact.org/what-is-gc/participants/search?utf8=%E2%9C%93&search%5Bkeywords%5D=&search%5Bcountries%5D%5B%5D=95&search%5Bper_page%5D=10&search%5Bsort_field%5D=&search%5Bsort_direction%5D=asc [Accessed 30 March 2016]
207. Van Wolferen (1989) *op. cit.* pp. 33, 145.
208. Krauss, E.S. (1989) *op. cit.* pp. 39, 52–53.
209. Hamai K. and Ellis T. (2008) '*Genbatsuka*: Growing Penal Populism and the Changing Role of Public Prosecutors in Japan?', *Japanese Journal of Sociological Criminology*, 33, pp. 67–92, p. 73.
210. Interview with two MOFA officials, Tokyo, 17 June 2011.
211. Garland, D. (1993) *Punishment and Modern Society: A Study in Social Theory*, Chicago: University of Chicago Press, pp. 99–100.
212. Johnson, D. & Zimring, F.E. (2009) *The Next Frontier: National Development, Political Change, and the Death Penalty in Asia*, Oxford University Press, USA, p. 62.
213. Johnson (2005) *op. cit.* p. 258; Hara (2001) *op. cit.* p. 60; and Yasuda, Y. (1998) '*Uchitsuzuku Tairyō Shikei Shikkō: 12 Gatsu Shikkō Soshi wo*' (Mass Executions: Calling for Blocking

Executions in December), *Nenpō Shikei Haishi* (Annual Report: Abolishing Capital Punishment), Tokyo: Impact Shuppan, p. 103.

214. Yasuda (1998) *Ibid.*
215. According to Article 98 (1) of the National Civil Service Law, it is senior staff of the Correction Bureau who are involved in the actual hanging procedure whilst a prosecutor, an assistant public prosecutor, and the Director and other staff of the Correction Bureau are present at the execution, along with a doctor of the Correction Bureau to confirm the inmate's death.
216. Hara (2001) *op. cit.* p. 17.
217. *Mainichi* (2010) '*Keijō Hatsukōkai: Sei to Shi Wakeru Fumi-ita Shikkōshitsu 14 Jō*'(First Public Exhibition of the Execution Ground: Square Plate which Divides Life and Death, 14-tatami-mat Death Chamber), 28 August 2010.
218. The execution is well rehearsed, the height and weight of the inmate being measured in advance (Hara (2001) *op. cit.* p. 25). The length of the rope that will go around the inmate's neck is adjusted so that it can hold his weight, and a solid metal block which is the same weight of the inmate is used to confirm that the square door on the ground falls instantly (Hara (2001) *Ibid*).
219. Using an exchange rate of ¥112.38 yen to $1, this amounts to $177.96. This exchange rate is used throughout the book.
220. Hara (2001) *op. cit.* p. 26.
221. Johnson (2005) *op. cit.* pp. 251–273, p. 259; FIDH (2008) 'The Death Penalty in Japan: The Law of Silence – Going against the International Trend', October 2008, p. 4. Available at: http://www.fidh.org/IMG/pdf/japon505a2008.pdf [Accessed 4 February 2016]; Some executions have recently been conducted between parliamentary sessions on the authorisation of pro-death-penalty Ministers including Ogawa Toshio (13 January 2012–4 June 2012) and Taki Minoru (4 June 2012–1 October 2012; 24 October 2012–26 December 2012) (see Chap. 7).
222. China, Vietnam, North Korea, India and Pakistan do not report execution statistics, and the true total number of executions may be higher than estimated. However, more than 95 per cent of all executions are believed to take place in China, and the estimates

range from 2,000 to 15,000 per year (Johnson and Zimring 2009, *op. cit.* p. 21).

223. Kakusho, T. (1991) *'Shikei Kakuteisha no Hōteki Chi-i to Jinken: Tsūtatsu "Shikei Kakuteisha no Sekken oyobi Shinsho no Hatsuju ni Tsuite" ni Kansuru Ichi Kōsatsu'*(The Legal Status and Rights of Prisoners Sentenced to Death), *Bulletin of Chiba and Keiai Junior College*, 13, pp. 13–30; Mori, T. (2008) *op. cit.*; Johnson and Zimring (2009) *op. cit.*
224. Mori, T. (2008) *op. cit.* p. 18.
225. Johnson and Zimring (2009), *op. cit.* p. 48; Mori, T. (2008) *Ibid.*
226. Kakusho (1991) *op. cit.* p. 13.
227. *Ibid*
228. Article 484 of the Code of Criminal Procedure stipulates that 'When a person who has been sentenced to death, imprisonment with or without work or a misdemeanor imprisonment without work is not under detention a public prosecutor shall summon that person. If that person does not respond to the summons, the public prosecutor shall issue a writ of commitment.'
229. Kakusho (1991) *op. cit.* p. 17.
230. Kakusho (1991) *op. cit.* p. 16.
231. Kawai, M. (2009) *Shūshinkei no Shikaku* (Blind Spot of Life Sentence without a Parole), Tokyo: Yōsensha, p. 234.
232. Hara (2001) *op. cit.* p. 198.
233. According to Article 36 of the Act on Penal Detention Facilities and Treatment of Inmates and Detainees, 'Treatment of an inmate sentenced to death shall be conducted in an inmate's room throughout day and night, except where it is deemed appropriate to conduct it in the outside of the inmate's room. (2) The room of an inmate sentenced to death shall be a single room. (3) No inmates sentenced to death shall be permitted to make mutual contacts even in the outside of the inmate's room, except where deemed advantageous in light of the principle of treatment prescribed in paragraph (1) of Article 32.'
234. Mori, T. (2008) *op. cit.* p. 216. For this reason, prison guards notify the inmate one or two hours before the execution in the morning. Therefore, death row inmates 'are given only enough time to clean their cells, write a final letter and receive last rites' (*New York Times* (2002) 'Secrecy of Japan's Executions is Criticized as Unduly Cruel', 30 June 2002. Available at: http://

www.nytimes.com/2002/06/30/world/secrecy-of-japan-s-executions-is-criticized-as-unduly-cruel.html?pagewanted=all&src=pm [Accessed 4 February 2016]). According to *Shi to Kabe: Shikei wa Kakushite Shikko Sareru* (Death and Wall: This is How Death Penalty is Executed), published in 1953 by Tamai Sakuro, a former Director-General of the Osaka Detention Centre, notification used to be given to inmates one or two days before the execution, and they could meet their family and order whatever they wanted to eat for the last supper. However, after 3 October 1975 when Tsuru Shizuo, then a death row inmate, committed suicide on the day of execution, the rule was amended. The Ministry of Justice believed that Tsuru's suicide was directly linked to the fact that he was notified of his execution in the late afternoon before the execution day (Menda S. (2004) *Menda Sakae Gokuchū Note: Watashi no Miokutta Shikeishū Tachi* (Menda Sakae's Notes on Death Row: Death Row Inmates Who I Saw Off), Tokyo: Impact Shuppan, p. 134).

235. According to Article 68 of the Act on Penal Detention Facilities and Treatment of Inmates and Detainees: 'The warden of the penal institution shall make efforts to make available the opportunities for inmates to participate in religious ceremonies presided over by religious leaders (limited to nongovernmental volunteers; hereinafter the same shall apply in this paragraph), or to receive religious teachings from religious leaders.'
236. Menda (2004) *op. cit.* p. 139.
237. Johnson (2005) *op. cit.* p. 260.
238. The case of a crime on 14 April 1999, when an 18-year-old male broke into a house in Hikari city in Yamaguchi prefecture, and murdered a woman and her baby.
239. Masuda, M. (2009) *Fukuda kun wo Koroshite Nani ni Naru?* (What is the Point of Killing Mr. Fukuda?), Tokyo: Incidents.
240. In the book his real name, several pictures and letters that Fukuda wrote to the author were disclosed, although disclosure of the name of the offender, who was a minor at the time of the crime, is usually withheld. His claim was that he had agreed to be interviewed by the author believing that publication of this book would help him avoid the death sentence. However, since his death sentence was confirmed regardless of the contents of the book, he sued the author and publisher, demanding a halt to

publication and financial compensation (*Nikkei* (2012) '*Moto Shōnen Jitsumei Bon no Shuppan Sashidome Mitomezu: Hikari shi Boshi Satsugai*'(Publication Ban of the Book, with Juvenile Offender's Name Disclosed, Disapproved: Hikari Murder Case), 23 May 2012. Available at: http://www.nikkei.com/article/DGXNASFK23013_T20C12A5000000/?uda=DGXZZO0207877015122009000000 [Accessed 4 February 2016])

241. *Ibid.*
242. McCargo (2004) *op. cit.* p. 103.
243. Krauss (1989) *op. cit.* pp. 39, 52–53.

CHAPTER 3

Governmental Justification for Capital Punishment and the *De Facto* Moratorium Periods Reconsidered

3.1 Introduction

Chapter 2 examined the elite-driven nature of Japan's capital punishment policy. It clarified that capital punishment has been dealt with by the Japanese government as an issue of law and order, and that important decisions regarding this policy are conducted by bureaucrats in selected governmental agencies. However, the Ministry of Justice tends to justify capital punishment not only on legal grounds but also on domestic and cultural grounds. The first section of this chapter critically examines the validity of the governmental justification for capital punishment. More precisely, through reconsidering the kind of cultural features that have been claimed to be associated with capital punishment in Japan, it will explore whether or not policy elites' narratives which make reference to culture have influenced the public and scholars in believing that capital punishment policy is domestically and culturally determined.

Firstly, it investigates the government's retention of capital punishment on the basis of its deterrent effect and public support for the system. Whilst governmental opinion poll results indicate that the vast majority of the Japanese public support capital punishment believing in its deterrent effect, comparison with other non-governmental opinion polls and an in-depth survey by an independent research body provides alternative views. This chapter raises methodological problems with the governmental opinion polls, and highlights the divergence between the public's and the state's official approach on capital punishment.

M. Obara-Minnitt, *Japanese Moratorium on the Death Penalty*,
DOI 10.1057/978-1-137-55822-0_3

Secondly, it clarifies the limited role that culture plays in capital punishment policy in Japan. After briefly reviewing theoretical research into the role of culture in rejecting particular international norms and in shaping legal punishment, it critically examines the application of a cultural value to justification of capital punishment. A former Minister of Justice, Moriyama Mayumi, claims that capital punishment is deeply embedded in the Japanese view of guilt. She invokes the example of a concept, *shinde wabiru*, which means atonement for one's crime or shameful behaviour by killing oneself;[1] and other Ministers of Justice such as Okuno Seisuke and Goto Masao also proclaim the same idea.[2] However, this section discusses the conceptual and methodological problem in application of this concept to capital punishment policy, highlighting the divergence between pro- and anti-death-penalty victim lobbies in their views on social justice.

Thirdly, it explores where public resistance to the abolition norm stems from. After investigating Japanese people's human rights and legal consciousness, it provides evidence that public resistance does not appear to stem from cultural features but from a lack of sympathy towards the activities of domestic anti-death-penalty groups. Through examining domestic and cultural factors comprehensively, this section illustrates that although there appears to exist a social norm that treats death as a price worth paying for serious crimes, decisions regarding capital punishment policy are made by selected elites independently of cultural factors. This is followed by a critical evaluation of the existing hypotheses about the government's retention of the system. It addresses the issue that existing approach to Japan's capital punishment policy tends to consider less relevant domestic or international factors without acknowledging the elite-driven nature of the system.

Finally, the second section of the chapter proposes a better approach to investigating the *de facto* moratorium periods in Japan. The existing literature places excessive emphasis on the causal relationship between the personal convictions of Ministers of Justice, or contemporary domestic or international events, and non-execution of people condemned to death; and it tends to overlook how consistently the Ministry of Justice has tried to justify the system during the moratorium periods. This section clarifies the point that investigation of these periods from the appropriate standpoint can provide a better understanding of the elite-driven capital punishment policy in Japan.

3.2 'Public Opinion' of the Capital Punishment System

The Japanese government frequently cites public opinion poll results to justify the capital punishment system. According to the results, 80.3 per cent of the Japanese public supported the system in 2014 and 85.6 per cent in 2009, with 57.7 per cent and 62.3 per cent respectively believing in its deterrent effect (see Appendix B). A former Minister of Justice, Ogawa Toshio (13 January 2012–4 June 2012), has claimed the voices of lay assessors in *saiban-in seido* to be 'public opinion'. In the Legal Affairs Committee on 28 March 2012, Ogawa stated that death sentences which have been imposed in *saiban-in seido* since its introduction in May 2009 demonstrate that lay assessors have been supporting the death penalty.[3] Thus, he tried to strategically incorporate the voices of lay assessors, who imposed death sentences, as 'public opinion', as if Ministers' refusal to authorise executions would go against 'the conclusion that ordinary citizens drew after going through the agony (of judging whether a person should live or die)'.[4]

Whilst the Japanese government claims that the majority of the Japanese public supports capital punishment, believing in its preventive effect, mainly through the results of the opinion polls, it does not provide any other data to underpin the claim. The following section provides an alternative view on the public opinion of capital punishment through examining the existing literature on the deterrent effect and analysing opinion polls conducted by governmental and non-governmental bodies.

3.2.1 *The Deterrent Effect of Capital Punishment*

The deterrent effect of capital punishment has been denied by various international scholars.[5] However, the debate is still open ended in Japan, and findings by Western scholars—in which some of the target periods date back to the 1920s—are still largely cited in the Japanese literature on comparative criminology. Torsten Sellin conducted a comparative analysis on homicide rates in US states with and without capital punishment from 1920 to 1958. According to the results, the homicide death rates trend was similar regardless of the availability of capital punishment.[6] On the other hand, Isaac Ehrlich and Gary S. Becker (1972),[7] Isaac Ehrlich (1973;1975),[8] Joanna Shepherd (2002),[9] and Hashem Dezhbakhsh and Paul Rubin (2003),[10] proclaim the deterrent effect of capital punishment.

In particular, Ehrlich challenged Sellin's findings by conducting similar research but with different methodology. He chose the target period of 1933–1969 and investigated the preventive effect of capital punishment, considering the role of social factors such as unemployment and per capita income.[11] Ehrlich claimed that a slightly negative relationship was observed between the execution rate and the murder rate.

In Japan, major scholars who deny the deterrent effect are Masaki Akira (1964; 1968)[12] and Tamiya Yu (2000).[13] For example, Masaki, a former Director-General of the Correction Bureau in the Ministry of Justice and a public prosecutor, calls the belief in the deterrent effect of capital punishment a superstition, and criticises the government's justification for the system through the example of the Second World War.[14] According to Masaki, prison guards' execution of death row inmates upon the order of the state authority is no different from wartime when state killing was justified: since Japan renounced war, it should also renounce the death penalty.[15] Meanwhile, others proclaim the preventive effect of capital punishment: Motoji Shinkuma (1939),[16] Ono Sei-ichiro (1950),[17] and Uematsu Tadashi (1958).[18] For example, Uematsu questions the credibility of the existing research on the correlation between the abolition of capital punishment and the decrease or non-increase in serious crimes. He argues that it is natural that no increase in serious crimes is observed right after the abolition of capital punishment, since the system is usually abolished when the crime rate is fairly low.[19]

Whilst there appears, therefore, to exist a fair amount of literature on the deterrent effect of capital punishment, two main concerns remain about the arguments made by proponents of the death penalty in Japan. It is not appropriate for Japanese scholars to try to apply decades-old Western findings to the contemporary Japanese context, as without empirical data collected in modern Japan, foreign research findings are not necessarily a sound evidence based upon which to proclaim the deterrent effect of Japan's capital punishment system.

The second concern is that most of the Japanese scholars who evaluate the deterrent effect of capital punishment tend to develop their arguments by focusing on its psychological effect without empirical data to underpin their claims. Proponents tend to claim that human fear of losing life has been constraining people from committing serious crimes,[20] but what makes their work appear unreliable is that some offenders commit crimes because they do not fear death.[21] In fact, Takuma Mamoru, who murdered eight pupils and wounded 15 others at Osaka Kyoiku University

Ikeda Elementary School on 8 June 2001, is reported to have declared that 'it is such a shame that I murdered *only* eight people. I should have murdered more if I get executed through capital punishment in any way'; and 'I wanted to be executed through capital punishment. I want to die sooner'.[22] Given that there are case examples, albeit rare ones, where the existence of capital punishment has been a motivating factor for people to commit serious crimes, the credibility of the deterrent effect of capital punishment is doubtful.

Although there is no systematic empirical research into the deterrent effect of the capital punishment system in Japan, governmental opinion polling indicates that the majority of the Japanese public believes in the deterrent effect. The question posed in the opinion poll was 'What do you think about the argument that serious crimes would increase or remain unchanged if capital punishment is abolished?', and 57.7 per cent and 62.3 per cent of the respondents answered that 'Crimes would increase', in 2014 and 2009 respectively (see Appendix B). Having said that, it is highly problematic that what the general public—most of whom are not experts in criminology or do not have basic knowledge of the capital punishment system—answered in the opinion poll has been used by government officials as a solid foundation to claim the preventive effect of capital punishment. The next section further investigates how the Japanese government shapes 'public opinion' in order to make its policy look democratic and legitimate.

3.2.2 Public Opinion on Capital Punishment Reconsidered

When capital punishment was declared constitutional by the Supreme Court of Japan on 12 March 1948, supplementary opinions about the role of public opinion with regard to the capital punishment system were provided by four judges: Shima Tamotsu, Fujita Hachiro, Iwamatsu Saburo and Kawamura Matasuke. According to them:

> The judgment of whether certain punishments are cruel is a question that should be decided *according to the feelings of the people* [..., and] what at one time may be regarded as not being a cruel punishment may at a later period be judged the reverse. In such a situation the interpretation of Article 31 of the Constitution will probably be limited as a matter of course and the death penalty will be eliminated as a cruel punishment which contravenes the Constitution.[23]

Supplementary opinions appear to allow public feelings to be a determining factor in discussing the cruelty of capital punishment in Japan. It may appear that capital punishment policy reflects public opinion, which is 'the prime mover in democracies'.[24] However, it is questionable whether the level of cruelty in punishment can be left to emotional argument by 'the man in the street',[25] who does not necessarily have sufficient knowledge in the area of crime and punishment. Furthermore, whilst the climate of public opinion on the capital punishment system in general can be found in the opinion polls, the credibility of findings regarding 'public opinion' needs re-evaluation before these findings can be considered as a crucial source of justification for capital punishment.

Although public support for capital punishment has been consistently high over a number of years, 'these are temperatures taken in a climate of death penalty secrecy and "censored democracy"'.[26] This support cannot be a major determinant in shaping capital punishment policy when the public are not fully informed about the system or the degree of the deterrent effect. As David T. Johnson and Franklin E. Zimring claim, 'If transparency and accountability are two hallmarks of a healthy democracy, then the secrecy and silence that surround capital punishment in Japan seem decidedly undemocratic'.[27] Public opinion can be influenced by governmental behaviour. As Sangmin Bae argues, '[p]olicy changes precede opinion changes, suggesting that the former cause the latter rather than vice versa'.[28] In order to explore how 'public opinion' is shaped and used for governmental justification of capital punishment, the following section examines public opinion polls conducted by the Prime Minister's Office and non-governmental agencies. Through examining the methodological problems in framing governmental opinion polls and comparing their results with those of polls conducted by non-governmental agencies, it will highlight the divergence between the public's and the state's approach to the capital punishment question.

3.2.2.1 'Public Opinion' in Governmental Opinion Polls

Since 1956, the Prime Minister's Office has been conducting *Kihonteki Hōseido ni Kansuru Yoron Chōsa* (Opinion Poll on Basic Legal System), every five years since 1994, surveying 3000 men and women aged 20 or older nationwide. The result in 2009 revealed that public support for capital punishment reached 85.6 per cent, the highest percentage ever, compared with 80.3 per cent in 2014, 81.4 per cent in 2004, 79.3 per cent in 1999 and 73.8 per cent in 1994.[29] Whilst these results appear to demonstrate strong public support for capital punishment, examination of the questions posed leaves room for doubt. In seeking public opinion, the poll required participants to choose between three choices: (1) 'it is unavoidable *in certain circumstances*', (2) 'it should be abolished *in all circumstances*' and (3) 'I do not know.' The results in 2014 were 80.3 per cent, 9.7 per cent and 9.9 per cent respectively; and the results in 2009 were 85.6 per cent, 5.7 per cent and 8.6 per cent respectively (see Appendix B). As Sato Mai analyses,[30] the first two answers appear to have been framed strategically in order to produce results which would justify governmental policy. In contrast to the second answer, the first one leaves some room for discussion regarding the level of public support for capital punishment. In other words, those who do not necessarily feel strong support for capital punishment may choose the first answer.[31]

Similarly, methodological problems in framing questions in public polls have also been pointed out by anti-death-penalty Diet members. For example, in the Legal Affairs Committee on 9 August 2000, Fukushima Mizuho, deputy leader of the Social Democratic Party, claimed that phrases used in the governmental opinion polls are heavily biased.[32] However, the then Minister of Justice, Yasuoka Okiharu, maintained the validity of the survey, and no change to the phrasing of the questions is planned. According to Yasuoka,

> the second answer that 'capital punishment should be abolished in all circumstances' exists as one of the opinions in the existing debate regarding this system. In order to grasp public opinion accurately, it is not necessarily inappropriate to set such answer.[33]

Nonetheless, if the Japanese government desires to grasp public opinion on the issue of capital punishment accurately, what is required is not 'for or against' types of questions or answers. Instead, attention needs to be paid to what degree of knowledge the Japanese public possess on the issue of capital punishment, and what factors can influence their opinion. For example, if the details of detention conditions and execution procedure are provided, or if miscarriage of justice cases are presented as an example of the downside of the capital punishment system, it would presumably generate different results.[34] Prevailing crime situations can heavily influence public opinion. If the survey dates are close to notable crimes or trials, it may make the public hesitant or resistant to choose the second answer.

Furthermore, the preconceived notion from the results of the governmental opinion polls that 'the majority of the Japanese public support capital punishment' may hinder respondents from going against the 'mainstream'. For example, results of the other questions in the same opinion poll appear to show the public's tendency to stick to the societal norms that they are familiar with. With regard to the second question, 'In case of abolishing capital punishment, which do you think is better?', the results were: 'abolish it straight away', 35.1 per cent; 'decrease the number of the use of capital punishment first', 63.1 per cent; and 'I do not know', 1.8 per cent (see Appendix B). Regarding the third question, 'Do you think Japan should not abolish capital punishment in the future; or can abolish the system when the situation changes?', the results were: 'Japan should not abolish the system', 60.8 per cent; 'Japan can abolish the system in the future', 34.2 per cent; and 'I do not know', 5.0 per cent (see Appendix B).

The public tendency to follow what is considered mainstream in society is not necessarily unique to the Japanese public. As Walter Lippmann argues, 'when a system of stereotypes is well fixed, our attention is called to those facts which support it, and diverted from those which contradict'.[35] When the governmental opinion polls show an increasing percentage of public support for capital punishment, it may make the abolitionists seem a tiny fraction of the public, which could affect public views on the existing legal system. 'Public opinion' can fluctuate depending on people's level of knowledge of the capital punishment system, the proximity of the survey dates to certain incidents and semi-established moods or ideas on the issue questioned.[36] In order to demonstrate the diversity in public opinion on the capital punishment system in Japan, the next section introduces the results of opinion polls conducted by newspapers and TV services, and an individual research group.

3.2.2.2 'Public Opinion' in Non-Governmental Opinion Polls

In opinion polls conducted by the *Yomiuri* newspaper in 1993, 1998 and 2006, surveying 3000 men and women aged 20 or older nationwide, respondents were asked for their opinion on the abolition or retention of capital punishment. The results in 2006 were: (1) It should be retained, 56.9 per cent; (2) I would rather think that it should be retained, 23.5 per cent; (3) I would rather think that it should be abolished, 9.3 per cent; (4) It should be abolished, 5.3 per cent; and (5) I would rather not answer, 5.0 per cent (see Appendix D). What makes this survey distinct from governmental opinion polls is that choices include neutral answers which start with 'I would rather think'. The Japanese public tend to answer that they 'feel neutral' or 'do not know' when they are asked about likes or dislikes concerning political matters,[37] and the survey appears to have been framed to allow some ambiguity in their answers. Having said that, those who support retention outnumbered the other choices in 2008, since the question itself was straightforward.

Whilst the survey conducted by *Yomiuri* did not investigate in what circumstances respondents would consider abolition, two other opinion polls presented the option of life imprisonment without parole as an alternative penalty to capital punishment. According to the results of the opinion poll conducted by the Japan Broadcasting Corporation (NHK) in 1994, surveying 1800 men and women aged 20 or older nationwide, 62.8 per cent of the respondents answered that the capital punishment system was necessary in Japan (see Appendix E). In the meantime, the second question, about the option of introducing life imprisonment without parole as an alternative to capital punishment, revealed that 40.5 per cent agreed whilst a slightly larger number of respondents, 42.9 per cent, called for the retention of capital punishment. Furthermore, in answer to the final question, 'Do you agree with the idea that we put executions on hold and discuss the issue of capital punishment fundamentally?', 37.6 per cent agreed whilst 28.9 per cent disagreed. Although the result of the first question tends to be primarily used by proponents in order to justify capital punishment policy, a second look at the rest of the results in this survey indicates a different perspective on the issue.

Another opinion poll was conducted by the anti-death-penalty *Asahi* newspaper in 1994, asking 509 members of the House of Representatives their views on capital punishment. *Asahi* offered five choices from which respondents chose: (1) It should be abolished right now (8.4 per cent); (2) It should be abolished with introduction of an alternative punishment such as life imprisonment without parole (19.6 per cent); (3) Executions should be put on hold and debate should be spurred meanwhile (19.2 per cent); (4) It should be as it is right now (40.2 per cent); and (5) Others/I do not know (12.6 per cent) (see Appendix F). Although 40.2 per cent of the respondents answered that the capital punishment system should be retained, it deserves some attention that 19.6 per cent showed support for the introduction of alternative punishment.

Opinion polls conducted by non-governmental bodies did not necessarily show a strikingly different result from the governmental one. The survey conducted by *Yomiuri* in 2006 showed 56.9 per cent public support for retention of the capital punishment system, and the NHK observed 62.8 per cent support in 1994. However, analysis of the other questions and answers can provide alternative views of public opinion of capital punishment in Japan. Whilst the governmental opinion poll tends to suggest that a vast majority of the Japanese public supports capital punishment, polls conducted by non-governmental bodies show that the public are not necessarily resistant to the idea of applying an alternative penalty to capital punishment or setting a moratorium period while discussing the future of the system (see Appendix F). This illustrates the fact that public opinion can vary depending on how questions are phrased and answers are set, and that it is also susceptible to the prevailing public mood.

3.2.2.3 'Public Opinion' Under the Secretive Policy of the Ministry of Justice

Finally, for a better analysis of the level of public understanding of the capital punishment system in Japan, findings of an in-depth survey conducted by the Japan–UK Deliberative Public Consultation Project are worthy of exploration. This project was organised by Mike Hough, Honjo Takeshi, Kimura Masato and Sato Mai, and it aims to examine the Japanese public's level of knowledge of the criminal justice system.[38] In 2009, the project team conducted a deliberative survey of 50 men and women aged between 20 and 58 who live in the Tokyo metropolitan area (Tokyo, Kanagawa, Chiba and Saitama). The purpose of the survey was to investigate how the capital punishment system has been construed by the Japanese public and to evaluate their level of knowledge, at the time of the introduction of *saiban-in seido* from 21 May 2009 in Japan.[39] Participants in the deliberative survey followed five main procedures:

(1) A survey was conducted among the participants online in order to examine their attitudes towards capital punishment;
(2) A leaflet was delivered shortly afterwards to the participants, including detailed information on the capital punishment system;
(3) Deliberative consultation on 4 April 2009 at Waseda University in Tokyo. It included a session to provide information about the system, two group discussions, and debate and Q&A sessions by guest speakers (both retentionists and abolitionists);
(4) A post-deliberation survey was conducted straight after the previous procedure in order to assess changes in attitudes towards the system; and
(5) Follow-up telephone interviews were conducted among ten participants who changed their views after the deliberative consultation.[40]

Some key findings from this survey are that: (1) 40 per cent of the participants' attitudes towards capital punishment were changed through the provision of information on the system, from retentionists to abolitionists and vice versa; and (2) participants stated that little information regarding capital punishment has been disclosed in Japan, and that they were not aware of its problematic nature before the deliberative consultation was conducted.[41] As briefly discussed in the Introduction, Japan's capital punishment policy is characterised by confidentiality and secrecy, and the general public appears to have been supporting the system without sufficient knowledge. According to Johnson:[42]

> Capital punishment in the United States has become increasingly hidden, privatized, and bureaucratized over the last 150 years, but the secrecy and silence that shroud Japan's death penalty are taken to extremes not seen in other nations.

As discussed briefly in Chap. 2, it was only from November 1998 that the Ministry of Justice started to disclose when executions took place and of how many convicts, and only from November 2007 that the names of those executed started to be disclosed. Until then, it was anti-death-penalty NGOs that were reporting the names of the executed through their own investigations. What is more, as previously mentioned, Japan does not usually conduct executions during parliamentary sessions or public and political holidays, with some exceptions.[43] These are the times when the Japanese public are distracted or anti-death-penalty Diet members or NGO members have difficulty voicing dissent.[44] This secretive policy in Japan is strikingly different from another retentionist country, the USA. Mori gives the example of the North Carolina Department of Correction: all the information about death row inmates is disclosed on its official website, including a convict's face, full name, age, race and date of sentence of death.[45] Whilst capital punishment policy is thus 'accessible' to the public there, it is largely hidden in Japan under the name of 'protect[ing] the "honor and privacy" of the offender's family'.[46]

From the opinion polls conducted by both governmental and non-governmental bodies and an in-depth survey by an independent research body, several findings must be noted for a better understanding of public opinion regarding capital punishment in Japan. Public and Diet members' support for the retention of capital punishment do not necessarily stem from enthusiastic support for the system. Rather, they appear to come from: (1) their aversion to a change in existing criminal justice, which they believe to have a deterrent effect; (2) a lack of options for discussing alternative penalties to capital punishment in the governmental opinion poll; and (3) a lack of knowledge of the capital punishment system. In fact, although results in the non-governmental opinion polls did not show a strikingly opposite view to that shown in the governmental opinion polls, it showed a variation when life imprisonment without parole was put forward as an alternative penalty. In other words, although the Japanese public tend to follow the existing mood and support the existing legal system, they do not necessarily strongly oppose the idea of halting executions to discuss the issue of capital punishment in detail. It appears that there are two important factors that have been hindering this discussion from gaining root in Japan: the bureaucratic decision-making, which puts emphasis on precedent, and ethical concerns about life imprisonment.

The capital punishment system has been justified as a legal penalty on the basis of: (1) Article 31 of the Constitution of Japan, which allows a legal punishment to deprive a person of life or liberty exceptionally; (2) Article 11 of the Penal Code, which specifies the execution method as hanging; (3) the Penal Code and the Nagayama Criteria, which specify crimes that are considered suitable for capital punishment according to nine main criteria; and (4) Articles 475 and 476 of the Code of Criminal Procedure, which stipulate the responsibility of Ministers of Justice regarding the timing of authorising and conducting executions. Whether the Ministry of Justice halts executions officially, abolishes the capital punishment system or installs an alternative penalty, it requires repealing or amending these existing legal provisions. Given that the bureaucrats endeavour to act on precedent, it is unlikely that they would initiate all the necessary legal changes.

Some disagreement can be observed within the anti-death-penalty lobby and among death row inmates regarding the option of introducing life imprisonment. For example, the Japan Federation of Bar Associations and Forum 90, the largest anti-death-penalty NGO in Japan, have been supporting the idea of introducing life imprisonment without parole as an alternative to capital punishment.[47] The Japan Federation of Bar Associations passed a resolution calling on the Japanese government to this effect in August 2012.[48] Both organisations acknowledge that the general public will not support the immediate abolition of capital punishment, believing in the myth that the system deters crimes. Therefore, these bodies claim that introducing a penalty that entails an equivalent amount of suffering can be a compromise and a firm step towards the abolition of capital punishment.[49]

By contrast, some NGOs such as the Centre for Prisoners' Rights do not support the introduction of alternative punishment as a temporary solution. Their argument is that: (1) imprisoning prisoners for life can be more cruel than capital punishment, since it deprives them of any chance to get rehabilitated and go back to society; and (2) it is not ethically right to impose another punishment in order to abolish capital punishment.[50] Furthermore, according to Fukushima Mizuho, deputy leader of the Social Democratic Party, who conducted surveys among death row inmates on this issue in 2012, opinions also vary amongst death row inmates. For example, one of their number, Kaneiwa Yukio, supports the introduction of life imprisonment without parole since it will relieve him from fearing every morning that the prison guard will stop at his door for the execution;[51] but another inmate, Okamoto Keizo, claims that such a penalty is more cruel as it will deprive inmates of a purpose to live.[52] Although the Japanese public are not necessarily resistant to an alternative penalty to capital punishment, the bureaucratic decision-making system and internal disagreement within the anti-death-penalty lobby appear to have been preventing constructive discussion of the subject.

This section has compared public opinion that is reflected in governmental and non-governmental opinion polls. Although great attention tends to be paid to the percentages of answers given by respondents, it is important to recognise with what intentions the questions and choices were framed, with what degree of knowledge the public chose particular answers, and the social incidents and atmosphere that can influence the results of the opinion polls. In order to measure public opinion accurately, it is necessary for the bodies conducting polls to add sufficient information about the capital punishment system and alternative punishments. However, the Japanese government has maintained that questions or answers in this survey are not biased, and no change has been made to date. It is very important to acknowledge the fact that public opinion has been shaped strategically and used as a primary source for justification of capital punishment policy, even though it can fluctuate depending on the phrases used and the timing of the survey.

The following section examines the validity of the government's justification for capital punishment with reference to Japanese culture.

3.3 Japanese Culture and the Capital Punishment System

Since capital punishment deprives people of their right to life, it cannot be simply justified as a domestic cultural manifestation or by reference to national sovereignty. Nonetheless, Japanese culture is another factor primarily cited by pro-death-penalty Ministers of Justice in order to make the policy appear to be culturally determined and to deter international pressures. First of all, a former Minister of Justice, Hatoyama Kunio, contends that capital punishment is an indigenous system deeply rooted in Japan's own history and culture.[53] Similarly, at the seminar 'Judiciary and Human Rights in Countries that Hold Observer Status with the Council of Europe', held on 28–29 May 2002, Moriyama Mayumi claimed that capital punishment is deeply embedded in the Japanese view of guilt, represented by a concept, *shinde wabiru*, meaning atonement for one's crime or shameful behaviour by killing oneself.[54] Related to this concept, the Japanese government claims that capital punishment functions as victim satisfaction. Government officials frequently use the phrase 'respecting the feelings of the victims' bereaved families' (*higaisha kanjō wo kōryo shite*), and cite a pro-death-penalty victim lobby's claim that it is a 'responsibility' for murderers to atone for crimes through death.[55] Furthermore, Sakata Michita argues that the Japanese culture of punishment and guilt developed over 2000 years as an introspective island nation without Western influence means compliance with international norms on abolition is not seen as high priority.[56] He argues therefore that outside parties should have no say.

The second section of this chapter critically examines the role that culture plays in the elite-driven capital punishment policy in Japan. It briefly reviews the existing theoretical research into the state's rejection of international norms for cultural reasons, and the relationship between legal punishment and culture. It then investigates Moriyama's claim that the concept of *shinde wabiru* has been widely accepted as a social norm and supports the retention of capital punishment. After recalling an actual occasion when an act of *shinde wabiru* was committed in Japan, it presents conceptual and methodological problems regarding the application of this cultural value to the justification of capital punishment. It also examines the divergence between pro- and anti-death-penalty victim lobbies in their views of this concept.

Finally, it clarifies where public resistance to the abolition norm stems from. It critically investigates the degree to which Japanese consciousness of human rights and legal questions has been contributing to shape the public pro-death-penalty sentiment or resistance to the abolition of capital punishment. Presenting the characteristics of the largest anti-death-penalty NGO in Japan, Forum 90, it argues that public resistance does not appear to stem from cultural features but from a lack of sympathy towards the activities of domestic anti-death-penalty groups.

3.3.1 Culture and Legal Punishment

Normative theory tries to offer a way of examining the state's reluctance to adhere to international norms, or 'collective expectations about proper behavior for a given identity'.[57] A national attachment to a competing norm and cultural factors have been raised as influential variables in this dynamic,[58] and some scholars find it useful to apply this framework to the state's non-compliance with the anti-death-penalty norm.[59] However, a fundamental question concerning the extent to which capital punishment policy is culturally determined in Japan has been overlooked in the theoretical approach. In order to investigate the degree to which a normative theory would help understand Japan's resistance to abolitionism, this section first introduces the mechanism through which international norms are transmitted to the domestic arena.

Thomas Risse and Kathryn Sikkink present step-by-step procedures of norm socialisation:[60] (1) processes of adaptation and strategic bargaining; (2) processes of moral consciousness-raising, shaming,[61] argumentation, dialogue and persuasion; and (3) processes of institutionalisation and habitualisation. These procedures can be explained in more detail with a 'life cycle' of norm transplantation that Martha Finnemore and Kathryn Sikkink present: norm emergence, norm cascades and norm internalisation. In the first stage, norm entrepreneurs/leaders—international organisations, transnational advocacy networks or NGOs and domestic elites—attempt to socialise other states so that they become norm followers/takers.[62] This is based on the assumption that the state's compliance with a norm depends on the domestic mobilisation of actors who socialise states to adhere to new norms and values.[63]

Norms then cascade in the second stage with 'a combination of pressure for conformity, a desire to enhance international legitimation, and the desire of state leaders to enhance their self-esteem'.[64] Although 'international society is a smaller group than the total number of states in the international system',[65] the embarrassment of not belonging to it and their desire to obtain a 'social proof' as a legitimate member of it are supposed to make states consider the acceptance of norms.[66] In other words, '[s]tates may obey international norms because doing so is right and moral, helps to shape and maintain an ordered international environment, and gains them respect in the eyes of the world'.[67] Finally, norm internalisation occurs when norms acquire a taken-for-granted quality that does not require a broad domestic debate, such as norms relating to women's voting rights and slavery.[68]

With regard to the denial of international norms in the domestic arena, Andrew P. Cortell and James W. Davis argue that it is not necessarily the case 'in advanced industrial democracies with a history of national attachment to a competing norm [...since] powerful states have strong material incentives to reject international norms'.[69] For example, Jeffery Checkel argues that diffusion is more rapid and smooth when a 'cultural match' exists to a great extent, which varies from positive (+), null (0) to negative (−), indicating a degree of congruence between international and domestic norms.[70] Under this assumption, '[i]nternational norms are more likely to have an impact if they resonate with established cultural understandings, historical experience, and the dominant views of domestic groups'.[71] Finally, Risse and Sikkink point out 'that denial of the norm almost never takes place in the form of open rejection of human rights, but is mostly expressed in terms of reference to an allegedly more valid international norm, in this case national sovereignty'.[72]

Normative explanation from cultural perspectives may appear useful when examining Japan's resistance to some international norms. For example, the anti-nuclear-proliferation norm is an example of a positive cultural match. Since the end of the Second World War, Japan has been preserving three main non-nuclear principles: not to make such weapons; not to possess them; and not to bring them into Japan.[73] As another example, the anti-whaling norm can be cited as a typical example of a negative cultural match between meat-eating and fish-eating countries.[74] Similarly, Japan's non-compliance with the anti-death-penalty norm may appear at first sight to be due to a cultural difference. The government tends to claim that this issue should be left to the national criminal justice system, the climate of public opinion and Japanese cultural assumptions regarding death and guilt. However, what is overlooked is that the issue of capital punishment is primarily elite-driven in Japan, and important decisions are made by policy elites irrespective of domestic or cultural factors.

As Sato argues, 'public opinion' can fluctuate depending on (1) people's level of knowledge of the capital punishment system, (2) the proximity of the survey dates to certain incidents and (3) semi-established moods or ideas on the issue questioned.[75] Furthermore, it is important to note that all these factors appear to have been influenced by the governmental approach to this issue. As already discussed, the secretive policy by the Ministry of Justice does not allow the public to have a correct understanding of the capital punishment system, and governmental opinion polls appear to have been strategically phrased in order to generate certain answers so that capital punishment is justified. 'Strong public support of capital punishment', which is generated from the governmental opinion poll results, can also affect respondents as a semi-established view.[76] Given that it is elite culture that precedes mass culture, it is inappropriate to assume that Japan's non-compliance with the anti-death-penalty norm has been driven by the climate of public opinion or the general public's cultural views about death and life.

Governmental justification of capital punishment on domestic and cultural grounds appears to have the intention of deterring external pressures by portraying them as an illegitimate intervention in internal affairs. Thus, normative theory from cultural perspectives does not fully account for the actual dynamic regarding Japan's capital punishment policy. Rather, more attention needs to be paid to Japan's institutional structure, where capital punishment policy is treated as an issue of law and order, and pressures from human rights perspectives are resisted.

Furthermore, David Garland's view of the influence of culture in shaping penal regulations and institutions should be noted:

> Penal laws and institutions are always proposed, discussed, legislated, and operated within definite cultural codes. They are framed in languages, discourses, and sign systems which embody specific cultural meanings, distinctions, and sentiments, and which must be interpreted and understood if the social meaning and motivations of punishment are to become intelligible.[77]

Since Garland contends that cultural sentiments can frame punishment, the capital punishment system may appear to be embedded in Japanese culture. However, the 'culture' associated with Japan's capital punishment system is not necessarily that of the general public. Rather, it is a routinely held institutional culture of the Ministry of Justice, which has been encouraging death row inmates to resign themselves to the inevitable,[78] and helping prison guards conduct executions in a smooth, efficient and uneventful manner away from public scrutiny. The following section reconsiders the validity of the governmental justification for capital punishment on the basis of Japanese culture, and argues that cultural sentiment among the general public is an independent variable in this system.

3.3.2 Capital Punishment as Social Justice and Victim Satisfaction Reconsidered

As noted above, a former Minister of Justice, Moriyama Mayumi, claims that capital punishment is deeply embedded in the Japanese view on guilt, represented by the concept *shinde wabiru*. This section examines whether or not such a social norm exists in Japanese civil society with an overwhelming public consensus, and whether the general public and the victim lobby believe that capital punishment functions as victim satisfaction. It recalls the actual occasion when an act of *shinde wabiru* was carried out in Japan, and the Japanese view of criminals relating to this concept. It then raises conceptual and methodological problems involved in the application of this concept to the capital punishment system, and also presents divergence within the victim lobby on how criminals should atone for their crimes.

3.3.2.1 The Social Norm of Atonement through Death, 'Shinde Wabiru'

General Nogi Maresuke and his wife committed *seppuku* following the state funeral of Emperor Meiji in 1912. His suicide note revealed that it was *junshi*—to commit *seppuku* upon the death of the lord—in order to expiate his disgrace in two main events: the Satsuma Rebellion in 1877, in which he lost the imperial banner to the enemy, and the devastating result of the Russo-Japanese War in 1904–1905 where 56,000 lives were lost, including his two sons. In the latter event in particular, although General Nogi was first stationed at Port Arthur with approximately 90,000 soldiers, the Commander in Chief, Oyama Iwao, sensed that defeat was imminent under Nogi's leadership. Therefore, Oyama appointed Kodama Gentaro as the Chief of General Staff of the Manchuria Army at the end of November 1904 instead.[79]

Since this decision was not announced to the public, Nogi was celebrated as a national hero following Japan's victory.[80] He took this as an undeserved honour, and a sense of shame made him plead that he deserved death on each occasion when he was granted an audience with the Emperor, and in his meetings with the major.[81] However, his death was not permitted since they both knew that Nogi genuinely meant to atone for his disgrace, and Emperor Meiji told him to live at least until his (the Emperor's) death.[82] On the day of the state funeral of Emperor Meiji in 1912, Nogi committed *seppuku* with his wife in order to atone for his disgrace.

Nogi's case drew a great deal of worldwide scholarly attention to the *seppuku* ritual; and this cultural value, *shinde wabiru*, may appear to still be accepted as a social norm in the contemporary era, relating to the Japanese view of criminals or death row inmates. For example, Komiya Nobuo claims that 'Japan is not a heaven for offenders in terms of rehabilitation because the reintegrative function of Japanese society is limited'.[83] According to Komiya, self-discipline is the virtue admired in Japan, and this has been a key factor not only in maintaining Japan's exceptionally low crime rate but also in 'expelling' criminals from society.[84] For example, schools in Japan are often inhospitable to original or critical thinkers since group harmony is highly stressed, and pupils learn to 'restrain selfish behaviour through various small group activities [...and to] continuously monitor[...] one another's behaviour within the group'.[85] Fearing 'deprivation of membership', pupils become submissive to authority, and this surveillance system also works in society after they grow up. In the meantime, 'one who neglects [...this repressive rule] is likely to be labelled as a social misfit and gradually excluded from one's group'.[86] In other words, whilst self-control makes the group members' bond stronger and contributes to the building of a crime-free society, once they become criminals it is less likely for them and their families to be integrated back into society.

These 'exclusive' attitudes of the public to offenders may imply that the Japanese public appreciates a social norm of *shinde wabiru* to some extent. However, three main concerns are aroused by Moriyama's claim that the capital punishment system has been underpinned by this Japanese concept in the modern period. The *seppuku* ritual is a particular historical and political event linked with a particular set of sociological phenomena, and Nogi's case was also a symbolic suicide, which aimed at appealing to the public in a traditional *samurai* spirit,[87] a sentiment not common amongst the contemporary Japanese public. In the contemporary context it has been overlooked by the Ministry of Justice, the pro-death-penalty lobby and the general public that spontaneity is required when an act of *shinde wabiru* is expected. The action is considered meaningful only when it is committed by people on their own initiative after a feeling of remorse has been generated from the bottom of their hearts.[88] If it is conducted on the state's authority on a date that the ministry bureaucrats chooses for their convenience, it is a mere state killing.

One should note that the existence of another Japanese proverb, '*tsumi wo urande hito wo uramazu*' (condemn the crime rather than the criminal), has been ignored in the governmental justification for capital punishment. If the government proclaims that capital punishment is deeply embedded in Japanese culture, it also needs to account for that proverb, contrasting to *shinde wabiru*. The following section further investigates this issue and introduces arguments by both pro- and anti-death-penalty victim lobbies. It summarises the main claims from both lobbies about how criminals should atone for their crimes, and critically examines how frequently the concept of *shinde wabiru* can be found in death sentences or the popular media as a widely accepted social norm.

3.3.2.2 The Pro-Death-Penalty Victim Lobby

In relation to this concept, it is also important to examine the pro-death-penalty lobby's claim that only capital punishment can bring social justice to the bereaved families. The Hikari case was a high-profile murder incident where the victims' bereaved family proclaimed such an opinion. On 14 April 1999, an 18-year-old male broke into a house in Hikari city in Yamaguchi prefecture. The offender, whose name was withheld until 2012,[89] since he was a minor at the time of the crime, raped and strangled a 23-year-old woman and strangled her baby daughter. What made this case distinct from other juvenile crimes was that: (1) Motomura Hiroshi, husband and father of the victims, called for the death sentence vocally; and (2) Yasuda Yoshihiro, an anti-death-penalty lobby activist and defence attorney for Asahara Shoko, leader of the Aum Shinrikyo responsible for the Aum gas attack on the Tokyo underground railway in 1995,[90] joined the defence team in the Hikari case from March 2006. The media coverage of these two helped to create a simplistic picture of a 'for or against' argument about capital punishment amongst the public. As Hamai and Ellis argue:

> Motomura had a very charismatic persona as the grieving husband and father that was well attuned to TV chat shows and tabloid styles of approach. In front of TV cameras and reporters, he has often produced emotional attacks on offenders and argued that he would kill the murderer in his own case, if he were released.[91]

Whilst Motomura's claim as a victim gained much sympathy from the public,[92] the argument of the defence team, which comprised 20 veteran attorneys including Yasuda, sounded poor and did not garner support from the public towards the offender. The team stressed that both victims died accidentally and that the offender even tried to revive both of them by raping the dead woman and leaving the dead baby in a cupboard so that *Doraemon*, a robotic cat *manga* character, could bring him back to life by using its powers.[93] The disclosure of the provocative letters which the offender wrote about the victims and Motomura also made the public doubt the credibility of the defence team's claim, and this murder case left an extremely negative image of the anti-death-penalty movement in Japan.[94] It was only the Broadcasting Ethics and Programme Improvement Organisation that vocally claimed that the excessive media coverage from the victims' perspective had been producing an unbalanced view of the case.[95]

The offender in the Hikari case was initially sentenced to life imprisonment, considering his age and the possibility that he could be rehabilitated. However, right before the ruling on 22 April 2008 when the offender was sentenced to capital punishment at the age of 27, Motomura stated that 'It's his responsibility to let society know about the consequences of killing someone'.[96] He implied that the death sentence passed on the offender could remind society that only capital punishment serves as social justice and can deter further serious crimes. On the other hand, Motomura's campaigns were not all about stirring up pro-death-penalty sentiment among the public. His appearance in the media appears to have helped to make other victims' bereaved families publicly visible, and brought several changes to the legal provisions.[97]

Cooperating with Okamura Isao, an attorney whose wife was murdered on 10 October 1997, Motomura established an NGO, *Zenkoku Higaisha no Kai* (The National Network for Victim Support), on 23 January 2000. Motomura spoke on behalf of victims' bereaved families who could not express their feelings openly, and the Basic Act on Crime Victims was enacted in order to protect their rights in November 2004. In the meantime, it appears that such victim-driven activism was also strategically used by the Public Prosecutor's Office to amend the Juvenile Law in November 2000 and May 2007. In particular, the amendment of the Juvenile Law in 2000 was the first since the Second World War,[98] and it lowered the minimum age for sending minors to reformatories from 16 to 14 in 2000 and from '14 to around 12 (in 2007), stirring concerns among lawyers and legal experts that tougher penalties might infringe on the rights of minors and might not lead to a reduction in juvenile delinquency'.[99] Harsher punishment of juvenile offenders was thus legalised as if it was influenced by the growing power of the victim lobby.

By contrast, when the Supreme Court rejected an appeal by the defendant and the death sentence was upheld on 20 February 2012, this appears to have put a brake on the pro-death-penalty mood in Japan. According to the judge, Kanetsuki Seiichi, 'Despite a severe sense of victimization by the bereaved family, sincere remorse is not seen as the defendant made irrational pleas', and the death sentence was inevitable.[100] Following this, an editorial in *Asahi* on 21 February 2012 posed an ethical question to the public, asking whether taking the life of one who had committed the crime as an 18-year-old boy was social justice and would bring happiness to Motomura:

> Death sentence was finalised to the defendant. However, if he had not reached the age 18 at the time of the crime, this court decision would not have been made. The decision was that *there is no other way than death for him to atone for the crime* even considering his immaturity and possibility of correction and rehabilitation. [...] Death sentence is challenging for the judges to give. A modern state, which aims to protect the individual life, deprives an individual of life under the name of law. This is the contradiction that anti-death penalty lobby claims.[101]

Asahi thus alarmed the public about the legal legitimacy issue regarding state killing. In fact, in contrast to Motomura, another victim lobbyist in a capital punishment case, Harada Masaharu, has been lecturing across the country proclaiming the importance of rehabilitation of offenders. The following section introduces an alternative voice to what the Japanese government cites as 'the feelings of victims' bereaved families'.

3.3.2.3 The Anti-Death-Penalty Victim Lobby

On 24 January 1983, Harada Akio, a 30-year-old truck driver, was killed in an incident that proved to be an insurance scam.[102] After Hasegawa was sentenced to death in two trials, he kept sending more than 100 letters to Harada Masaharu, the victim's brother, from death row; most of them were filled with words of apology and hope for the best for his family. He also sent some drawings; Hasegawa's self-portraits.[103] It was not until around 1986 that Harada finally started reading Hasegawa's letters, and he visited Hasegawa in the detention centre in 1993. Facing Hasegawa, who was apologising sincerely, Harada felt a sense of comfort and healing for the first time, if not forgiveness.[104] Harada also got to know that

Hasegawa's sister and son had committed suicide, as they were so ashamed that Hasegawa had been arrested. Harada began to believe that another unnatural death should be avoided, and that Hasegawa should compensate for his wrongdoings by living and by expressing remorse to Harada for the rest of his life.[105]

Since Hasegawa had already exhausted the appeals process and the death sentence had been finalised, on 18 April 2001 Harada handed a petition to the then Minister of Justice, Komura Masahiko, calling on him to halt Hasegawa's execution. Komura declared in front of a TV crew that Hasegawa's execution would not be authorised so soon.[106] However, despite Harada's pleas, Hasegawa was executed on 27 December 2001 under the authorisation of the next Minister of Justice, Moriyama Mayumi. Although the Japanese government often claims that capital punishment is carried out considering the feelings of the victims' families in Japan, Hasegawa was executed against Harada's feelings.

Because of this experience, Harada claims that executing offenders through capital punishment does not necessarily bring closure or satisfaction to the bereaved families.[107] Similarly, Katayama Tadaari, who lost his eight-year-old son in a traffic accident on 28 November 1997, has declared that:

> It should be realized that each bereaved family has different views [...,] and within a family the father, mother, or the victim's brothers and sisters have their own opinions. We cannot refer to 'victims' or 'bereaved families' in a lump. [...] I want to see a system where victims are fully supported financially and psychologically and they could have a venue for dialogue with offenders, who will return to society in the future, rather than feuding with each other.[108]

Harada describes crime victims as those who were pushed off a cliff by criminals, and the rest of the Japanese citizens as those who live peacefully on the cliff: the latter never say, 'Hang in there! We will lift you up!' but only shout from above, 'You must be hurt. We will also push the criminal off the cliff so you feel better.'[109] Harada claims that third parties usually seek to promote more severe punishment for the criminals without being aware of what they can really do to heal the bereaved families' mental wounds. Thus, there exists some divergence within the victim lobby on the ways in which criminals should atone for crimes. Whilst the government proclaims that capital punishment is deeply embedded in cultural values concerning death and life, and functions as victim satisfaction, some victim lobby campaigners do not share the same idea. It is only the voice of the pro-death-penalty victim lobby that is used as a primary source for the governmental justification of capital punishment. The following section explores how the media have been contributing to build 'public opinion on capital punishment'.

3.3.2.4 *The Influence of the Media in Shaping Pro-Death-Penalty Sentiment Amongst the Public*

At first glance, it appears that the media allow the public to make up their minds whether to support Motomura's vocal pro-death-penalty campaigns or Yasuda's anti-death-penalty campaigns. The media usually report only when an incident occurs, the offender is arrested and capital punishment is imposed on offenders. These reports, however, give only basic information, yet enough for the public to build up the myth that capital punishment is social justice, and to help develop public fear about abolition of the system. In comparison, the media infrequently feature detention conditions or details about the exact method of execution. As a result, it is difficult for the public to observe psychological changes in offenders' feelings towards the bereaved families or the crimes they committed, as the Harada case shows. The public have therefore supported capital punishment over years without being provided with sufficient information about the death row inmates to inform a balanced opinion.

It is not necessarily the media's fault that the public are not fully informed about the capital punishment system. Rather, this closely relates to the secretive policy of the Ministry of Justice that hinders the media from gaining access to Ministry officials for investigation. However, in my interviews with writers of two main newspaper agencies, they both stated that writers tend to develop sympathy towards the bereaved families in the process of getting to know about the victims through interviews, and articles tend to be written from the victims' perspectives.[110] Although it is not impossible for them to interview offenders, writers cannot usually spend the same amount of time doing this as they spend interviewing bereaved families; in any case, it is usually impossible once the offender is detained. It is also crucial that the media allows some minority victim lobby voices to be heard by the public, in order to demonstrate that capital punishment does not necessarily bring justice to all the victims' bereaved families.

Motomura's and the general public's support for capital punishment appears to come from a simple reason rather than complex cultural factors: it comes from lack of understanding about the second heaviest penalty, or life imprisonment with parole. According to Article 28 of the Penal Code:

> When a person sentenced to imprisonment with or without work evinces signs of substantial reformation, the person may be paroled by a disposition of a government agency after that person has served one-third of the definite term sentenced or 10 years in the case of a life imprisonment.

Therefore, the public tend to perceive life imprisonment with parole as a fairly mild penalty, considering that those convicted of serious crimes can be released within ten to 15 years. However, statistics from 2007 showed that offenders have been released in 31 years and ten months on average; and 'the chances of release on parole among lifers have almost disappeared and a life sentence really does mean "until death" in Japan'.[111] In order to reduce the gap between the heaviest and the second heaviest penalty, there exists a movement promoting the introduction of life imprisonment without parole.[112] However, as discussed in the previous section, domestic discussion has not yet advanced. Governmental opinion polls do not pose such questions, and the ethical debate about whether life imprisonment without parole would be as cruel as capital punishment, or more so, has not been resolved amongst legal experts or within the anti-death-penalty lobby. Therefore, public support for capital punishment does not appear to stem from a definite reliance on and understanding of the capital punishment system itself. Rather, it is heavily influenced by the media coverage of serious crimes and incorrect understanding of the second heaviest punishment in Japan, which stems from a fundamental lack of governmental effort to discuss the issue.

To sum up, what makes the 'retributive' sentiment look Japanese appears to be strategic narratives by the policy elites. Whilst social norms around atonement through death may exist in civil society, influenced by the Japanese public's possession of self-discipline and their views on criminals and death row inmates, the existence of such a norm does not necessarily lead the state to retain capital punishment. Given that the issue of capital punishment is elite-driven, it is the governmental discourse, which refers to historical and cultural practice, that has made Japanese culture look like a determining factor for justification of the system. Having examined the cultural features that have been proclaimed by the Japanese government to support capital punishment, the next section investigates the other cultural factors that appear to be hindering the Japanese public from complying with the anti-death-penalty norm.

3.3.3 Public Resistance to the Anti-Death-Penalty Norm Reconsidered

Whilst the cultural value of *shinde wabiru* may not be appreciated by the contemporary Japanese public, other cultural features may also appear to be associated with public support for capital punishment. This section critically examines the extent to which Japanese legal and human rights consciousness have contributed to public resistance to abolitionism. It contends that it is not necessarily Japanese cultural values that have been hindering the abolitionism movement, but the principles and characteristics of domestic anti-death-penalty NGOs that have been failing to garner widespread public support.

3.3.3.1 Japanese Human Rights and Legal Consciousness

First of all, retention of capital punishment in Japan might at first sight imply that the Japanese public have lower human rights consciousness than occurs in Western countries. However, in reality, since the Japanese government has been treating the issue of capital punishment from the perspective of criminal justice, the Japanese public do not appear to have been given or initiated opportunities to discuss the subject from a human rights perspective in the first place.

Jinken Yōgo ni Kansuru Yoron Chōsa (The Public Survey on Defence of Human Rights) is conducted by the Prime Minister's Office every five years; and 1776 out of 3000 people aged 20 or older responded in 2007. With regard to the question: 'Which of the following human rights issues are you concerned with?', 19 issues are listed as possible choices (see Appendix G). However, domestic human rights issues as defined/raised by the Prime Minister's Office are mostly different from what international society has mainly been concerned with in Japan, for example: (1) treatment of prisoners; (2) lack of an independent national human rights institution; (3) historical responsibility for the *ianfu* (comfort women) system during the wartime; and (4) the rights of minorities and foreigners.[113]

Of course, it is natural that domestic concerns raised by the national government tend to be daily or local issues, whilst those raised by international society tend to be more internationally critical issues. Having said that, since treatment of prisoners is not listed in the survey, there is little chance that the public would spontaneously initiate discussion on related issues such as detention conditions and execution methods for death row inmates as human rights issues in Japan. Excluding these issues from the opinion polls appears to be preventing the public from engaging in a domestic debate on capital punishment. Therefore, it is a difficult task to statistically observe the Japanese public's attitude towards human rights of prisoners or death row inmates in particular, or to claim that retention of capital punishment stems from low human rights consciousness among the Japanese public.

Similarly, the state of Japanese legal consciousness may appear to explain why the general public do not show much sympathy towards domestic anti-death-penalty activities. In other words, if the Japanese public has low legal consciousness, they may not necessarily show particular interest in activists' campaigns which try to challenge the existing legal system. For example, a low litigation rate in Japan, in comparison with other industrialised countries,[114] may make it appear as though the Japanese public have a low level of legal consciousness and do not support the anti-death-penalty lobby, which tries to challenge the existing legal provisions. According to Meryll Dean, the Japanese public tends to 'regard law like an heirloom samurai sword, something to be treasured but not used', and prefers to settle disputes informally through mediation.[115]

A legal sociologist, Kawashima Takeyoshi, agrees on this point, and also claims that the Japanese public do not appear to assert their legal rights. Whilst duty or norms are emphasised in Japanese society, terms such as *kenri* (rights) did not exist when Japan imported a Western legal system, which has made translation work challenging.[116] Kawashima also claims that once a contract is made in any profession, a master–servant relationship arises: when troubles occur in this power dynamic, mediation is preferred and any hard feeling is expected to be *mizu ni nagasu* (washed away) through apology or small compensation. If someone still tries to bring a lawsuit, this behaviour is seen as morally wrong, subversive and rebellious; and it is this ingrained social mindset that appears to have been contributing to low litigation rates in Japan.[117] This also relates to Wagatsuma Hiroshi and Arthur Rosett's work on the apology culture in Japan. According to them, the Japanese tend to apologise even when it is not entirely their fault, and this derives from their wish to maintain community harmony and stability.[118] Such a cultural preference might not appear to motivate the Japanese public to support the anti-death-penalty lobby's vocal campaigns, which try to urge the government to repeal or amend legal provisions.

However, as with human rights consciousness, it is not easy to evaluate Japanese legal consciousness on a scale from low to high in the first place. Reflecting the informal way that is preferred for solving problems, it is worth noting the conciliation methods employed in Japan. For example, companies usually provide employees with a mediation service in the case of traffic accidents, and there is no need for the individual to bring a lawsuit. Legal procedures come in only after exhausting all available conciliation methods, and by the time this is done, the problem has normally been solved peacefully by mediators' efforts. Therefore, the low litigation rate in Japan does not necessarily stem from 'low' legal consciousness among the Japanese public, but from what is preferred as an alternative conciliation method. More precisely, the legal consciousness of the Japanese public cannot be examined through the lens of culture *or* institutions, but should rather encompass both study areas.[119]

The next section examines the characteristics of one of the largest anti-death-penalty NGOs, which appears to be playing a more significant role than any cultural factors in failing to gain sympathy from the majority of the public for the cause of abolition.

3.3.3.2 Characteristics of Anti-Death-Penalty NGOs in Japan

Currently, Forum 90, which was founded in 1990, is the largest anti-death-penalty NGO in Japan. Yasuda Yoshihiro is one of the key founders of Forum 90, and as already discussed, he is a criminal lawyer widely known for his activities in high-profile murder cases. He was one of the defence counsel for Asahara Shoko, who was responsible for the Aum gas attack on the Tokyo underground railway in 1995, and of the offender, then a minor, in the Hikari case in 1999.

The former case was the biggest security threat in Japan in a decade, in which massive numbers of the Self-Defence Forces (SDF) with approximately 60,000 policemen were deployed.[120] Aum Shinrikyo was not only a religious group with approximately 10,000 members, led by Asahara Shoko, but also an organisation that sought to protest against the government by committing crimes; 58 SDF members had been identified as Aum members by the autumn of 1995. This sect's commitment to organising crimes from the late 1980s to the early 1990s is abundantly clear.[121] Some core members were among the brightest scientists in Japan, and the gas attack was planned using their skills to achieve the maximum impact.[122] The media portrayed this organisation as an atrocious murder group or a brainwashed cult group, and getting rid of it from society became a high priority for restoring public safety in Japan.[123] The public consensus was that Asahara should be sentenced to death and executed as soon as possible, and the trial for the Aum gas attack commenced even though most psychiatrists diagnosed that Asahara did not have the mental capacity to stand trial.[124]

Whilst the Aum gas attack created an extremely negative image of the anti-death-penalty movement,[125] the public resistance to abolitionism became more pronounced after Yasuda joined the defence team of the Hikari case. As highlighted earlier, the defence team claimed that the perpetrator, who was a minor at the time of the offence, tried to revive both victims using the magic power of the *Doraemon*, a robotic cat manga character.[126] However, as soon as the media featured the defence team's claim, Yasuda received a tremendous amount of criticism. For example, the Japan Federation of Bar Associations received more than 8000 requests from the public demanding the disbarment of Yasuda,[127] and Forum 90 received daily harassment calls and threats.[128]

In my interview, an anonymous NGO member stated that Yasuda's activities as a defence attorney directly set back their anti-death-penalty campaigns.[129] Because of his professional position and his passion to bring abolitionism to Japan, Yasuda tends to argue from the perspectives of the criminals, and not in line with those of the victim lobby or the general public.[130] Since Yasuda is a key figure of a well-known anti-death-penalty NGO, the abolitionist lobby tends to be collectively labelled as putting an extreme emphasis on the human rights of criminals but undervaluing the feelings of victims or their bereaved families.[131] As a result, the public tend to show resistance to abolitionism activities, which appear in their eyes to go against the public good.

Cultural explanations for the Japanese public's failure to show sympathy towards anti-death-penalty NGO activities—for example, that the Japanese public have a distinctive view of death and life or possess 'low' human rights or legal consciousness—do not necessarily tell the full story. Rather, it is the distinctive characteristics of key high-profile anti-death-penalty NGOs that appear to have caused their failure to win support amongst the public for different ideas of social justice, simply because of those campaigners' professional activity and their passion about bringing abolitionism to Japan.[132]

This chapter has thus clarified the limited role that culture plays in the bureaucratic decision-making mechanism. Applying the analytical framework presented so far, the following section evaluates the validity of the existing hypotheses regarding Japan's retention of capital punishment.

3.3.4 *Existing Hypotheses About Governmental Retention of Capital Punishment Reconsidered*

As explored in Chap. 2, Johnson demonstrates the existing hypotheses that Japan's retention of capital punishment relates to the following historical factors: (1) the US occupation; (2) the characteristics of Japanese political parties; and (3) Japan's geographical position and its stability as a democratic country.[133] Regarding the first hypothesis, it is not impossible to assume that Japan would have abolished the system if that had been included in post-war US policy. However, no literature has systematically examined the causal relationship between the US occupation and the retention of capital punishment. Johnson himself expresses caution about the validity of this claim and emphasises the necessity for further research.[134]

With regard to the characteristics of Japanese political parties and their resistance to political changes, including the abolition of capital punishment, this appears to go some way to explain Japan's retention of the system. Since the pro-death-penalty the Liberal Democratic Party (LDP) ruled for approximately 54 years from its foundation in 1955 until 2009 (with 1993 as an exception), the relationship between bureaucrats and LDP politicians became highly interdependent over these years. In the meantime, it is unrealistic to assume that a change in the ruling party can bring about a shift in capital punishment policy. Of course, after the Democratic Party of Japan took over from the LDP in August 2009, several changes were observed: the issue of capital punishment was 're-discovered' by Ministers of Justice such as Chiba Keiko, Eda Satsuki, Hiraoka Hideo and Ogawa Toshio, and executions were put on hold for approximately 20 months. Furthermore, it is worth noting that politicians in other parties have different views on capital punishment. For instance, Fukushima Mizuho, deputy leader of the Social Democratic Party, is an outspoken anti-death-penalty advocate and has been showing a particular interest in human rights protection. As already discussed in earlier sections, she consistently claims that phrases used in the governmental opinion polls on the issue of the death penalty are heavily biased, and she has conducted surveys among death row inmates in 2012 regarding the issue of whether or not life imprisonment without parole can be an alternative punishment to the death penalty. Kamei Shizuka, leader of the People's New Party and a former police officer, is also against capital punishment and published a book, *Shikei Haishi Ron* (Debate on the Abolition of the Death Penalty), in 2002. No matter how outspoken Diet members are about the capital punishment system, they tend to be sensitive to public opinion and reluctant to include the abolition of capital punishment in their manifestos at election time, but Kamei is an exception. Therefore, a change in the ruling political party may appear a significant factor for the future of capital punishment policy in Japan.

Having said that, as Chap. 2 has demonstrated, it is employed-for-life bureaucrats who are in charge of the actual decision-making irrespective of any change in the ruling party. Although some Ministers of Justice in the Democratic Party of Japan contributed to the domestic debate on the rights and wrongs of capital punishment, to date executions have been resumed by pro- and anti-death-penalty Ministers of Justice. Therefore, whilst a strong link between the perpetual dominance of the LDP and retention of capital punishment can be observed, it is doubtful if a change in the ruling political party could bring a rapid shift towards abolition of the capital punishment system.

Regarding the claim that Japan's geographical independence does not make the EU's anti-death-penalty norm appealing to the Japanese government,[135] it is again important to acknowledge where exactly its disagreement with international human rights stems from. Japan's resistance to international pressures from organisations such as the UN, the EU, Amnesty International and the Council of Europe may appear on a simple map as 'Japan v. the West' at first sight. Whilst Europe is currently a death-penalty-free zone, Japanese governmental officials tend to proclaim that those outside its sphere should have the right to choose their own criminal justice system without interference from international society.[136] What is more, one academic points out that the anti-death-penalty norm appears to be considered by the Japanese government as a mere 'European ideology'.[137]

However, being outside the Western sphere of influence does not necessarily mean that Japan defies all pressures from outside. Japanese social and political norms have the capacity to be heavily influenced by external actors, although such 'external actors' are often limited to the USA as a result of its unique and intimate relationship since the end of the Second

World War. Rather, it is important to acknowledge the Japanese government policy that treats capital punishment as an issue of law and order, not of human rights. Hence it is not necessarily the case that the Japanese government's refusal to comply with the internationally recognised anti-death-penalty norm is based upon disagreement with the human rights norm. Instead, it is the Ministry of Justice's commitment to actions based on legal precedents combined with its unwillingness to countenance international criticism from a human rights perspective or abolish this historically held governmental policy by amending legal provisions. This, however, does not justify the retention of capital punishment. Given that 'institutional ambivalence' and legitimacy issues are observed (see Chap. 2), the validity of the governmental claim that it does not consider international criticism from a human rights perspective needs to be challenged.

A related hypothesis that Japan's stability as a democratic state would prevent international society from sanctioning Japan for not complying with international norms must hold true to some extent. Japan obtained observer status in the Council of Europe in 1996, and is entitled to participate in the Committee of Ministers and all intergovernmental committees. However, Japan has not met the requirement declared in the Statutory Resolution (93) that those who acquire observer status should be 'willing to accept principles of democracy, the rule of law and of the enjoyment by all persons within its jurisdiction of human rights and fundamental freedoms'.[138] In 2001, the Parliamentary Assembly of the Council of Europe warned both Japan and the USA that the possession of observer status would be threatened if any significant progress in the implementation of the resolution could not be made by 1 January 2003.[139] The Japanese government did not respond to this. The lack of sanction on Japan on this policy appears to reflect the hesitant approach of economic and political partners in the West.

Ideas that Japan's external relations with the USA, South Korea and Asia as a whole can affect Japan's capital punishment policy need caution,[140] given that capital punishment is a criminal justice issue in Japan. As already discussed above, Japan's social and political norms have the capacity to be heavily influenced by its close ally, the USA, and it is not impossible to imagine that an initiative by the USA could determine the future course of capital punishment in Japan. However, as Johnson himself discusses, the USA and Japan have not employed a similar approach in legitimising the use of capital punishment. In the USA, greater communication between death row inmates and their families has been secured and most states have been employing lethal injections to kill inmates more humanely with less pain.[141] In Japan, on the other hand, death row inmates' communication remains limited, the execution date is not given to the families in advance and hanging is the only execution method, regardless of the debate about whether it infringes Article 36 of the Constitution, which forbids cruel punishment. Given that Japan has not mirrored its counterpart in detention and execution method, or in the strategy of legitimising state killing, it is doubtful that the USA can set a future course for Japan. Similarly, the Japanese government does not appear to be affected by changes in other Asian countries' capital punishment policies, since it proclaims that each country has the right to retain a capital punishment system depending on public sentiment and the domestic crime situation.[142]

Finally, regarding three internal factors, (1) strong public support for capital punishment, (2) a unique Japanese view on sin and human rights, and (3) a 'punitive' way of thinking among Japanese from the perspective of victims' bereaved families, this chapter has claimed that they are independent of the actual governmental decision-making. Comparison of opinion polls by the government and non-governmental bodies, and an in-depth survey by an independent research body, have provided alternative views. Although opinion polls conducted by non-governmental bodies did not necessarily show a strikingly different result from the governmental one, they highlighted a divergence between the public's and the state's official approach on capital punishment. Depending on the questions posed, the public showed some understanding and interest in suspending executions in order to debate the issue of capital punishment and alternative penalties, such as life imprisonment without parole.

Whilst the social norm regarding atonement through death appears to exist in civil society, influenced by the Japanese public's possession of self-discipline and their views on criminals and death row inmates, the existence of such a norm does not necessarily lead the state to retain capital punishment. The issue of capital punishment is elite-driven, and it is governmental narratives, which refer to historical and cultural practice, that have created the impression that Japanese culture is a determining factor for justification of the system. This chapter has presented contrary perspectives to the governmental claim that the victim lobby as a whole demands *shinde wabiru* for criminals. Whilst the government tends to justify capital punishment as victim satisfaction, and the media sensationally feature a pro-death-penalty victim lobby, there also exists an anti-death-penalty victim lobby, which poses an ethical question about whether state killing can bring closure to a crime. The next section examines how investigating the *de facto* moratorium periods can inform scholars and activists about the elite-driven nature of capital punishment policy.

3.4 The *De Facto* Moratorium Periods Reconsidered

As already explained, the Japanese government tends to justify capital punishment policy on domestic and cultural grounds, and endeavours to conduct executions annually. However, at times executions do not take place for years, and some scholars and anti-death-penalty lobby supporters to refer to such pauses as *de facto* moratorium periods. As mentioned in the Introduction, discussions in the existing literature revolve around the causal relationship between the personal convictions of Ministers of Justice and the non-authorisation of executions. However, there has not been any serious attempt to define this phenomenon or investigate its implications. This section looks at one such pause in executions, the period from 1989 to 1993, to clarify whether there was a moratorium period at this time. In order to investigate this, the following factors will be discussed: (1) what the nature of a moratorium period is; (2) who tends to describe, or refuse to describe, an execution-free period as a *de facto* moratorium period; and (3) what factors tend to make an execution-free period look like a moratorium period. In order to do this, political and non-academic debate will be reviewed.

3.4.1 *The Political Debate*

As discussed in the Introduction, the Japanese government has not treated any of the *de facto* moratorium periods as a political event, and there has been no official statement setting out a dominant governmental discourse on the subject. For example, when executions were resumed for the first time in three years and four months in 1993, press conferences were not held to explain why executions had been put on hold or why they had been resumed; and Ministry bureaucrats did not make official comments in the Diet meetings. Whilst it is difficult to trace the governmental and ministerial discourse around this event, one minister and two officials in the Ministry of Foreign Affairs (MOFA) provided me with some unofficial views.[143] Their main claims were that: (1) this period was independent from the influence of the international anti-death-penalty movement; and (2) it is doubtful if there existed an internationally recognised anti-death-penalty norm during this period in the first place.

Regarding the international anti-death-penalty movement, the UN's initiative can be cited as an example. Recalling Article 3 of the Universal Declaration of Human Rights and Article 6 of the International Covenant on Civil and Political Rights (ICCPR), the Second Optional Protocol to the ICCPR, aiming at the abolition of the death penalty,[144] was adopted on 15 December 1989 and entered into force on 11 July 1991. In the voting, 59 states voted for, 26 voted against and 48 abstained; Japan and the USA voted against the protocol. In an interview, an anti-death-penalty MOFA minister stressed that no matter how hard international society tries to urge Japanese governmental agencies to abolish capital punishment, the Ministry of Justice and the Public Prosecutor's Office resist such pressures, and it must have been the same during this *de facto* moratorium period.[145]

With regard to the two MOFA officials, they asked me the following questions: (1) whether or not there was a '*de facto* moratorium period' from 1989 to 1993; (2) whether or not the anti-death-penalty norm was already firmly established worldwide in the late 1980s; and (3) why the Japanese government was and still is required to follow the international trend in the first place.[146] Using the figures for voting on the resolution, in which 26 voted against and 48 abstained whilst 59 states voted for, government officials often point out that the sum of those who voted against and abstained outnumbered those who voted in favour.[147] Therefore, their argument is that there is still a divergence in this ethical principle in a substantial number of countries; and that there was no such thing as an internationally supported anti-death-penalty norm in the 1980s. Interviewees also denied that the adoption of the UN resolution led Japanese bureaucrats to refrain from conducting annual executions,[148] and two MOFA officials, in particular, implied that the anti-death-penalty norm was and still is a mere European or Western ideology.[149]

In short, MOFA officials argued that since not all states share identical political cultures, it is not appropriate for Western countries to seek by one-sided pressure to impose such values on Japan.[150] Such responses sounded like a model answer that is used when they are questioned about capital punishment policy. Throughout the interviews, they appeared to be reluctant to answer questions about international criticism of Japanese policy from a Western perspective. One of the academics whom I interviewed concluded that this may stem from the resistance of Japanese governmental officials to 'Western arrogance', which tries to impose Western values on other countries.[151]

3.4.2 *The Non-Academic Debate*

Whilst the Japanese government does not treat the *de facto* moratorium periods as politically significant, it is worth considering the events that have been suggested by a TV agency and anti-death-penalty NGO staff as possible factors that have contributed to this *de facto* moratorium period: (1) the death of Emperor Shōwa in 1989; and (2) an international anti-death penalty initiative in the same year.

Firstly, the death of Emperor Shōwa (Hirohito) was briefly mentioned in a broadcast in an educational television series broadcast by NHK on 27 February 2011. The main focus of the programme, entitled '*Hōmu Daijin no Kunō*' (Agony of Ministers of Justice), was to examine what led a former anti-death-penalty Minister of Justice, Chiba Keiko, to decide to authorise executions for three death row inmates in July 2010, before one year of a *de facto* moratorium period had passed. The *de facto* moratorium period from 1989 to 1993 was briefly presented as a comparison, and NHK made a correlation with the death of Hirohito: 'Since Emperor Shōwa died in 1989, executions were put on hold for the first time after the war.'[152] One anti-death-penalty MOFA minister supported this hypothesis, though he could not explain exactly how that event affected the capital punishment system in Japan.[153]

The proponents of this hypothesis appear to argue that the death of Emperor Shōwa made the then Ministers of Justice refrain from hanging death row inmates. However, it is not empirically proved that this event had a specific effect on the capital punishment policy. Of course, the social and political impact that the death of the Emperor had on Japanese government and civil society should not be underestimated. As an example, consider Japan's two calendar systems: one is Western, the other is the *nengō* system, where the name of the era changes with the death of an emperor and succession by his eldest son. *Shōwa* (enlightened peace or harmony) was the name of the era during which Hirohito served as emperor, and he was called 'Emperor Shōwa'. Moreover, Emperor Shōwa is associated with historical events such as the Second World War and the pacifism and economic miracle that Japan achieved during the post-war period. Therefore, the psychological impact of his death should not be underestimated as the mere end of an era under the *nengō* system.

However, the suggestion that the Emperor's death was connected with a halt in executions appears to be based on hearsay rather than empirical evidence. There is no record that a reprieve was granted to any death row inmates at this time. One of the former Ministers of Justice during this *de facto* moratorium, Sato Megumu, did not mention that the event affected his decision concerning authorisation of executions, or induced a mood of voluntary restraint within the Ministry of Justice.[154] Similarly, an academic, who is one of the most consistent writers on capital punishment policy in Japan, also showed a sceptical attitude towards this hypothesis.[155] Given that the media have a potentially enormous role in shaping the public understanding of political events, it was wrong to speak of a correlation between the death of Emperor Shōwa and the beginning of the *de facto* moratorium as an established fact, without support from empirical research.

An anti-death-penalty NGO worker, who has been acting on behalf of innocent death row inmates, spoke of the impact that international pressure must have had on the Japanese government at that time.[156] The UN initiative was not a one-off event that grabbed worldwide attention just on the day it was adopted. Since the resolution entered into force on 11 July 1991, those who voted against or abstained have begun to adopt it. Given that Japan halted executions from 10 November 1989 for three years and four months, this informant claimed that the UN's initiative had an indirect influence upon Japanese policy-making, even if the government did not feel impelled to adopt the resolution.[157]

By contrast, most NGO staff denied that there was an international influence on the non-execution period, considering the elite-driven nature of the policy. For example, another NGO worker, who was interviewed at the same time as the one just cited, disagreed with her, and argued that the *de facto* moratorium took place totally independently of any international movement.[158] This second NGO worker is one of the editors of *Nenpō Shikei Haishi* (Annual Report: Abolishing Capital Punishment), which has been following the domestic trend of capital punishment in Japan, and he appeared confident in his denial of any causal relationship. In his opinion, it is doubtful that any international event influenced Japanese government bureaucrats to consider where international society was heading or what political price the Japanese government would pay by going against such a global initiative.[159] However, the gap between these two interviewees was bridged by other anti-death-penalty NGO workers, who said it was not necessarily a single event or person that had an impact on pro-death-penalty sentiment, but rather a combination of domestic and international events, such as the disclosure of four major miscarriage of justice cases in the 1980s; the adoption of the UN Resolution Concerning Abolition of the Death Penalty in 1989; and anti-death-penalty campaigns by NGOs at the time.[160]

These hypotheses on the beginning of the *de facto* moratorium period are promulgated by some MOFA officials, TV programme producers and anti-death-penalty advocates, and appear to have been partly accepted as important in approaching the *de facto* moratorium periods. However, other important topics have been overlooked in this discussion. Firstly, the issue of capital punishment is the province of a narrow elite in the Ministry of Justice and the Public Prosecutor's Office, and it is incorrect to argue that domestic or international factors influenced capital punishment policy-making during this period. Secondly, the hypotheses put forward here are based on the presumption that this was a *de facto* moratorium period (caused by internal or external factors), but without further investigation of the nature of the moratorium period, or whether the execution-free period was actually a moratorium. Clarifying these conceptual issues, the following section highlights the importance of investigating how the Ministry of Justice has consistently promoted the pro-death-penalty actors norm during execution-free periods.

3.4.3 *The* De Facto *Moratorium Periods in Japan's Capital Punishment Policy*

The significant fact about moratorium periods is that executions are put on hold temporarily. Even if inmates are still detained on death row, it is guaranteed that they will not be executed for a certain period. The Japanese government has never officially set a moratorium period. Therefore, during the eras which are referred to as *de facto* moratorium periods in the existing literature, no significant change was observed in the status of death row inmates, and they were in constant fear of execution.

Despite this fact, some scholars, anti-death-penalty NGOs and the media tend to treat this period as worthy of close attention, as if there was a change in the government's policy. Discussion in the existing literature stresses the causal relationship between the personal convictions of Ministers of Justice and their non-authorisation of executions.[161] It tends to suggest that the issue of capital punishment is heavily dependent on who is serving as Minister of Justice.

Anti-death-penalty NGOs tend to treat the *de facto* moratorium periods as a politically significant phenomenon, and view them as part of a smooth transition towards abolition. Indeed, they consider execution-free periods as a stage when the Japanese government has abolished capital punishment in practice, and seek to make these periods last as long as possible, expecting that the Ministry of Justice will abolish capital punishment in law.[162] For example, they tend to strengthen their anti-death-penalty campaigns during these periods, for example by collecting signatures from supporters and submitting them to Ministers of Justice as an alternative voice to 'public opinion' found in governmental opinion polls.[163]

Furthermore, the media tend to highlight the length of time during which executions have been put on hold, citing Ministers' personal views on capital punishment. For example, in light of the recent *de facto* moratorium period which lasted for one year and eight months from 28 July 2010 to 29 March 2012, most of the newspapers put the phrase 'no execution for the first time in 19 years' in their article titles,[164] in order to stress the 'abnormality' of this period.

How these three groups of commentators treat the *de facto* moratorium periods appears to vary. Scholars tend to try to account for the central fact that executions are put on hold; anti-death-penalty NGOs tend to use this period as an opportunity to promote abolition as a final aim; and the media tend to alert the public that this form of legal punishment has not been used. Despite the difference in their intentions and implications, what they overemphasise is that this time period is 'different' in nature, and that the personal convictions of individual Ministers of Justice change capital punishment policy. In reality, no significant change can be observed in capital punishment policy during these periods.

As discussed in Chap. 2, important decisions regarding capital punishment are made by elites in the Ministry of Justice and the Public Prosecutor's Office. Therefore, one should not try to overestimate the characteristics of Ministers of Justice, who do not stay in office for more than a year on average and cannot get involved in the crucial part of the decision-making process. Similarly, whilst contemporary domestic and international events tend to be instantly linked to explanations of why executions were put on hold, it is wrong to consider that these events led the Japanese government to take a political initiative with the intention of discussing abolition. Rather, it is important to acknowledge that the moratorium equivalent periods were not set by the Japanese government with political intentions, but that the non-authorisation of executions by Ministers of Justice appeared to have created a 'gap' in capital punishment policy. More precisely, various factors including the personal convictions of Ministers of Justice and contemporary domestic or international events appear to have made these times look like moratorium periods. Therefore, trying to investigate what leads to a *de facto* moratorium is not a suitable approach for understanding Japan's capital punishment policy, as in policy terms no such period has existed. Rather, it is important to investigate how and why the Japanese government has consistently justified its policy even during the *de facto* moratorium periods.

3.5 Conclusion

Through a comprehensive examination of domestic and cultural factors, this chapter has investigated the governmental claim that capital punishment is culturally determined. Public opinion is cited by the government as a primary justification for capital punishment. However, comparison of the opinion polls conducted by the government and non-governmental bodies indicates that 'wide public support' for the capital punishment system mainly stems from strategically phrased questions in governmental opinion polls. Indeed, analysis of the results of opinion polls conducted by non-governmental bodies and an in-depth survey by a research team has suggested that: (1) the majority of the Japanese public is not fully informed about the human rights issues of death row inmates; and (2) the public have shown some understanding of and interest in introducing life imprisonment without parole as an alternative punishment. Besides the fact that 'public opinion' can fluctuate depending on the level of knowledge of the capital punishment system, and how questions are phrased in the questionnaire, it is important to acknowledge that in reality important decisions regarding the policy are made by elites, irrespective of public opinion.

Secondly, the chapter has investigated the cultural features that have been claimed by the government to be associated with and to support capital punishment. It has challenged the theoretical approach to governmental and public non-compliance with the anti-death-penalty norm on cultural grounds. Existing literature indicates that culture has an influence on shaping legal punishment and that national attachment to a contrasting domestic norm can hinder the importing of international norms. However, this chapter has argued that it is policy elites' recurring use of narratives that make reference to culture that has influenced the public and scholars in their belief that capital punishment policy is domestically and culturally determined.

For example, although a concept of *shinde wabiru* appears to have been accepted as a social norm in Japanese society, a problem emerges when the government seeks to use it as a reason to legitimise state killing. Not all the victim lobby believes that capital punishment functions as social justice; and the fact that *shinde wabiru* requires spontaneous acceptance by convicts has been overlooked. Moreover, the existence of a proverb that strongly contrasts with *shinde wabiru* has been completely ignored in the governmental narratives. The act of *shinde wabiru* can be appreciated as a virtue, since it symbolises that convicts have a sincere feeling of remorse towards the victims and their bereaved families. However, given that capital punishment is conducted at the convenience of the Ministry of Justice and the Public Prosecutor's Office, under the ill-defined criteria that govern how some inmates are chosen out of dozens, it appears inconceivable that capital punishment policy has been designed to reflect death row inmates' will to atone for crimes through death.

Thirdly, this chapter has outlined the methodological problems concerning the measurement of Japanese human rights and legal consciousness relating to support for capital punishment. Capital punishment has been conceived by the public as an issue of criminal justice because of the government's approach, and it is wrong to conclude that the Japanese public have a weaker human rights consciousness than the global norm and therefore support capital punishment. The chapter has argued that the state of Japanese legal consciousness may partially account for the public's 'indifferent' attitude towards campaigns that demand the government repeal or amend the existing legal provisions. However, it appears that public reluctance to comply with the anti-death penalty norm largely stems from a lack of sympathy towards the activities of domestic anti-death penalty NGOs. Since a key figure in a well-known anti-death-penalty NGO puts extreme emphasis on the human rights of criminals or death row inmates, the public appears to tend to perceive their activities as undervaluing the feelings of victims or their bereaved families.

Finally, this chapter has suggested that further investigation of the *de facto* moratorium periods from appropriate perspectives can provide scholars and activists with a better understanding of Japan's capital punishment policy. Scholars and activists have paid tremendous attention to a wide range of domestic or international factors that affect the *de facto* moratorium periods; and the media also highlight the length of the execution-free periods. However, it is important to acknowledge the fact that the *de facto* moratorium periods were not implemented by the Japanese government with political intentions. Rather, non-authorisation of executions by Ministers of Justice caused by the frequent cabinet reshuffles has created 'gaps' in capital punishment policy, which has created the false impression of a change in government policy. Execution-free periods should not be treated as a politically significant phenomenon out of line with government policy, and there should be no attempt to specify what has led to the *de facto* moratorium periods. Rather, it is more beneficial to focus on the Ministry of Justice's consistent justification of capital punishment policy, even when executions are put on hold.

The following chapters empirically examine all of the *de facto* moratorium periods, applying the analytical framework presented in Chap. 2. Although various domestic and international factors have been considered as influential factors contributing to the *de facto* moratorium, the following case study illuminates the fact that capital punishment policy is primarily elite-driven, and the Japanese government has consistently justified the system even during execution-free periods.

Notes

1. *Japan Times* (2002) 'Diet Group against Death Penalty to Make Its Move, 4 October 2002'. Available at: http://www.japantimes.co.jp/text/nn20021004b1.html [Accessed 17 March 2016]
2. Okuno S. (1980) *The 93th Legal Affairs Committee of the House of Councillors*, 18 December 1980, p. 8; Goto, M. (1989) *The 116th Legal Affairs Committee of the House of Councillors*, 5 December 1989, p. 3.
3. Ogawa, T. (2012) *The 180th Legal Affairs Committee of the House of Councillors*, 28 March 2012, pp. 8–9; After the introduction of *saiban-in seido*, nine people were sentenced to death in the first court in 2009, four in 2010 and nine in 2011 (Japan Federation of Bar Associations (2012) '*Shikei wo Kangaeru Shiryō*'(Documents to Discuss Death Penalty). Available at: http://www.nichibenren.or.jp/activity/criminal/deathpenalty/shiryou.html [Accessed 17 March 2016]; Supreme Court (2012) *Nenpō Shihō Tōkei* (Annual Report of Justice Statistics). Available at: http://www.courts.go.jp/search/jtsp0010

[Accessed 17 March 2016]). The cases involved include the Pachinko parlour murder case where Takami Sunao, 41 at the time of the crime, set fire to a *pachinko* parlour in Osaka on 5 July 2009, killing five people and leaving ten injured. Takami was sentenced to death in the first court on 31 October 2011 (*Nikkei* (2011) '"*Kōshukei wa Gōken*": *Pachinko Ten Hōka de Shikei Hanketsu, Osaka Chisai*' (Hanging in Constitutional: Death Sentence for Setting Fire to the Pachinko Parlour, Osaka District Court), 31 October 2011).

4. Wakasa quoted in *Japan Times* (2012) 'Ogawa Has No Qualms about Executions Justice Minister Says Lay Judges, Public Call Shots on Inmates' Fate', 6 April 2012. Available at: http://www.japantimes.co.jp/text/nn20120406b5.html [Accessed 17 March 2016]
5. Major classical works that deny the deterrent effect of capital punishment are: Bye, R.T. (1919) *Capital Punishment in the United States*, Philadelphia: the Committee on Philanthropic Labor of Philadelphia Yearly Meeting of Friends; Sutherland, E.H. (1925) 'Murder and the Death Penalty', *Journal of the American Institute of Criminal Law and Criminology*, 15(4), pp. 522–529; Kirkpatrick, C. (1925) *Capital Punishment*, Philadelphia: Committee on Philanthropic Labor of Philadelphia Yearly Meeting of Friends; Vold, G.B. (1932) 'Can the Death Penalty Prevent Crime?', *Prison Journal*, 12, pp. 3–7, Sellin, J.T. (1959) 'The Death Penalty: A Report for the Model Penal Code Project of the American Law Institute', American Law Institute.
6. Sellin (1959) *Ibid*; Lamperti, J. (2008) 'Does Capital Punishment Deter Murder? A Brief Look at the Evidence', Retrieved 8 October, pp. 1–10, p. 4. Available at: http://www.dartmouth.edu/~chance/teaching_aids/books_articles/JLpaper.pdf [Accessed 17 March 2016]
7. Ehrlich, I. & Becker, G.S. (1972) 'Market Insurance, Self-insurance, and Self-protection', *The Journal of Political Economy*, 80(4), pp. 623–648.
8. Ehrlich, I. (1973) 'Participation in Illegitimate Activities: A Theoretical and Empirical Investigation', *The Journal of Political Economy*, 81(3), pp. 521–565; (1975) 'The Deterrent Effect of Capital Punishment: A Question of Life and Death', *American Economic Review*, 63(3), pp. 397–417.

9. Shepherd, J.M. (2002) 'Fear of the First Strike: The Full Deterrent Effect of California's Two-and Three-Strikes Legislation', *Journal of Legal Studies*, 31 (1), pp. 159–201.
10. Dezhbakhsh, H., Rubin, P.H. & Shepherd, J.M. (2003) 'Does Capital Punishment have a Deterrent Effect? New Evidence from Postmoratorium Panel Data', *American Law and Economics Review*, 5(2), pp. 1–47.
11. Ehrlich (1975) *Ibid*; Lamperti (2008) *op. cit.* p. 6.
12. Masaki, A. (1964) *Shikei: Kieyuku Saigo no Yaban* (Death Penalty: Ultimate Barbarity Disappearing), Tokyo: Nihon Hyōron Sha; (1968) *Gendai no Chijoku: Watakushi no Shikei Haishi Ron* (Contemporary Shame: My Abolitionism), Tokyo: Kyōsei Kyōkai. Masaki was one of the main contributors to the awakening of abolitionism in the 1950s through his activities. Masaki issued a magazine, *Shakai Kairyō* (Social Reform), to spread his anti-death-penalty beliefs, conducted informal meetings for prison guards and death row inmates, respectively, and published the meetings' outcomes in *Keisei*', a monthly magazine from the Correction Association (Yasuda, Y., Kikuta, S. and Tsushima, S. (1996) '*Shikei Haishi e Mukete Dōsuruka: Kono 5 Nen no Ayumi to Tenbō*' (What We should do towards the Abolition of Death Penalty: Paths over the Five Years and Prospect), Tokyo: Impact Shuppan, pp. 106–143, p. 107).
13. Tamiya, Y. (2000) *Keijihō no Riron to Genjitsu* (Theory and Reality of the Criminal Law), Tokyo: Iwanami Shoten.
14. Masaki (1968) *op. cit.* pp. 70–72.
15. *Ibid.*
16. Motoji, S. (1939) *Nihon Keihō Ron: Gekan* (Theory of Japanese Criminal Law: Part 2), Tokyo: Yuhikaku.
17. Ono, S, (1950) *Keihō Kōgi Sōron* (Lectures on Criminal Law, General Part), Tokyo: Yuhikaku.
18. Uematsu T. (1958) *Keihō Sōron* (Criminal Law, General Part), Seirin Shoin; (1990) *Shikei Haishi Ron no Kanshō o Kirau* (*Shikei Seido Sonpai Mondai o Kangaeru—Nagayama Jiken Sashimodoshi Jōkokushin hanketsu o Keiki to Shite <Tokushū>*) (Hating the Sentimentality of Anti-Death-Penalty Argument—Discussion of Retention and Abolition of Death Penalty: Case Study of Remand of the Nagayama Case <Special Issue>), *Hōritsu no Hiroba*, 43 (8), pp. 11–15.

19. Uematsu (1990) *Ibid*; However, this contradicts the fact that France abolished capital punishment in 1981 despite the fact that murders of children were occurring successively and there was high public support (63 per cent) for the system at the time (Badinter, R., Roth, K. & Mercer, J. (2008) *Abolition: One Man's Battle Against the Death Penalty*, Boston: Northeastern University Press, p. 169).
20. Motoji (1939) *Ibid*, Ono (1950) *Ibid* and Uematsu (1990) *Ibid*.
21. Bye, R.T. (1919) *op. cit.* p. 98.
22. Quoted in Mori, T. (2008) *Shikei: Hito wa Hito wo Koroseru, Demo Hito wa Hito wo Sukuitai tomo Omou* (Death Penalty: People Could Kill People, but People Also Feel Like Saving People), Tokyo: Asahi Shuppan Sha, p. 118; Shinoda, H. (2008) *Document Sikeishū* (Documentary of Death Row Inmates), Tokyo: Chikuma Shinsho, p. 185.
23. Translated in Maki, J.M. (1964) *Court and Constitution in Japan: Selected Supreme Court Decisions, 1948–60*, Seattle: University of Washington Press, pp. 161–162.
24. Lippmann, W. (1997) *Public Opinion*, New Brunswick, NJ: Transaction Publishers, p. 161.
25. Bring, O. (2009) 'The Death Penalty from a European View', EUIJ Conference 'Reflections on Life: European and Asian Perspectives on Capital Punishment', Tokyo: Waseda University, p. 2. Available at: http://www.euij-waseda.jp/common/pdf/Prof._Ove_Bring.pdf [Accessed 17 March 2016]
26. Johnson, D. & Zimring, F.E. (2009) *The Next Frontier: National Development, Political Change, and the Death Penalty in Asia*, Oxford University Press, USA, p. 85.
27. Johnson & Zimring (2009) *op. cit.* p. 62.
28. Bae, S. (2008) *When the State No Longer Kills: International Human Rights Norms and Abolition of Capital Punishment*, Albany: State University of New York Press, p. 119.
29. Prime Minister's Office (1994; 1999; 2004; 2009 and 2014) '*Kihonteki Hōseido ni Kansuru Yoron Chōsa*' (Opinion Poll on Basic Legal System).
30. Sato, M. (2008) 'Public Opinion and the Death Penalty in Japan', *Centre for Capital Punishment Studies*, 4, pp. 1–39, p. 17.

31. *Ibid.*
32. Fukushima, M. (2000) *The 149th Legal Affairs Committee of the House of Councillors*, 9 August 2000, p. 12.
33. Yasuoka, O. (2000) *The 149th Legal Affairs Committee of the House of Councillors*, 9 August 2000, p. 12.
34. Sato, M. (2009) 'Deliberative Survey on the Japanese Death Penalty System', *Institute for Contemporary Asian Studies, Temple University*, pp. 1–2. Available at: http://www.tuj.ac.jp/icas/pdf/icjs_090616.pdf [Accessed 17 March 2016]
35. Lippmann (1997) *op. cit.* p. 78.
36. Sato (2009) *Ibid.*
37. Richardson, B. (1998) *Japanese Democracy: Power, Coordination, and Performance*, New Haven: Yale University Press, p. 25.
38. Sato (2009) *op. cit.* p. 3.
39. *Ibid.*
40. Sato (2009) *op. cit.* p. 5.
41. Sato (2009) *op. cit.* p. 7.
42. Johnson, D. T. (2006) 'Japan's Secretive Death Penalty Policy: Contours, Origins, Justifications, and Meanings', *Asian-Pacific Law & Policy Journal*, 7, pp. 62–124, p. 70.
43. The International Federation for Human Rights (2008) 'The Death Penalty in Japan: The Law of Silence - Going against the International Trend', October 2008, p. 4. Available at: http://www.fidh.org/IMG/pdf/japon505a2008.pdf [Accessed 17 March 2016]. As briefly touched upon in Chap. 2, there are some exceptions where executions were conducted during parliamentary sessions. This includes the terms of pro-death-penalty Ministers Ogawa Toshio (13 January 2012–4 June 2012) and Taki Minoru (4 June 2012–1 October 2012; 24 October 2012–26 December 2012) (see Chap. 7).
44. Johnson, D.T. (2005) 'The Death Penalty in Japan: Secrecy, Silence, and Salience' in A. Sarat & C. Boulanger (eds) *The Cultural Lives of Capital Punishment: Comparative Perspectives*, Stanford: Stanford University Press, pp. 251–273, p. 259.
45. Mori (2008) *op. cit.* p. 75; North Carolina Department of Public Safety (2012) 'Offender Public Information'. Available at: http://webapps6.doc.state.nc.us/opi/offendersearch.do?method=view [last accessed 17 March 2016]

46. Johnson (2005) *op. cit.* p. 260.
47. Japan Federation of Bar Associations (2008) '*Ryōkei Seido wo Kangaeru Chōtōha no Kai no Keihō nado no Ichibu wo Kaisei suru Hōritsuan* (*Shūshinkei Dōnyū Kankei*) *ni Taisuru Ikensho*' (Written Opinion on the Legislative Bill which Nonpartisan Association Proposes the Partial Amendment of the Criminal Law (Introduction of Life Sentence without Parole), 18 November 2008. Available at: http://www.nichibenren.or.jp/library/ja/opinion/report/data/081118.pdf [Accessed 17 March 2016]; Interview with two NGO workers, Tokyo, 17 May 2011.
48. *Japan Times* (2013) 'Opinion Divided on Life Term without Parole', 21 February 2013. Available at: http://www.japantimes.co.jp/news/2013/02/21/national/opinion-divided-on-life-term-without-parole/#.UU-ChRwZFBM [Accessed 17 March 2016]
49. Japan Federation of Bar Associations (2008) *Ibid.*
50. Interview with an NGO member, Tokyo, 12 April 2011.
51. *Japan Times* (2013) *Ibid.*
52. *Ibid.*
53. Hatoyama, K. (2008) *The 169th Legal Affairs Committee of the House of Representatives*, 11 April 2008.
54. *Japan Times* (2002) *Ibid.*
55. Moriyama quoted in *Japan Times* (2002) *Ibid*; Métraux, D.A. (2009) 'The Nagayama Criteria for Assessing the Death Penalty in Japan: Reflections of a Case Suspect', *Southeast Review of Asian Studies*, 31, pp. 282–289, p. 282.
56. Sakata, M. (1982) *The 96th Legal Affairs Committee of the House of Councillors*, 23 March 1982, p. 20.
57. Katzenstein, P. J. (1996) *The Culture of National Security: Norms and Identity in World Politics*, Columbia University Press, p. 54.
58. Checkel, J.T. (1999) 'Norms, Institutions, and National Identity in Contemporary Europe', *International Studies Quarterly*, 43(1), pp. 84–114; Hawkins, D.G. (2001) 'The Domestic Impact of International Norms and Transnational Networks', The Annual Meeting of the American Political Science Association, San Francisco, 30 August–2 September 2001,

p. 11; Cortell, A.P. & Davis, J.W. (2005) 'When Norms Clash: International Norms, Domestic Practices, and Japan's Internalisation of the GATT/WTO', *Review of International Studies*, 31(01), pp. 3–25, p. 4.

59. Checkel, J.T. (2012) 'Norm Entrepreneurship: Theoretical and Methodological Challenges', Workshop 'The Evolution of International Norms and "Norm Entrepreneurship": The Council of Europe in Comparative Perspective', 11 January 2012, Wolfson College, University of Oxford; Sithole, K. (2012) 'The Council of Europe and the Death Penalty: Intergovernmental Legitimation as Enabling and Constraining' in Workshop 'The Evolution of International Norms and "Norm Entrepreneurship": The Council of Europe in Comparative Perspective', 11 January 2012. Wolfson College, University of Oxford.
60. Risse, T. & Sikkink, K. (1999) *'The Socialisation of International Human Rights Norms into Domestic Practices: Introduction'*, in Risse, T., Ropp, S.C., and Sikkink, K.(eds) *The Power of Human Rights, International Norms and Domestic Change*, Cambridge: Cambridge University Press, pp. 1–38, p. 11.
61. Shaming here means creating a tension between norm-abiding and norm-violating countries to make the latter realise that international norm compliance has now become one of the crucial constitutive elements of modern statehood or a member of international society (Risse and Sikkink (1999) *op. cit.* p. 8, 15; Risse, T. & Ropp, S.C. (1999) 'International Human Rights Norms and Domestic Change: Conclusions' in Thomas Risse, S.C. Ropp, & K. Sikkink (eds) *The Power of Human Rights, International Norms and Domestic Change.* Cambridge: Cambridge University Press, pp. 234–278, p. 234.
62. Finnemore, M. & Sikkink, K. (1998) 'International Norm Dynamics and Political Change', *International Organization*, 52(04), pp. 887–917, p. 895.
63. Moravcsik, A. (1997) 'Taking Preferences Seriously: A Liberal Theory of International Politics', *International Organization*, 51(04), pp. 513–553; Hafner-Burton, E.M. & Tsutsui, K. (2005) 'Human Rights in a Globalizing World: The Paradox of Empty Promises', *American Journal of Sociology*, 110(5), pp. 1373–1411, p. 1380. Available at: https://umdrive.

memphis.edu/rblanton/public/POLS_7508_Fall_2009/hafner_paradox.pdf [Accessed 17 March 2016]

64. Finnemore and Sikkink (1998) *Ibid.*
65. Risse and Sikkink (1999) *Ibid.*
66. Axelrod, R. (1986) 'An Evolutionary Approach to Norms,' *American Political Science Review*, 80(4), pp. 1095–1111, p. 1105. Available at: http://www-personal.umich.edu/~axe/Axelrod%20Norms%20APSR%201986%20%282%29.pdf [Accessed 17 March 2016]
67. Bae (2008) *op. cit.* pp. 111, 126. Bae takes an example of Ukraine and argues that its 'policy change regarding the death penalty was mainly based on strategic means-ends considerations at both domestic and international levels'.
68. Finnemore and Sikkink (1998) *Ibid*; Hafner-Burton and Tsutsui (2005) *op. cit.* p. 1385.
69. Cortell, A.P. & Davis, J.W. (2005) *Ibid.*
70. Checkel (1999) *op. cit.* p. 6.
71. Hawkins (2001) *Ibid.*
72. Risse and Sikkink (1999) *op. cit.* pp. 23–4.
73. However, it should be added that this can also be construed as a socialised norm as a product of the American security guarantee, given that the renunciation of war was included in the US occupation policy (Johnson & Zimring (2009) *op. cit.* pp. 60–1).
74. Hirata, K. (2004) 'Beached Whales: Examining Japan's Rejection of An International Norm', *Social Science Japan Journal*, pp. 177–197, p. 188. Available at: http://ssjj.oxfordjournals.org/cgi/reprint/7/2/177 [Accessed 17 March 2016]
75. Sato (2009) *op. cit.* pp. 1–2.
76. Lippmann (1997) *Ibid.*
77. Garland, D. (1993) *Punishment and Modern Society: A Study in Social Theory*, Chicago: University of Chicago Press, p. 198.
78. Menda, S. (2004) *Menda Sakae Gokuchū Note: Watashi no Miokutta Shikeishū Tachi* (Menda Sakae's Notes on Death Row: Death Row Inmates Who I Saw Off), Tokyo: Impact Shuppan, p. 139.
79. Lifton, R.J. (1977) *Nihonjin no Shiseikan Jō* (Japanese View on Death Penalty, Part 1), Tokyo: Iwanami Shoten, p. 65.
80. Lifton (1977) *op. cit.* p. 66.
81. Lifton (1977) *op. cit.* p. 53.
82. *Ibid.*

83. Komiya, N. (1999) 'A Cultural Study of the Low Crime Rate in Japan', *British Journal of Criminology*, 39(3), pp. 369–390, p. 387.
84. *Ibid*
85. Komiya (1999) *op. cit.* p. 383.
86. Komiya (1999) *op. cit.* p. 373.
87. Lifton (1977) *op. cit.* pp. 73, 79, 92.
88. Interview with an attorney, Tokyo, 13 April 2011.
89. When several media agencies disclosed the name of the offender in the Hikari case in 2012, the Japan Federation of Bar Associations voiced concerns, stressing that he was a minor at the time of the crime (*Kyōdō* (2012) '*Jitsumei Hōdō 'Kiwamete Ikan' to Nichibenren: Hikarishi Jiken Hanketsu de Kaichō Seimei*' (Media Coverage Disclosing Minor Offender's Name: 'Extremely Regrettable' Says the Japan Federation of Bar Association: Chairman's Statement on the Hikari Case Ruling), 24 February 2012). *Sankei*, *Asahi*, *Yomiuri* and *Nikkei* disclosed the name when the death sentence was finally upheld in February 2012. It had been withheld considering that he was a minor (the legal age of adulthood is 20 in Japan) and would go back to civil society after correction or rehabilitation. However, these newspaper agencies concluded that the opportunity for that had been lost and there was no need to hide his identity (*Sankei* (2012) '*13 Nen go no Shinpan: Keiji Bengo no Arikata Tou "Doraemon" no Shōgeki*' (Trial after 13 Years: Shock of 'Doraemon' which Questions What Criminal Defence Should be), 22 February 2012). In the meantime, the *Mainichi* and *Tokyo* newspapers withheld it, considering that it was still important for the offender to be corrected and show remorse towards the bereaved family, and leave the possibility of retrials or a reprieve as well (*Sankei* (2012) *Ibid*).
90. Sarin gas was spread by the Aum Shinrikyo Sect in the Tokyo underground on 20 March 1995—the biggest security threat in Japan in decades, in which massive numbers of the Self-Defence Forces with approximately 60,000 policemen were deployed.
91. Hamai, K. & Ellis, T. (2008a) '*Genbatsuka*: Growing Penal Populism and the Changing Role of Public Prosecutors in Japan?', *Japanese Journal of Sociological Criminology*, 33, pp. 67–92, p. 80.
92. *Ibid*

93. *Japan Times* (2010) 'Writer: Juvenile Killer not a 'Devil' First Sentenced to Life, then Death, Accused was Abused, Name-Naming Book Says', 6 January 2010. Available at: http://www.japantimes.co.jp/text/nn20100106f2.html [Accessed 17 March 2016]
94. *Sankei* (2012) *Ibid.*
95. *Sankei* (2008) '*Hikari shi Boshi Satsugai: TV Hōso wa Kanjōteki, BPO Kenshōi ga Ikensho*' (Hikari Murder Case: TV Coverage is Emotional: Opinion Statement by the Broadcasting Ethics & Program Improvement Organisation), 16 April 2008.
96. Quoted in Hamai and Ellis (2008a) *op. cit.* p. 81.
97. Hamai and Ellis (2008a) *op. cit.* p. 79.
98. Hamai and Ellis (2008b) 'Japanese Criminal Justice: Was Reintegrative Shaming a Chimera?', *Punishment & Society*, 10(1), pp. 25–46, p. 33. Available at: http://www.port.ac.uk/departments/academic/icjs/staff/documentation/filetodownload,73687,en.pdf [Accessed 17 March 2016]
99. *Japan Times* (2008) 'Experts Doubt Wisdom of Proposal to Let Victims Attend Juvenile Trials', 11 April 2008. Available at: http://www.japantimes.co.jp/text/nn20080411f2.html [Accessed 17 March 2016]
100. *Mainichi* (2012) 'Death Penalty to Stand for Man over 1999 Murders of 2 as Minor', 20 February 2012.
101. *Asahi* (2012) '*Tensei Jingo*' (The Voice of Heaven is the Voice of People), 21 February 2012.
102. Although his death was initially believed to be a traffic accident, it was discovered on 2 May 1984 that the president of his company was involved in the murder (Harada, M. (2004) *Otōto wo Koroshita Kare to Boku* (He, Who Killed My Brother, and I), Tokyo: Popura, pp. 76–77).
103. Mori (2008) *op. cit.* p. 51.
104. Harada (2004) *Ibid.*
105. Harada (2004) *op. cit.* p. 104.
106. Harada (2004) *op. cit.* pp. 108–109.
107. Harada (2004) *Ibid.*
108. *Japan Times* (2007) 'Victims' Trial Role to be Avengers?', 21 November 2007. Available at: http://www.japantimes.co.jp/text/nn20071121f3.html [Accessed 17 March 2016]
109. Harada (2004) *op. cit.* pp. 51–52.

110. Interview with a senior writer at a newspaper agency, Tokyo, 12 May 2011; postal correspondence with a senior writer at a newspaper agency, 21 May 2011.
111. Hamai and Ellis (2008a) *op. cit.* p. 73; Kiriyama, K. (2008) '*Susumu Shūshinkeika: Mukichōueki no Genjitsu*'(Growing Trend Towards Life Sentence Without Parole: Reality of Indefinite Imprisonment), *Sekai*, Tokyo: Iwanami Shoten, p. 171.
112. Japan Federation of Bar Associations (2008) *Ibid.*
113. Amnesty International (2008) 'Japan: Amnesty International Submission to the UN Human Rights Committee', 92nd session of the UN Human Rights Committee, 17 March—4 April 2008, Pre-sessional meeting of the Country Report Task Force on Japan, February 2008. Available at: http://www2.ohchr.org/english/bodies/hrc/docs/ngos/AIJapan92.pdf [Accessed 17 March 2016]; UN Human Rights Committee (2008) *Concluding Observations of the Human Rights Committee: Japan*, 18 December 2008, CCPR/C/JPN/CO/5. Available at: http://www.adh-geneva.ch/RULAC/pdf_state/states-reports-2008-civil-ccpr2.pdf [Accessed 17 March 2016]
114. Kawashima, T. (1967) *Nihonjin no Hōishiki* (Japanese Legal Consciousness), Tokyo: Iwanami Shoten; Cole, T. (2007) 'Commercial Arbitration in Japan: Contributions to the Debate on Japanese 'Non-Litigiousness', *New York University Journal of International Law and Politics*, 40(1), pp. 29–114.
115. Dean, M. (2002) *Japanese Legal Syste*m 2nd ed., Abingdon: Routledge-Cavendish, p. 4.
116. Kawashima (1967) *op. cit.* p. 15.
117. Kawashima, T. (1963) 'Dispute Resolution in Contemporary Japan' in A.T. Von Mehren (ed) *Law in Japan: The Legal Order in a Changing Society*, Cambridge (MA): Harvard University Press, pp. 41–72, p. 45.
118. Wagatsuma, H. and Rosett, A. (1986) 'The Implications of Apology: Law and Culture in Japan and the United States', *Law and Society Review*, 20(4), pp. 461–498.
119. Feldman, E. (2007) 'Law, Culture, and Conflict: Dispute Resolution in Postwar Japan', *Scholarship at Penn Law*, pp. 50–79, p. 63. Available at: http://lsr.nellco.org/cgi/viewcontent.cgi?article=1158&context=upenn_wps [Accessed 17 March 2016]

120. Katzenstein, P.J. (1996) *Cultural Norms and National Security: Police and Military in Postwar Japan*, Ithaca: Cornell University Press, p. 192.
121. They include: (1) the Sakamoto family murder on 4 November 1989; (2) the Matsumoto gas attack on 27 June 1994; (3) the shooting of the National Police Agency Chief, Kunimatsu Takaji, on 21 June 1995; and (4) a case of a letter bomb sent to the Tokyo Governor on 16 May 1995 (Katzenstein (1996) *op. cit.* pp. 71–72).
122. Katzenstein (1996) *op. cit.* p. 71.
123. Osawa, M. and Mori, T. (2008) '*Taidan: Wareware wa Tasha no Shi ni Mukiaeru ka: Akihabara Jiken to Shikei wo Megutte*' (Dialogue: Whether or not We can Face Strangers' Death: Regarding Death Penalty for the Akihabara Case), *Sekai*, Tokyo: Iwanami Shoten, p. 157.
124. Kaga, O. and Yasuda, Y. (2008) '*Taidan: Shikei wa Shakai wo Yaban ni suru*' (Dialogue: Capital Punishment Makes the Society Uncivilised), *Sekai*, Tokyo: Iwanami Shoten, p. 133; The trial started on 24 April 1996, and Asahara was sentenced to death on 27 February 2004 after 257 trial sessions (Nakamura, J. (2006) 'The Present Situation of Aum Trials', *Zeitschrift für Internationale Strafrechtsdogmatik*, 8, pp. 378–379, p. 378. Available at: http://www.zis-online.com/dat/artikel/2006_8_60.pdf [Accessed 17 March 2016]
125. *Sankei* (2012) *Ibid.*
126. *Japan Times* (2010) *Ibid.*
127. *Sankei* (2012) *Ibid.*
128. Interview with two NGO members, Tokyo, 17 May 2011.
129. Interview with an NGO member, Tokyo, 12 April 2011.
130. *Ibid.*
131. *Ibid.*
132. *Ibid.*
133. Johnson, T. D. (2011) *Nihon ga Shikei wo Sonchi suru Riyū: Kokonotsu no Kasetsu* (Why Japan Retains Capital Punishment: Nine Hypotheses) in A. Fukurai (ed) *Shikei to Mukiau Saibanin no Tame ni* (For Lay Judges who Handle Capital Punishment Sentencing), Tokyo: Gendai Jinbun Sha, pp. 141–144.
134. Johnson (2011) *op. cit.* pp. 142–143.
135. Johnson (2011) *op. cit.* p. 144.
136. Moriyama, M. (2001b) *The 153rd Legal Affairs Committee of the House of Representatives*, 19 October 2001, p. 8.

137. Interview with an academic, Tokyo, 12 April 2011.
138. The Council of Europe (1993) *Statutory Resolution (93) 26 on Observer Status*, p. 1. Available at: http://conventions.coe.int/Treaty/en/Treaties/Html/Resol9326.htm [Accessed 17 March 2016]
139. The Council of Europe (2001) *Resolution 1253: Abolition of the Death Penalty in Council of Europe Observer States*, p. 3. Available at: http://assembly.coe.int/Main.asp?link=/Documents/AdoptedText/ta01/ERES1253.htm [Accessed 17 March 2016]
140. Johnson (2011) *op. cit.* pp. 145–148.
141. Johnson (2005) *op. cit.* p. 259.
142. Moriyama (2001b) *Ibid.*
143. Interview with a MOFA minister, Tokyo, 9 May 2011; and with two MOFA ministers, Tokyo, 17 June 2011.
144. It is called the UN Resolution Concerning Abolition of the Death Penalty in a short form.
145. Interview with a MOFA minister, Tokyo, 9 May 2011
146. Interview with two MOFA officials, Tokyo, 17 June 2011.
147. According to the result of the Second Protocol of the ICCPR, aiming at the abolition of the death penalty, 55 voted for, 28 voted against and 45 abstained on 22 November 1989. In the Legal Affairs Committee on 5 December 1989, Ishigaki Yasuji in the MOFA combined the number of the latter two, and denied that the anti-death-penalty norm was not widely supported in the world yet (Ishigaki, Y. (1989) *The 116th Legal Affairs Committee of the House of Councillors*, 5 December 1989, p. 3).
148. Interview with a MOFA minister, Tokyo, 9 May 2011; and with two MOFA officials, Tokyo, 17 June 2011.
149. Interview with two MOFA officials, Tokyo, 17 June 2011.
150. *Ibid.*
151. Interview with an academic, Tokyo, 13 April 2011.
152. NHK (2011) '*Hōmu Daijin no Kunō*' (Agony of Justice Ministers), broadcast on 27 February 2011.
153. Interview with a MOFA minister, Tokyo, 9 May 2011.
154. Postal correspondence with a former Minister of Justice, 8 February 2011.
155. Interview with an academic, Tokyo, 13 April 2011.
156. Interview with an NGO staff(a), Tokyo, 27 May 2011.

157. *Ibid.*
158. Interview with an NGO staff(b), Tokyo, 27 May 2011.
159. *Ibid.*
160. Interview with two NGO staff members, Tokyo, 17 May 2011.
161. Schmidt, P.(2002) *Capital Punishment in Japan*, Brill Academic Publishers, pp. 45, 55; Johnson (2006) *Ibid.*
162. *Ibid.*
163. *Ibid.*
164. *Asahi* (2011b) '*19 nen buri Shikei Zero, Shinchō na Hōshō, Zehi no Giron wa Fukamarazu* (No Death Penalty for the First Time in 19 Years, Careful Minister of Justice, No Deep Discussion on the Rights and Wrong of the Penalty), 31 December 2011. Available at: http://www.asahi.com/special/minshu/TKY201112280771.html [Accessed 17 March 2016]; *Nikkei* (2011) '*Shikei Shikkō 19 nen buri ni Zero no Mitōshi, Kotoshi Ichinen kan no Saiban-in Saiban, Shikei 9 nin, Muzai 10 nin*'(Zero Execution for the First Time in 19 Years, Quasi-Jury Trials This Year, Death Penalty to Nine People, Innocence to 10 People), 28 December 2011; *Yomiuri* (2011) '*Shikei Shikkō, 19 nen buri Zero, Mishikkō Saita 129 nin*'(Zero Execution for the First Time in 19 Years, Largest Death Row Inmates, 129 People), 28 December 2011.

CHAPTER 4

An Honourable Death? Governmental Justification for Capital Punishment 1980–1989

4.1 Introduction

The previous chapters have analysed the capital punishment system in Japan, highlighting the tightly knit institutional mechanism within which selected elites in the Ministry of Justice and the Public Prosecutor's Office operate. This chapter and the following three will focus on how the Ministry of Justice has consistently sought to construct a dominant discourse on this system. As already discussed, the government frequently cites public opinion as a primary reason for retaining capital punishment. Therefore, the first section of each chapter briefly examines the prevailing social climate surrounding capital punishment at certain times, which was often a result of media coverage of, and the governmental response to, contemporary crime situations. The second section of each chapter investigates the official comments on capital punishment by Ministers of Justice in press conferences and Diet meetings. This clarifies how the Ministry of Justice continuously tried to justify the capital punishment system, citing domestic factors as 'legitimate' reasons.

This chapter examines the period from 1980 to 1989, that is, the ten years before the *de facto* moratorium period. Initially, it introduces several key events that aroused domestic discussions about the Japanese criminal justice system during this period: disclosure of miscarriage of justice cases and successive serious murder cases. Through examining media coverage of and governmental response to these incidents, and the absence of effective anti-death-penalty NGO activities at the time, it clarifies why

M. Obara-Minnitt, *Japanese Moratorium on the Death Penalty*,
DOI 10.1057/978-1-137-55822-0_4

these events did not necessarily cause a setback to retentionism in civil society. The second section explores the governmental discourse on capital punishment by pro-death-penalty actors, or Ministers of Justice and bureaucrats in the Ministry of Justice. It investigates how the Japanese government dealt with cases where there was a miscarriage of justice, in order to legitimate the retention of capital punishment even at the risk of detaining and executing innocent people.

4.2 Persistent Pro-Death-Penalty Mood Among the Public?

According to governmental poll results, 62.3 per cent of the Japanese public supported capital punishment in 1980 and 66.5 per cent in 1989 (see Appendix B). Although there exists a methodological problem regarding the governmental opinion polls (see Chap. 3), Japanese civil society in the 1980s did not appear a fertile ground for the discussion of abolitionism. The following section examines key events during this period and investigates why they did not become major impediments to the prevailing argument that capital punishment functions as social justice.

4.2.1 Public Reaction to the Disclosure of the Four Main Miscarriage of Justice Cases in the 1980s

During the 1980s there were four major retrials that revealed miscarriages of justice, resulting from forced confessions by police and prosecutors: these were the Menda case, the Saitagawa case, the Shimada case and the Matsuyama case. As Petra Schmidt argues:

> [a]ll [the four cases] occurred during the postwar turmoils, when the violent investigation methods of prewar times were still applied. Police, prosecutors and judges had been trained under the old system, and a confession was still regarded as the most important and absolute evidence. Moreover, the techniques of forensic science had not yet been very highly developed.[1]

In the Menda case, Menda Sakae, a 23-year-old black market rice dealer, was detained for 34 years and seven months until 15 July 1983, on a false charge of murdering a priest and his wife with a knife and an axe on 29 December 1948. Although Menda had an alibi, that he stayed at a guesthouse with a prostitute on the day of the crime, a policeman made her testify that it was on 30 December 1948 that Menda stayed with her, and by torturing Menda continuously for a number of nights he forced him to confess.[2] Menda's death sentence was upheld on 5 January 1952 on the basis of two pieces of 'evidence': (1) a confession extracted by torture and (2) Menda's axe with some type O blood on.[3] Although the three other murder cases are different in nature,[4] some similarities can be observed in how suspects were chosen and forced to confess: the defendants were either not engaged in professional work of high social status or had previous crime records. In order to achieve a higher success rate in 'solving' murder cases, the police appear to have charged socially and economically vulnerable people after insufficient investigation.

Disclosures of miscarriages of justice were widely featured in the media in the 1980s, and this could have become a setback to the 'persistent' pro-death-penalty sentiment amongst the Japanese public. However, at no point was there a full public debate on whether or not capital punishment functions as social justice when there is a risk of detaining and killing innocent people. Most of the interviewees for this book, including governmental ministers, NGO staff and attorneys who specialise in capital cases, argued that this was closely linked to the fact that the Japanese government and the media dealt with these serious miscarriages of justice as a separate issue from capital punishment, and did not encourage domestic debate on the immediate abolition of capital punishment.[5]

For example, as is discussed in the following section in detail, the then Minister of Justice claimed that erroneous judgements should not happen in the Japanese criminal justice system since it is equipped with a fair three-tiered judicial system,[6] so that even if human errors are made in the first or second trial, they will be rectified in the Supreme Court following a careful investigation of the case. The media coverage of the four main miscarriage of justice cases emphasised the violent interrogation methods in *daiyō kangoku* (police detention) and an inadequate forensic approach, with poor blood tests or the lack of adequate DNA test technology in the late 1940s and early 1950s. Despite the 'fatal' outcome for those falsely convicted, the media did not reflect on the context of these catastrophic errors by questioning the existence of the capital punishment system itself.[7]

Besides the lack of fundamental efforts by the government or the media to tackle miscarriages of justice, it should be noted that anti-death-penalty NGOs were still in their inception, and lacked the social impact to advance domestic discussion of the issue at this time. During the 1980s individual activities gradually started to develop into collective action. For example, it was a chaplain, Shiotani Soichiro, who acted on behalf of Menda for approximately 30 years at his request, not a group of activists.[8] Various anti-death-penalty NGOs started to be founded in the 1980s,[9] and it was after the disclosure of these miscarriages of justice that they began to act systematically on behalf of other wrongly convicted death row inmates. However, anti-death-penalty NGOs constantly received complaints from the public, indicating that they should not mix advocating on behalf of particular innocent convicts with advancing anti-death-penalty campaigns.[10]

Considering the methodological issues regarding the governmental opinion polls (see Chap. 3), the results of those polls cannot be taken as showing that the Japanese public during this period was pro-death-penalty.[11] However, the public showed aversion to the emergence of collective anti-death-penalty actions. A similar view also appears to have been shared by the attorneys who specialised in wrongful conviction cases. Whilst they strongly denounced the efficiency-centred public prosecutors' work, where priority was given to obtaining confessions from suspects, not many of them supported the idea of abolishing capital punishment immediately.[12] As Yasuda points out, their professional mission was to save innocent convicts through retrials, and most of them believed that convicted criminals must be punished legally and deserved death to make atonement when appropriate.[13]

4.2.2 Public Reaction to Serious Murder Cases and Two Capital Cases in the 1980s

Another reason why disclosure of wrongful conviction cases did not particularly advance abolitionism in Japanese society in the 1980s appears to relate to sensational media broadcasting of serious murder cases and inappropriate governmental responses to them. These cases were (1) the Shinjuku bus arson attack case, (2) the Miyazaki Tsutomu case, (3) the Nagoya murder case and (4) the Ayase murder case.

Regarding the Shinjuku bus arson attack case,[14] it was first mis-reported that the offender was mentally disabled. Expressing concern that mentally disabled people tend to be exempted from death sentences and become repeat offenders, the then Minister of Justice, Okuno Seisuke, called for harsher punishment of mentally disabled people:[15] this is discussed further in the following section. In the second incident Miyazaki Tsutomu, 26 or 27 at the time of the crimes, molested and strangled four primary school girls in Tokyo and Saitama prefectures between 1988 and 1989. Because of the abnormality of the crimes that he committed, there was a national outcry.[16]

The third and fourth incidents were both committed by juvenile offenders, and the media sensationally featured their brutality. The Nagoya murder case arose from a murder-robbery and gang-rape incident in Nagoya in Aichi prefecture on 23–25 February 1988. Five out of the six criminals were teenagers; one of them was first sentenced to death on 28 June 1989.[17] Similarly, the Ayase murder was committed by seven juvenile offenders: they kidnapped and tortured a 17-year-old high school girl for 41 days from 25 November 1988 in Ayase, a suburb of Tokyo. What aroused public attention was not only the cruel nature of the crime, but also the media's response to it. The identities of juvenile offenders are usually hidden in court, and the media do not disclose them, respecting Article 61 of the Juvenile Law, which 'prohibits the publication of information that reveals the identity of suspects or convicted criminals below the age of 20'. However, a weekly magazine, *Shūkan Bunshū*, revealed the offenders' real names in its issue of 20 April 1989, claiming that 'beasts do not deserve human rights'.[18]

According to an interview conducted by *Asahi* with Hanada Kazuyoshi, the then editor of *Shūkan Bunshū*, this decision was made in order to: (1) impose a 'social sanction' on the offenders, who were protected by the Juvenile Law; (2) denounce the responsibility of the educational institution and parents of the offenders, and call for amendment of the Juvenile Law; and (3) pose a question to Japanese journalism, which customarily did not disclose the names of juvenile victims or offenders.[19] Despite Article 61, the law does not provide for any punishment or fine for violating the right of juveniles to anonymity, and in practice decisions about this are at the discretion of media agencies.[20] According to Hanada, the editorial team realised how brutal the case was as they proceeded with their investigation, and they decided to treat it as an exception.[21]

In the meantime, whilst juvenile crimes were featured sensationally in the media, one death row inmate at the time, Nagayama, who had also been a minor at the time of his crime, grabbed public attention as a novelist in the 1980s–1990s. He published a book *Kihashi* (Wooden Bridge) in 1984 and was granted the New Japanese Literature Award; and his *Muchi no Namida* (Tears of Ignorance) of 1990 became a best-selling book, with over 270,000 copies in print. Claiming that his poverty and ignorance had led him to commit a series of serious murders, 'From prison, he pleaded for tolerance and sought to win sympathy with his novels and poetry.'[22]

Nonetheless, virtual interaction with a death row inmate through his literature did not necessarily help to promote the idea of abolishing capital punishment amongst the public. The *New York Times* (26 April 1990) suggested that the Japanese media were not necessarily sympathetic to Nagayama, but supported the Supreme Court decision:[23]

> Several newspapers warned last week that capital punishment should be imposed carefully but that it was appropriate in this case because of what one called 'the coldbloodedness of the slayings, the motives for the crimes and the great pain suffered by the families of the victims.'

Indeed, the Hidaka murder case highlighted the lack of public interest in the legal rights of death row inmates.[24] Hidaka Yasumasa and Nobuko, a married couple, had been appealing since they were sentenced to death on 4 March 1987, but they withdrew their appeal on 11 October 1988 after hearing that a reprieve would possibly be granted. Emperor Shōwa (Hirohito) was very ill at that time, and there was a rumour in the prison that a reprieve from execution would be handed down at his death only if the final verdict had been delivered.[25] Article 6 (4) of the International Covenant on Civil and Political Rights (ICCPR) stipulates the right to plead for reprieve,[26] as do Articles 3 and 4 of the Pardon Act,[27] and Article 337 (3) of the Code of Criminal Procedure.[28] However, reprieves for death row inmates in Japan have been very rare, except for some special events such as when the San Francisco Peace Treaty came into effect in 1952. Although anti-death-penalty NGOs tried repeatedly to convince the Hidakas not to give up their right to appeal, they did so.[29] Emperor Shōwa died on 7 January 1989, but no reprieve was issued.[30]

Although anti-death-penalty activists protested against this, claiming that decisions on amnesty or reprieve are ill defined and can mislead convicts into give up their rights to appeal or seek retrials, this case did not necessary make the general public look at the Hidakas sympathetically.[31] There was no public movement to reconsider the legal rights of death row inmates.[32] Just as anti-death-penalty NGOs faced protests from the public, which called on them not to mix the two issues of advocating for wrongfully convicted people and abolishing a legal system thought to uphold social justice, Nagayama's contribution to the literary world did not necessarily make the public reconsider the ways in which criminals convicted in serious murder cases could atone for their crimes.

To summarise, even though the four wrongful convictions were exposed and publicised, they did not necessarily lead the public to call for abolition of capital punishment. This appears to be because: (1) the media and the Japanese government framed these events as a negative legacy of the immediate post-war era, which would be less likely to happen in the future; and (2) the media sensationalised serious murder crimes. In addition, the 1980s was a period when individual abolitionist activities began to gradually evolve into collective actions, but they still lacked social impact across the nation.[33] NGOs acting on behalf of the victims of miscarriages of justice were viewed by the public as conflating the two ideas of fighting for the innocent and abolishing the capital punishment system.[34] Furthermore, Nagayama's success as a novelist did not help to advance the public debate about whether depriving a man of life is merely judicial killing, or lead to an examination of the possibility of alternative punishment. As the Hidaka case illustrates, whilst anti-death-penalty activists criticised the Ministry of Justice for the ill-defined criteria regarding reprieve for death row inmates, the issue did not become a central concern for the general public.[35]

The next section focuses on the governmental discourse on capital punishment, and examines the government's strategic use and manipulation of public opinion in order to add legitimacy to the retention of the system.

4.3 Governmental Justification for Capital Punishment

The successive disclosure of miscarriage of justice cases could have caused a setback to Japan's justification of its capital punishment policy. Even if capital punishment appears to function as social justice for victims' bereaved families, executing innocent people is nothing but injustice. However, in order to maintain public support for the system, the Ministry of Justice endeavoured to stress that these miscarriages of justice stemmed from a pre-war criminal justice system, and amended the compensation system instead of halting executions, which could have avoided further deaths following wrongful conviction. For examination of the measures that the government took, this section divides the time period into three phases: (1) 1980–1984, when the first three wrongful convictions were disclosed; (2) 1984–1987, when the issue of a decades-long-serving death row inmate was raised; and (3) 1987–1989, when the Criminal Compensation Act was amended and the fourth miscarriage of justice case was disclosed.

4.3.1 Governmental Response to Miscarriage of Justice/Wrongful Conviction Cases (1980–1984)

The Minister of Justice Okuno Seisuke's (17 July 1980–30 November 1981) pro-death-penalty approach was first observed in the Legal Affairs Committee on 27 August 1980, when he proposed amendment of the Penal Code following the Shinjuku bus arson attack case. According to Okuno, harsher punishment must be imposed on mentally disabled people, since it was not fair to the public that this group tended to be exempted from death sentences and remain free to become repeat offenders.[36] He proclaimed the deterrent effect of capital punishment when he was questioned on the retention of the death penalty in the Legal Affairs Committee on 16 October and 18 December 1980. He stressed that the Japanese public believed that criminals of serious murder cases should atone for the crimes with death, and that the capital punishment system had been working as a deterrent.[37]

With regard to the miscarriages of justice, he emphasised the existence of a fair trial system in Japan. When the Menda Sakae case started to be examined as a possible miscarriage of justice by attorneys and anti-death-penalty advocates, Okuno was asked his opinion in the Legal Affairs Committee on 18 December 1980. He commented that cases of wrongful conviction could usually be avoided since Japan was equipped with a fair three-tier judicial system.[38] Thus, Okuno: (1) proposed an amendment to the legal provisions so that death sentences would also be imposed on mentally disabled people; (2) proclaimed the retention of capital punishment referring to a cultural value, *shinde wabiru*, and capital punishment's deterrent effect; and (3) denied the possibility that convicts could be wrongly convicted in the Japanese criminal justice system.

On the other hand, it is worth noting that Okuno commented in the Legal Affairs Committee on 16 October 1980 that he was unwilling to be given such a difficult decision (authorising execution orders) during his term.[39] That is, he showed some reluctance to become involved in state killing. However, given that Okuno did authorise an execution during his term, he appears to have chosen to separate his personal feelings from his official duty. A similar attitude was observed from the subsequent Minister of Justice, Sakata Michita (30 November 1981–27 November 1982). Sakata indicated that his official responsibilities overrode his personal convictions, and he also tried to justify capital punishment on cultural grounds.[40] In the Legal Affairs Committee on 23 March 1982, he claimed that the Japanese had nurtured their own culture as an island nation for over 2000 years: abolishing capital punishment could go against it.[41]

It was during the term of Hatano Akira (27 November 1982–27 December 1983) that Menda Sakae was found not guilty on 15 July 1983 after being detained on death row for 34 years and seven months. Therefore, it was expected by anti-death-penalty Diet members that the Ministry of Justice would engage in a constructive discussion and take appropriate measures to prevent further miscarriages of justice. However, Hatano tried to legitimise the retention of capital punishment, denying the necessity of reforming the criminal justice system. In the Legal Affairs Committee on 10 August 1983, the international anti-death-penalty trend was discussed, citing the example of the UK.[42] However, Hatano argued that the issue of whether or not states should abolish capital punishment depended on the quality of the national criminal justice system, the climate of public opinion and cultural practices.[43]

Regarding the first factor in particular, Hatano argued that Japanese criminal justice was 'superior' to that of the USA or the UK, referring to the findings by B.J. George, Jr.[44] According to George, Japan is both 'number one and unique' since 'public prosecutors in Japan are committed to a standard of objectively fair administration of justice to a far greater extent than all but a handful of federal and state prosecutors in the United States'.[45] George is an expert in comparative criminal law, but it cannot be ignored that the majority of scholars agree that whilst public prosecutors pursue 'exceptional efficiency' in solving the cases,[46] their activities are not directed by the principle of *in dubio pro reo* ('when in doubt, favour the accused').[47] As Johnson argues, forced confessions lie at the heart of Japanese criminal justice.[48] In fact, in the Menda case, it was the criminal justice system that 'delayed' and 'denied' justice for more than three decades.[49] Nevertheless, citing a single source that admires the 'fair' work of Japanese public prosecutors, Hatano claimed that disclosure of a single miscarriage of justice case cannot necessarily be a significant factor in advancing abolitionism in Japan.[50]

To sum up, Hatano insisted that wrongful convictions rarely occur in Japan, and it is not necessary to abolish capital punishment since: (1) prosecutors do an outstanding job compared with those in other countries; (2) defendants can prove their innocence through the legal process from first to third trials; and (3) death row inmates can submit pleas for retrials if they are falsely convicted. However, in reality, human errors are inevitable, even with improved DNA test technology compared with the poor quality of blood testing in the late 1940s and early 1950s, and it is not easy for death row inmates to prove their innocence. Prosecutors tend to make defendants confess in order to keep their investigative efficiency high; they are involved in the rulings from the first to third trials; and they possess the right to submit immediate appeals against retrials.

In fact, contrary to Hatano's confidence in the Japanese criminal justice system, two more serious miscarriages of justice were disclosed during the term of the subsequent Minister of Justice, Sumi Eisaku (27 December 1983–1 November 1984): Taniguchi Shigeyoshi was found not guilty on 12 March 1984 after 33 years and 11 months, and Saito Yukio on 11 July 1984 after 28 years and seven months. The issues of wrongful conviction and capital punishment were frequently discussed in the Diet meetings, and several proposals were made by anti-death-penalty Diet members.

Hayashi Hyakuro proclaimed the rights of death row inmates to retrial in the Legal Affairs Committee on 2 March 1984.[51] He proposed that once retrials are permitted, death row inmates must be treated as 'defendants' who may be proved innocent, and should be released from death row temporarily. In response, the Director-General of the Criminal Affairs Bureau, Kakei Eiichi dismissed the proposal,[52] referring to Article 11 (2) of the Penal Code, which provides that 'A person who has been sentenced to the death penalty shall be detained in a jail until its execution.' However, Hayashi's proposal aroused a great amount of sympathy amongst some Diet members, and on 17 May 1984 Terada Kumao proposed a bill to amend a part of the Code of Criminal Procedure with other abolitionist Diet members.[53] According to the proposed bill:

(1) criteria for opening of retrials must be softened;
(2) executions must be halted once death row inmates have started to appeal for retrials;
(3) attorneys' rights must be secured in the process of opening retrials (secret communication between death row inmates and attorneys, and attorneys' rights to access to necessary information must be secured);
(4) public prosecutors' immediate appeals against retrials must be forbidden; and
(5) the costs of appeals for and opening of retrials must be covered by the government.[54]

Since the three wrongful conviction cases had already been disclosed by then, this proposal was a constructive action towards ensuring fairer trials in the Japanese criminal justice system. However, the bill did not pass in the Diet and to date no similar measures have been introduced by the Ministry of Justice. Given that approximately 80 per cent of all legislation passed is drafted by bureaucrats (see Chap. 2), it was unlikely from the start that measures drafted by Diet members who are not in favour of government policy would pass.

Although Sumi sought to avoid the issue of wrongful convictions, he made further conservative remarks justifying capital punishment in the Legal Affairs Committee on 27 March 1984: (1) views on capital punishment depend on individuals; (2) the government must respect the feelings of the Japanese nation, which can be observed in public opinion polls; and (3) it is a legal duty of Ministers of Justice to authorise executions.[55] Even though two more wrongful convictions were disclosed during his term after the Menda case, and initiatives to improve the rights of death row inmates and ensure a better chance for them to open retrials were taken by Diet members, Sumi authorised an execution of a death row inmate during his term. Like Okuno, Sumi showed some reluctance to authorise executions, but chose to carry out his official duty on the basis of law and public opinion.[56]

4.3.2 *Governmental Response to a Long-Serving Death Row Inmate (1984–1987)*

Following the disclosure of a number of wrongful convictions, the main discussion topic during the term of Shimasaki Hitoshi (1 November 1984–28 December 1985) was shifted to an inmate at the time, Hirasawa Sadamichi. Hirasawa had been on death row for 30 years since 1950, on a charge of poisoning 12 people and committing a bank robbery on 26 January 1948. Hirasawa had submitted 17 pleas for retrials and five pleas for clemency by that time, none of which had been accepted. What deserves particular attention is that he was the last defendant sentenced to death under the old Code of Criminal Procedure used in the pre-war period, whereby only a confession was required to charge defendants with a capital offence. Therefore, Diet members such as Miura Takashi, Akiyama Chozo and Inokuma Shigeji raised two main concerns: (1) Hirasawa might have been forced to make a confession by torture; and (2) years of detention in constant fear of execution is an inhuman punishment, which cannot be justified by the Penal Code.

In the Legal Affairs Committee on 11 December 1985, Miura questioned whether Hirasawa would be granted a reprieve considering his age, which was 94.[57] However, the Director-General of the Criminal Affairs

Bureau, Kakei, explained that no exception could be allowed to the elderly unless they suffered from a serious mental disorder as specified in Article 479 (1) and (2) of the Code of Criminal Procedure.[58] With regard to Shimasaki, he took no initiatives. He merely mentioned that the case was not an easy one given that approximately 30 years had passed since the incident occurred, and few public prosecutors knew the details of the case.[59] Given that Shimasaki believed in *Jōdo Shinshū* Buddhism, which teaches that every single person's life is precious, one may conjecture that he was personally sensitive to the issue of depriving death row inmates of life. Indeed, it has been disclosed that a later Minister of Justice, Sato Megumu (29 December 1990–5 November 1991), refused to authorise executions out of respect for the teaching of *Jōdo Shinshū* Buddhism, and this is discussed further in Chap. 5. However, rather than sticking to his religious beliefs, Shimasaki appears to have chosen to fulfil his official responsibility. He authorised executions of two death row inmates during his term.

Regarding the term of Suzuki Seigo (28 December 1985–22 July 1986), what merits some attention is not necessarily his own remarks. Rather, it is a drastic change in the opinion of the former Minister of Justice, Hatano, regarding the Japanese criminal justice system. During his term as Minister of Justice (27 November 1982–27 December 1983), Hatano stuck to his argument that the Japanese criminal justice system was superior to those in Western countries, and that there were only a handful of wrongful convictions in Japan.[60] However, Hatano argued in the Legal Affairs Committee on 25 March 1986 that public prosecutors' role must be altered to achieve fairer trials in Japan.[61] According to him, whilst public prosecutors were considered as judicial officers in the prewar period, they became administrative officers after the war.[62] The Public Prosecutor's Office accordingly became the administrative authority, and the judges became the only judicial officers. Despite this change, prosecutors continued to exert tremendous power in the Japanese criminal justice system and were involved in the crucial part of capital punishment policy. Furthermore, Hatano claimed that the criminal justice system was originally an import from Germany, and now that it had taken root in Japan it was time to adjust it to the Japanese way so that it could function better.[63]

Whilst Hatano sought to legitimise and justify Japanese criminal justice when he was in the post of the Minister of Justice, later he criticised deficiencies in exactly the same system. Given that these criticisms were made only three years or so after he left his post, one may doubt that such concerns suddenly occurred to him after such a short time. This could indicate that Ministers of Justice tend to act on precedents and, as the top authority of the Ministry of Justice, seek to legitimise the existing legal system, even if their personal convictions are contrary. In response to Hatano's suggestion about the role of public prosecutors, Suzuki merely stated that he would respect Hatano's opinion and continue to make an effort for the future of the Japanese criminal justice system.[64] Invoking the feelings of Japanese citizens on capital punishment in the Legal Affairs Committee on 27 March 1986, Suzuki authorised executions of two inmates during his term.

In the meantime, the natural death of Hirasawa Sadamichi at the age of 95 was confirmed on 10 May 1987, and a subsequent Minister of Justice, Endo Kaname (22 July 1986–6 November 1987), and bureaucrats in the Ministry of Justice were accused by the anti-death-penalty lobby of ill treatment in his case. However, the Ministry of Justice endeavoured to: (1) legitimate the non-execution, allowing some room around the interpretation of Article 475 of the Code of Criminal Procedure, which specifies the responsibility of the Minister of Justice regarding the timing for authorising and conducting executions; and (2) stress that there was no possibility that Hirasawa was innocent.[65] In the Legal Affairs Committee on 14 May 1987, a Diet member, Inokuma Shigeji, voiced concerns regarding the non-execution of Hirasawa against the legal provisions. According to him, Hirasawa's 32 years of life in detention could imply that Japan used a system of life imprisonment without parole with no legal backing, and this could be more inhuman than hanging.[66]

In response, Okamura Yasutaka, the Director-General of the Criminal Affairs Bureau, provided three main explanations of why the Ministry of Justice had failed to take appropriate measures in dealing with the case: (1) shortage of competent public prosecutors; (2) low efficiency caused by an outstanding number of pleas from Hirasawa; and (3) the advisory nature of Article 475 of the Code of Criminal Procedure. According to Okamura, whilst the number of applicants for public prosecutor posts had been decreasing,[67] Hirasawa submitted pleas for retrials 18 times and for reprieves five times in total, which heavily hindered the Bureau's efficiency in dealing with the case.[68] What is more, Okamura tried to justify Hirasawa's 32-year detention, claiming that it was reasonable for Ministers of Justice to have dealt with the case very carefully and postponed the execution orders.[69] More precisely, he argued that it was not strictly necessary for Ministers of Justice to be bound by Article 475 (2): whilst it requires the Minister to order the execution of the death penalty 'within six months from the date when the judgment becomes final and binding', this excludes the period during which applications or requests for a retrial or pardon are being made.[70]

This is strikingly different from Ministry bureaucrats' usual claim in justifying the capital punishment system. It is usually the Ministry of Justice that contends that executions must be authorised on the basis of Article 475 in order to keep Japan's status as a *hōchi kokka* (a law-abiding country), whilst constitutional scholars tend to interpret this provision in wider terms and claim that it is mandatory for Ministers of Justice to be extraordinarily careful with decisions that relate to matters of life and death.[71] In order to justify the fact that Hirasawa was not executed despite the legal provisions, Okamura thus implied legal ambivalence in Article 475, which was not consistent with the Ministry's usual legitimation of capital punishment on the basis of law.

Endo also supported Okamura's explanation regarding this case, and claimed that it was not necessarily unusual that more than 30 years should pass without parole or execution while the Ministry of Justice and the Public Prosecutor's Office were handling each plea one by one.[72] Furthermore, both Okamura and Endo stressed that there was no possibility whatever that Hirasawa was innocent;[73] and Endo provided detailed information on how he had tried to deal with the case. According to Endo, doubting whether the non-execution of Hirasawa indicated a neglect of the Ministry of Justice's duties, he had set up several meetings with senior bureaucrats in the Ministry.[74] He claimed that the Ministry appeared to have been extraordinarily careful, in case the Japanese public might wonder whether the government had killed an innocent person before Hirasawa's retrials were permitted.[75]

Given that Ministers of Justice rarely talk about internal communication within their Ministry, Endo appeared at first sight enthusiastic about being engaged in this issue. However, stressing that there was no possibility whatever that Hirasawa was innocent and that the Ministry of Justice cared about the public view of the legitimacy of capital punishment policy, Endo appeared to have evaded a fundamental question about whether it is appropriate to retain capital punishment at the risk of detaining or executing innocent people.

The Ministry of Justice thus endeavoured to defend the non-execution of Hirasawa on the grounds of: (1) the shortage of competent prosecutors; (2) the tremendous number of pleas from Hirasawa; (3) the 'rights' of Ministers of Justice to postpone executions when appropriate; and (4) careful investigation in order not to raise public doubt about wrongful conviction. However, a further remark by Endo raised controversy in the Diet. In light of the Hirasawa case, he suggested in the Legal Affairs Committee on 14 May 1987 that it would be better to limit the number of retrials for each inmate, since it could give the public the incorrect understanding that there was a loophole that death row inmates could use in order to postpone execution.[76] What is more, Toyoshima Eijiro, Superintendent Public Prosecutor in the High Public Prosecutor's Office in Nagoya, made a similar comment at his inauguration speech on 18 May 1987, only four days after Endo's statement. Since Toyoshima stated that 'it appears that submitting pleas for opening retrials are currently "in fashion"', Negoro Yasuchika, the Chief Cabinet Secretary, had to comment in the Legal Affairs Committee on 27 August 1987 that Toyoshima's remark referred to those who submit pleas without valid reasons repeatedly, and did not necessarily refer to Hirasawa.[77]

The Hirasawa case thus revealed the 'institutional ambivalence' of the capital punishment system. The Ministry of Justice consistently treats capital punishment as an issue of law, and justifies executions on the basis of Article 475 of the Code of Criminal Procedure. However, it tried to legitimate non-execution of a death row inmate who had been sentenced to death decades ago, using the same legal provision as justification. Endo authorised executions of two inmates during his term, justifying his approach in the Legal Affairs Committee on 15 May 1987 by arguing that the validity of the system's deterrent effect depends on national characteristics.[78]

4.3.3 Governmental Response to the Criminal Compensation Act and Disclosure of Another Wrongful Conviction Case (1987–1989)

It was during the term of Hayashida Yukio (6 November 1987–27 December 1988) that an amendment was made to the Criminal Compensation Act relating to those detained on death row following wrongful convictions. Given that Menda, Taniguchi and Saito were found not guilty in 1983–1984, and Hirasawa died in 1987, leaving the possibility that he was innocent, significant attention was paid in the Diet meetings to the improvement of criminal compensation. Originally, criminal compensation for those detained on death row as a result of a miscarriage of justice was from ¥1000 ($8.90) up to ¥7200 ($64.10) per day, while for those who were executed following a wrongful conviction it was up to ¥20 million ($177,962.54), this having been set in 1980.[79] Hayashida proposed a new bill in the Legal Affairs Committee on 25 March 1988 which would increase the amounts to ¥9400 ($83.64) and ¥25 million ($222,453.18), respectively.[80]

In the following Legal Affairs Committee on 29 March 1988, scholars and attorneys were called to the Diet to give unsworn testimony. Discussions ranged from raising the amount of the compensation money more than the Ministry of Justice proposed to a fundamental question of whether or not it was appropriate to set a limit to the amount in the first place. For example, Yokoyama Koichiro, professor of law at Kyushu University, used the example of the Compensation Act in West Germany in 1971. There was no upper limit in West Germany, and those who were detained following wrongful conviction could claim any amount as long as they could prove the loss they had incurred.[81] Considering the psychological damage that inmates had to go through from the first trial to the third, and financial loss during their life in detention, Yasuoka Okiharu, a Diet member and a later Minister of Justice, also disagreed with an upper limit to compensation.[82] Despite these criticisms in the Diet discussions, the proposed bill, which presumably had already been agreed amongst governmental officials, passed in the Legal Affairs Committee on 28 April 1988.

The Diet discussion agenda then moved back to whether or not Japan should retain capital punishment. Chiba Keiko, later Minister of Justice, argued in the Legal Affairs Committee on 26 April 1988 that abolishing capital punishment was as important as securing criminal compensation for those detained on death row or executed after a wrongful conviction.[83] This was because amendment of the Act appeared to have been made as an alternative to discussing a temporary halt to executions or the abolition of the capital punishment system. In response, Hayashida merely commented that the death sentence had only been given to those convicted of significantly serious crimes, with very careful consideration.[84] This sounded like a claim that capital punishment policy only involves a small fraction of criminals and does not deserve fundamental consideration.

A similar attitude was observed throughout this period. For example, the Ministry of Justice tried to deny the possibility of more wrongful conviction cases and to justify capital punishment on three grounds: (1) the three-tier judicial system, (2) death row inmates' rights to retrials, and (3) the improved financial compensation system.[85] However, the Ministry of Justice did not try to explain why capital punishment needed to be retained even at the risk of detaining and executing innocent people. It left aside the ethical concerns about depriving a person of life, and dealt with the issue of wrongful convictions by increasing the amount of financial compensation. The Ministry of Justice thus tried to retain a historically held policy acting on precedents, and Hayashida authorised executions of two inmates as an annual practice.

With regard to the subsequent three Ministers of Justice, each resigned within a short period, and active discussions did not take place on the issue of capital punishment or miscarriage of justice cases. For example, Hasegawa Takashi (27–30 December 1988) resigned within four days over an insider trading scandal: the so-called Recruit Scandal. A former Supreme Court judge, Takatsuji Masami (30 December 1988–3 June 1989), took over from him, and it was during his term that Akahori Masao was found not guilty on 11 February 1989 after 34 years and eight months. However, the Legal Affairs Committees met only five times during his term, and death row inmates' rights to retrials and the rights and wrongs of capital punishment were not discussed. The subsequent Minister of Justice, Tanikawa Kazuo (3 June 1989–10 August 1989), resigned within approximately two months because of the Prime Minister Uno Sosuke's resignation, which was brought about by his womanising. Successive replacements of Ministers of Justice did not allow active discussions on human rights issues in the Diet, and executions did not take place during these periods either.

During the term of Goto Masao (10 August 1989–28 February 1990), he did not show any particular initiatives on the issue of capital punishment. In the Legal Affairs Committee on 5 December 1989, Chiba Keiko questioned Japan's position towards the international anti-death-penalty initiatives such as the Second Protocol of the ICCPR, the aim of which was to bring about the abolition of the death penalty.[86] However, Ishigaki Yasuji of the Ministry of Foreign Affairs (MOFA) stressed that: (1) such an initiative is a mere recommendation and legally non-binding; and (2) an internationally recognised norm on the death penalty does not exist yet.[87] Although Goto was also questioned on his policy on capital punishment, he only replied that the decision on whether or not Japan should comply with such initiatives must be made considering various domestic factors such as public opinion that those committing serious crimes deserve death.[88] Goto authorised an execution of one death row inmate during his term.

4.3.4 *Governmental Justification for Capital Punishment (1980–1989)*

To sum up, Ministers of Justice during this term separated their personal views or emotions from the performance of their official duties, and execution orders were authorised upon the basis of law, public opinion and the *shinde wabiru* social norm. Given that there were a maximum of two executions per year during this period, which was exceptionally low by comparison with other retentionist countries,[89] the dutiful manner in which the Ministry carried out its duty was observed. Furthermore, what merits particular attention regarding this period is that: (1) executions were not hindered even after several controversial events, such as disclosure of wrongful convictions; and (2) the Ministry of Justice invoked the 'advisory' nature of legal provisions on executions once it was accused of the imprisonment of a death row inmate until death. The Ministry of Justice treated miscarriages of justice as exceptional incidents which occurred during the post-war turmoil, and it downplayed their importance and relevance as crucial incidents that might bring about reconsideration of the possible abolition of capital punishment. A politicians-led bill to provide death row inmates with better treatment in the process of opening trials did not pass the bureaucratic decision-making mechanism, and instead the Compensation Act was amended as a temporary alternative to such a proposal. The amendment of the Act did not mean that the Ministry of Justice reflected on the issue of capital punishment or sought to introduce additional safeguards to avoid miscarriages of justice. Rather, the amendment appears to have been used to support the idea that abolition of capital punishment was unnecessary, since Japan was equipped with a three-tier judicial system and a retrial system.

Although the death row inmate Hirasawa was not permitted to open retrials and was detained for approximately three decades until his death, a ministry bureaucrat, Okamura, claimed that it was mandatory for Ministers of Justice to be extraordinarily careful with decisions.[90] Whilst Ministry bureaucrats usually criticise refusals by anti-death-penalty

Ministers of Justice to authorise executions as a neglect of official duty, Okamura justified this action when the Ministry was accused of practically giving someone life imprisonment without parole without legal backing. Consequently, instead of clarifying why Japan should retain capital punishment even at the risk of detaining and executing innocent people, the Ministry of Justice chose to justify the existing criminal justice system by: (1) using legal provisions, public opinion and cultural factors as prime sources; (2) stressing the available measures to avoid miscarriages of justice, and increasing the amount of financial compensation for those falsely charged or executed; and (3) implying the ambiguity of legal provisions regarding executions.

4.4 Conclusion

This chapter has investigated how the Ministry of Justice consistently justified capital punishment and conducted executions on an annual basis from 1980 to 1989. With regard to the social dynamic in the 1980s, there did not appear to exist a mood to fundamentally re-examine the issue of capital punishment. It was a time when individuals gradually started to take collective action, and anti-death-penalty NGOs were still in the early stages of development. Following the successive disclosure of wrongful conviction cases, newly formed anti-death-penalty NGOs began to act on behalf of inmates who had been wrongfully convicted. However, their campaigns were criticised by the public for mixing two different issues: (1) resolving judicial injustice by trying to prove the innocence of particular inmates, and (2) denying social justice by calling for the abolition of capital punishment. Such protests appear to have arisen from the public mainly because the Japanese government and the media had been hindering them from acknowledging the correlation between the two issues of wrongful conviction and capital punishment.

The media sensationalised several serious murder cases during this period. Although Japan had an exceptionally low crime rate, as it still has today, the media coverage of these cases may have led the public to believe that a heavy punishment through death was still required. Exceptionally, Nagayama's activities as a novelist on death row grabbed public attention to some extent; but this did not advance the idea of abolitionism across society. For example, whilst the Hidaka case made anti-death-penalty activists criticise the Ministry of Justice over the ill-defined criteria for reprieves for death row inmates, this did not become a central concern amongst the general public. Although wrongful convictions aroused sympathy towards the victims of miscarriages of justice to some extent, and Nagayama raised public awareness about death row inmates, this did not necessarily lead the public to reconsider how death row inmates should and could atone for their crimes.

On the government side, the Ministry of Justice consistently endeavoured to justify capital punishment on the basis of law and domestic factors such as the climate of public opinion. For example, although wrongful convictions were successfully exposed and publicised, the Ministry of Justice treated them as exceptional incidents which occurred during the post-war turmoil, not as 'systematic injustice' inflicted by police and public prosecutors.[91] It endeavoured to proclaim that Japan was equipped with a three-tiered judicial system and retrial system, and dealt with criticisms by amending the financial compensation policy. In other words, the Ministry did not take any particular measures to prevent further miscarriages of justice or to have a fundamental discussion about the existence of capital punishment, but reiterated the measures already in place for the wrongfully convicted.

Moreover, with regard to the Hirasawa case, the Ministry of Justice showed an ambiguous attitude towards the legal provisions. Whilst the Ministry of Justice usually claims that Article 475 of the Code of Criminal Procedure, which specifies the responsibility of Ministers of Justice regarding executions, must be respected in order to keep Japan *hōchi kokka*, a Ministry bureaucrat suggested that it was not necessarily required for Ministers of Justice to strictly comply with the relevant legal provision. The Ministry of Justice also tried to consistently justify the capital punishment system with reference to domestic factors such as the presumed deterrent effect, public opinion and cultural values. However, it failed to account or avoided accounting fully for why Japan is required to retain the system even at the risk of detaining or executing innocent people. The following chapter examines the *de facto* moratorium period from 1989 to 1993, and investigates how the Ministry of Justice justified the capital punishment system even while executions were put on hold for three years and four months.

Notes

1. Schmidt, P. (2002) *Capital Punishment in Japan*, Brill Academic Publishers, p. 148.
2. Foote, D. H. (1992a) 'From Japan's Death Row to Freedom', *Pacific Rim Law & Policy Association*, 1, pp. 11–103, p. 20; Schmidt *op. cit.* p. 143. Menda happened to know that a policeman, Masuda, was tolerating a minor prostitution business, and Masuda felt a strong urge to make Menda a suspect for this crime (Menda, S. (2004) *Menda Sakae Gokuchū Note: Watashi no Miokutta Shikeishū Tachi* (Menda Sakae's Notes on Death Row: Death Row Inmates Who I Saw Off), Tokyo: Impact Shuppan; Shiotani, S. (1994) *Shikei Shū 34 Nen: Fukutsu no Otoko, Menda Sakae no Saigetsu* (Death Row Inmate for 34 Years: A Man with Great Fortitude, Years Menda Sakae Has Spent), Tokyo: East Press, p. 48).
3. Shiotani (1994) *op. cit.* p. 21. Given that Menda's grandmother, who had often used the same axe, also had type O blood, what was found was not necessarily the blood of the victims. However, further investigation was not conducted since the confession was used as prime evidence.
4. (1) In the Saitagawa case, the police forced Taniguchi Shigeyoshi, a 19-year-old unemployed man with a few previous criminal convictions, to make a confession under torture. Taniguchi was detained for 33 years and 11 months until 12 March 1984 on a charge of stabbing a 62-year-old black market rice dealer (Foote (1992a) *op. cit.* p. 30). (2) In the Shimada case, 24-year-old Akabori Masao, who had mental disabilities and two previous criminal convictions for theft, was forced to confess to kidnapping a six-year-old girl, and was detained for 34 years and eight months until 11 February 1989 (Schmidt (2002) *op. cit.* p. 146). (3) In the Matsuyama case, 24-year-old Saito Sachio, who had been arrested for causing bodily harm a few weeks before, was forced to confess to murdering four members of the Ohara family and setting fire to their house, and was detained for 28 years and seven months until 11 July 1984 (Schmidt (2002) *op. cit.* p. 145).
5. Interview with: (1) a MOFA official, Tokyo, 9 May 2011; (2) an NGO worker, Tokyo, 12 April 2011; and (3) two NGO workers, Tokyo, 17 May 2011.
6. Okuno, S. (1980a) *The 93th Legal Affairs Committee of the House of Councillors*, 18 December 1980, pp. 3, 19.

7. Yasuda, Y., Kikuta, S. and Tsushima, S. (1996) '*Shikei Haishi e Mukete Dōsuruka: Kono 5 Nen no Ayumi to Tenbō*' (What We should do towards the Abolition of Death Penalty: Paths over the Five Years and Prospect), Tokyo: Impact Shuppan, p. 112.
8. Postal correspondence with a former death row inmate, Menda Sakae, 8 March 2011; and interviews with two NGO workers, Tokyo, 17 May 2011.
9. They include: (1) *On-na no Kai* (Women's Anti-Death Penalty Group); (2) *Shikei Shikko Teishi Renraku Kaigi* (Liaison Conference for Suspending Death Penalty); (3) *Mugi no Kai* (Group of Straw, or an anti-death-penalty group with death row inmates as full members); (4) *Shikei Jiken Tantō Bengoshi no Kai* (Attorney Group that Specialises in Capital Cases); and (5) *Kyūen Renraku Centre* (Rescue Liaison Centre).
10. Yasuda et al. (1996) *op. cit.* p. 116.
11. According to the government opinion polls, 62.3 per cent of the Japanese public supported capital punishment in 1980 and 66.5 per cent in 1989 (see Appendix B).
12. Yasuda et al. (1996) *op. cit.* pp. 112–113.
13. *Ibid.*
14. Maruyama Hirofumi, 38 at the time of the crime, threw some burning newspaper and a bucket of petrol into a bus in Shinjuku, Tokyo on 19 August 1980; six people died and 14 were seriously injured.
15. Okuno, S. (1980b) *The 92nd Legal Affairs Committee of the House of Councillors*, 27 August 1980, p. 5.
16. He burned a four-year-old girl's body and sent her bones and teeth to her parents, and he is also reported to have eaten her flesh and drunk her blood (*Japan Times* (2008) 'Lawmakers Slam Hatoyama over Executions', 18 June 2008. Available at: http://search.japantimes.co.jp/cgi-bin/nn20080618a6.html [Accessed 17 March 2016]).
17. His death sentence was reduced to life imprisonment on 16 December 1996.
18. Hanada cited in Tanihara, K., Kojima, S., Nakajima Y. and Mizuno T. (2005) '*Moto Shōnen' Satsujin Han no Saihan to Jitsumei Hōdō: Jyoshi Kōsei Konkurito Zume Satugai Jiken no Jun Shuhan Kaku wo Meguru Mass Media no Hōdō (Zenpen)*' (The Media Naming of Adult Criminals with Juvenile Criminal Records: The 1989 Concrete-Packing Murder Case and 2004 Assault Case (Part 1)), *Jyōhō Kenkyū*, 33, pp. 331–344, p. 334. Available at: http://www.

bunkyo.ac.jp/faculty/lib/slib/kiyo/Inf/if33/if3311.pdf [Accessed 17 March 2016].

19. Tanihara, K. et al. (2005) *Ibid.*
20. Brislin, T. & Inoue, Y. (2005) 'Youth Crime Coverage in Japan and the U.S.: A Comparative Study of Naming Juveniles in Youth Crime Coverage', presented at The Association for Education in Journalism and Mass Communication, San Antonio, Texas, August 2005, pp. 1–15, p. 3. Available at: http://list.msu.edu/cgi-bin/wa?A3=ind0602a&L=AEJMC&E=8bit&P=4542176&B=--&T=text%2Fplain;%20charset=iso-8859-1 [Accessed 17 March 2016].
21. Hanada cited in Tanihara, K. et al. (2005) *Ibid.*
22. Métraux, D.A. (2009) 'The Nagayama Criteria for Assessing the Death Penalty in Japan: Reflections of a Case Suspect', *Southeast Review of Asian Studies*, 31, pp. 282–289, p. 286.
23. *New York Times* (1990) 'Death Sentence Fuels Japan's Soul-Searching', 26 April 1990.
24. Hidaka Yasumasa and Nobuko, committed an murder for insurance-related reasons in Yubari, Hokkaido, on 5 May 1984. It was first dealt with as a fire accident, but after a conspirator turned himself in, the Hidakas were arrested on 19 August 1984.
25. Yasuda, Y. (1998) '*Uchitsuzuku Tairyō Shikei Shikkō: 12 Gatsu Shikkō Soshi wo*' (Mass Executions: Calling for Blocking Executions in December), *Nenpō Shikei Haishi* (Annual Report: Abolishing Capital Punishment), Tokyo: Impact Shuppan, p. 98.
26. It provides that 'Anyone sentenced to death shall have the right to seek pardon or commutation of the sentence. Amnesty, pardon or commutation of the sentence of death may be granted in all cases' (UN Human Rights Committee (1966) *International Covenant on Civil and Political Rights*, 16 December 1966).
27. According to Article 3, 'Except as otherwise specially provided for by the Cabinet Order of the preceding Article, general pardon shall have the following effect with respect to crimes for which general pardon has been granted: (i) In the case of a person against whom a judgment of conviction has been rendered, the rendition thereof shall cease to have effect; (ii) In the case of a person against whom a judgment of conviction has not yet been rendered, the power to prosecute shall be extinguished.' Moreover, Article 4 stipulates that 'A special pardon shall be granted with respect to a specific person against whom a judgment of conviction has been rendered.'

28. According to Article 337, 'The court shall, by a judgment, render a dismissal for judicial bar when: (i) The case has gone through a final and binding judgment; (ii) The punishment is repealed by laws and regulations established after the crime; (iii) There is a general pardon; (iv) There is a lapse of the statue of limitations.'
29. Yasuda (1998) *Ibid.*
30. The Hidakas were both executed on 1 August 1997.
31. Yasuda (1998) *Ibid.*
32. Yasuda (1998) *Ibid.*
33. Postal correspondence with a former death row inmate, Menda Sakae, 8 March 2011; and interviews with two NGO staff, Tokyo, 17 May 2011.
34. Yasuda et al. (1996) *op. cit.* p. 116.
35. Yasuda (1998) *Ibid.*
36. Okuno (1980b) *op. cit.* p. 5.
37. Okuno (1980a) *op. cit.* p. 8.
38. Okuno (1980a) *op. cit.* pp. 3, 19.
39. Okuno, S. (1980c) *The 93th Legal Affairs Committee of the House of Councillors*, 16 October 1980, p. 24.
40. Sakata, M. (1982) *The 96th Audit Committee of the House of Councillors*, 20 January 1982, p. 29.
41. Sakata, M. (1982) *The 96th Legal Affairs Committee of the House of Councillors*, 23 March 1982, p. 20.
42. In the UK, a motion to reintroduce capital punishment was rejected in the House of Commons on 13 July 1983 in the face of strong public support corresponding to an increase in serious crimes.
43. Hatano, A. (1983) *The 99th Legal Affairs Committee of the House of Representatives*, 10 August 1983, p. 23.
44. *Ibid.*
45. George Jr, B.J. (1984) 'Discretionary Authority of Public Prosecutors in Japan', *Law in Japan*, 17, pp. 42–84, p. 72.
46. Consistent writers on this issue include: Johnson, C. (1972) *Conspiracy at Matsukawa*, Berkeley and Los Angeles: University of California Press; Clifford, W. (1976) *Crime Control in Japan*, Lanham, MD: Lexington Books; Aoyagi, F. (1986) *Nihonjin no Hanzai Ishiki* (Japanese Consciousness on Crimes), Tokyo: Chūo Kōronsha; Foote, D.H. (1992a) *Ibid*; (1992b) 'From Japan's Death Row to Freedom', *Pacific Rim Law & Policy Association*, 1, pp. 11–103; Haley, J.O. (1992) 'Criminal Justice in Japan', *Journal*

of Japanese Studies, 18(2), pp. 553–556; Mukherjee, S. (1994) 'What is So Good about The Low Crime Rate in Japan', *Australian Rationalist*, 37, pp. 7–19; Johnson, D.T. (2002) *The Japanese Way of Justice: Prosecuting Crime in Japan*, New York: Oxford University Press.

47. Van Wolferen, K. (1989) *The Enigma of Japanese Power: People and Politics in a Stateless Nation*, New York: Macmillan, p. 222.
48. Johnson (2002) *op. cit.* p. 39.
49. Van Wolferen (1989) *op. cit.* p. 190.
50. Hatano (1983) *Ibid.*
51. Hayashi, H. (1984) *The 101st Legal Affairs Committee of the House of Representatives*, 2 March 1984, p. 38.
52. Kakei, E. (1984) *The 101st Legal Affairs Committee of the House of Representatives*, 2 March 1984, p. 38.
53. Terada, K. (1984) *The 101st Legal Affairs Committee of the House of Councillors*, 17 May 1984, p. 1.
54. *Ibid.*
55. Sumi, E. (1984) *The 101st Legal Affairs Committee of the House of Councillors*, 27 March 1984, p. 8.
56. Sumi (1984) *op. cit.* p. 32.
57. Miura, T. (1985) *The 103rd Legal Affairs Committee of the House of Representatives*, 11 December 1985, p. 6.
58. Kakei, E. (1985) *The 103rd Legal Affairs Committee of the House of Representatives*, 11 December 1985, p. 6.
59. Shimasaki, H. (1985) *The 103rd Legal Affairs Committee of the House of Representatives*, 11 December 1985, p. 7.
60. Hatano (1983) *op. cit.* p. 23.
61. Hatano, A. (1986) *The 104th Legal Affairs Committee of the House of Councillors*, 25 March 1986, p. 11.
62. *Ibid.*
63. *Ibid.*
64. Suzuki, S. (1986) *The 104th Legal Affairs Committee of the House of Councillors*, 25 March 1986, p. 12.
65. Okuno (1980a) *op. cit.* pp. 3, 19; Endo, K. (1987a) *The 108th Legal Affairs Committee of the House of Councillors*, 14 May 1987, p. 8; Okamura, Y. (1987) *The 108th Legal Affairs Committee of the House of Councillors*, 14 May 1987, p. 8.
66. Inokuma, S. (1987) *The 108th Legal Affairs Committee of the House of Councillors*, 14 May 1987, p. 14.

67. Okamura explained that whilst there were more than 50 applicants for prosecutor posts in the previous year, less than 40 applied in 1987.
68. Okamura (1987) *op. cit.* p. 5, 6, 14.
69. Okamura (1987) *op. cit.* p. 14.
70. *Ibid.*
71. Interview with two constitutional scholars, Tokyo, 13 May 2011.
72. Endo (1987a) *op. cit.* p. 15.
73. Okamura (1987) *op. cit.* p. 8; Endo (1987a) *op. cit.* p. 8.
74. Endo (1987a) *op. cit.* 15.
75. Endo (1987a) *op. cit.* p. 8.
76. *Ibid.*
77. Negoro, Y. (1987) *The 109th Legal Affairs Committee of the House of Councillors*, 27 August 1987, p. 3.
78. Endo, K. (1987b) *The 108th Legal Affairs Committee of the House of Representatives*, 15 May 1987, p. 6.
79. Hayashida, Y. (1988a) *The 112th Legal Affairs Committee of the House of Representatives*, 25 March 1988, p. 1.
80. Hayashida, Y. (1988b) *The 112th Legal Affairs Committee of the House of Councillors*, 26 April 1988, p. 1. The amount was originally up to ¥1 million ($8898.13) in 1964; ¥3million ($26,694.38) in 1968; ¥5million (44,490.64) in 1973; ¥15 million ($133,471.91) in 1975; and ¥20 million ($177,962.54) in 1980. It is currently up to ¥30 million ($266,943.81) since the bill was passed in 1992 (Shigitani, J. (2007) '*Korekara no Enzai Hoshō wo Kangaeru*' (Debating Future False Charge Trials), *Rippō to Chōsa*, 270, Tokyo: The House of Councillors, pp. 64–75, p. 72).
81. Yokoyama, K. (1988) *The 112th Legal Committee of the House of Representatives*, 29 March 1988, p. 2.
82. Yasuoka, O. (1988) *The 112th Legal Affairs Committee of the House of Representatives*, 29 March 1988, p. 5.
83. Chiba, K. (1988) *The 112th Legal Affairs Committee of the House of Councillors*, 26 April 1988, p. 6.
84. Hayashida, Y. (1988b) *op. cit.* p. 6.
85. Okuno (1980a) *Ibid*; Okamura *Ibid*; Endo (1987a) *Ibid*; Hayashida (1988b) *Ibid.*
86. Chiba, K. (1989) *The 116th Legal Affairs Committee of the House of Councillors*, 5 December 1989, p. 3.

87. Ishigaki, Y. (1989) *The 116th Legal Affairs Committee of the House of Councillors*, 5 December 1989, p. 3. In voting on the Second Protocol of the ICCPR, aiming at the abolition of the death penalty, 55 voted for, 28 voted against and 45 abstained on 22 November 1989. Ishigaki combined the number of the latter two and denied that the anti-death-penalty norm was not widely supported.
88. Goto, M. (1989) *The 116th Legal Affairs Committee of the House of Councillors*, 5 December 1989, p. 3.
89. More than 95 per cent of all executions are believed to take place in China; the estimates range from 2000 to 15,000 per year (Johnson, D.T. & Zimring, F.E. (2009) *The Next Frontier: National Development, Political Change, and the Death Penalty in Asia*, Oxford University Press, USA, p. 21).
90. Okamura (1987) *op. cit.* p. 14.
91. Van Wolferen (1989) *op. cit.* p. 188.

CHAPTER 5

Conscience or Chaos?: Governmental Justification for Capital Punishment During the *De Facto* Moratorium Period 1989–1993

5.1 Introduction

Through examining the period from 1980 to 1989, Chap. 4 clarified that the Ministry of Justice consistently justifies capital punishment on legal, domestic and cultural grounds, and conducts executions annually. However, no executions took place for three years and four months from 1989 to 1993, and it may appear at first sight that domestic or international events during this period made the bureaucrats at that time refrain from applying capital punishment. Nonetheless, as earlier chapters have discussed, capital punishment policy is primarily elite-driven, and it is not appropriate to consider that executions were put on hold as part of a political initiative. Instead, this chapter examines how the Japanese government continued to present the dominant governmental discourse on capital punishment during the *de facto* moratorium period from 1989 to 1993.

The first section of this chapter critically investigates public opinion of capital punishment, which the Japanese government frequently cites in order to justify its policy. Whilst governmental opinion polls tend to suggest that the majority of the Japanese public supports capital punishment, no significant protest from the public was observed during the *de facto* moratorium period. This section investigates whether or not some domestic factors softened the public attitude, or if there was no persistent public support for capital punishment in the first place.

M. Obara-Minnitt, *Japanese Moratorium on the Death Penalty*,
DOI 10.1057/978-1-137-55822-0_5

The second section explores how the Japanese government justified the capital punishment system while 'institutional ambivalence' was observed and executions did not take place for three years and four months. Since it has been revealed that the then Minister of Justice, Sato Megumu, refused to authorise executions owing to his religious belief, the role that he played in bringing about the execution-free period tends to be over-represented in the existing literature. Although this chapter investigates the social climate of the time and the personal convictions of Ministers of Justice, it does not aim to investigate the extent to which these factors contributed to the *de facto* moratorium period. Rather, it illuminates the fact that: (1) the period of 40 months without executions mainly stemmed from a frequent change in Ministers of Justice, and not from a changed view amongst bureaucrats on the policy; and (2) the capital punishment system is consistently justified by the Ministry of Justice on the basis that the current law allows it to exist.

5.2 A Softened Pro-Death-Penalty Mood Among the Public?

It is noteworthy that the general public was not particularly concerned that executions were put on hold during this time period. As Johnson argues, no significant protests by pro-death-penalty bodies were observed, whilst the government claims consistently that capital punishment has been retained on the basis of strong public support.[1] This section investigates whether the increase and decrease in certain media coverage raised the public's awareness of capital punishment and helped soften the pro-death-penalty sentiment or, on the other hand, whether public opinion on capital punishment was always more neutral in the first place, in contrast to the findings of governmental poll results.

5.2.1 Media Influence of the Public View of Capital Punishment

In contrast to the previous period (1980–1989), there appears to have been a change in the media coverage of issues related to capital punishment: (1) an increase in media coverage of the issue of capital punishment; (2) a decrease in media coverage of serious murder cases; and (3) well-known novelists' action for the basic rights of death row inmates. The media appear to have helped spur a domestic debate on the retention of capital punishment following the disclosure of a number of miscarriage of justice cases in the 1980s. Japan's major newspapers such as *Asahi*, *Yomiuri*, *Mainichi* and *Nikkei* became very active in calling for a national debate.[2] Asahi TV also broadcast a debate on the issue of capital punishment on 30 March 1989 and 18 June 1992; and Mainichi TV broadcast a documentary on the system in Osaka on 28 July 1989. Furthermore, the *Chūnichi* newspaper, a local newspaper in the Tokai area, and *Shūkan Josei*, a weekly magazine, displayed an anti-death-penalty mood.[3] A lack of sensational media coverage of serious murder cases may not have particularly encouraged the public to demand that the government resume executions. Of course, it is not that serious incidents did not occur during this period, but there was no high-profile case that remained in the news for any length of time.

A number of famous writers called for equal opportunities for death row inmates in 1990. Recommended by novelists such as Akiyama Shun and Kaga Otohiko, the then death row inmate, Nagayama, applied to be a member of the Japan Writers' Association (*Nihon Bungeika Kyōkai*). However, his application was rejected on 5 March 1989 'given his status as a convicted killer'.[4] To protest against that decision, novelists such as Nakagami Kenji, Tsutsui Yasutaka, Karatani Kojin and Iguchi Tokio withdrew from the association.[5] They held Nagayama's talent as a writer in high regard and proclaimed the need to 'accommodate' death row inmates as normal citizens in civil society like everyone else.

Thus, the absence of a particularly strong pro-capital-punishment protest from the public during this period may have stemmed from the aforementioned three factors: media coverage on the rights and wrongs of capital punishment, lack of sensational media reports on murder cases and some novelists' action to call for basic rights to be given to death row inmates. However, this does not automatically mean that an anti-death-penalty mood surged amongst the public at this time. Whilst media agencies, regardless of size or popularity, may have helped raise public awareness of the issue of capital punishment and wrongful conviction cases, lack of media coverage of serious murder cases does not appear to have motivated the public to doubt the deterrent effect of capital punishment or call for abolition.

Similarly, it is important to highlight that novelists who supported Nagayama's membership in the association were not anti-death-penalty advocates. What they called for was an equal opportunity for talented novelists regardless of criminal record, since they believed it inappropriate to draw lines between those on death row and outside it.[6] They did not necessarily intend to discuss the rights and wrongs of the capital punishment system fundamentally, and their protest action does not appear to have generated a drastic and conscious change in thinking about how those now sentenced to death should atone for their crimes. Just as acting on behalf of death row inmates who were the victims of miscarriages of justice and advancing abolitionism were treated separately in the 1980s (see Chap. 4), so the call for Nagayama's rights as a writer appears to have been conceived by the public as a distinct issue.

Moreover, it is not impossible to conjecture that public opinion was more neutral in the first place than was suggested in the governmental opinion polls. Given that there was no particular public protest against the absence of executions, which lasted for more than three years, a mixture of the aforementioned factors may appear at first sight to have softened strong public support for capital punishment. However, it is unsafe to argue that there was originally 'strong' or 'persistent' public support for capital punishment, which some domestic factors dampened down. As the other opinion poll conducted by NHK indicated in 1994, 40.5 per cent of the public supported the introduction of alternative punishment such as life imprisonment without parole (see Appendix E), so it is important to acknowledge that answers can vary depending on how the questions are phrased. The next section examines the prominence of an anti-death-penalty NGO in Japan and its social impact.

5.2.2 *Emergence of Collective Anti-Death-Penalty Activities*

Whereas abolitionism was still in the making in civil society in the 1980s, anti-death-penalty activities started to be recognised from 1990 with the foundation of Forum 90, one of the largest anti-death-penalty NGOs in Japan. According to Yasuda Yoshihiro, criminal attorney and key founder of Forum 90, it was the adoption of the UN Resolution Concerning Abolition of the Death Penalty in 1989 that motivated the existing anti-death-penalty groups to become a stronger force in Japan.[7] They believed that abolition could be achieved in the country if they succeeded in raising awareness amongst the public about the international abolitionist movement. They felt they could help to mobilise a more enlightened public through their grass-roots campaigns to increase pressure upon the Japanese government.[8] Forum 90 was thus established in 1990, with a unique vision. The founders did not try to create a formal organisation with official members, but instead an informal gathering for those who shared the same vision.[9] This is because they wanted the group to be open to supporters of any social, political and academic background, and to make their activities long-lasting, avoiding any friction amongst members concerning the direction of anti-death-penalty activities.[10] In addition to existing supporters from the 1980s, several associations and individuals joined: (1) the Japan Federation of Bar Associations; (2) Setouchi Jakuchō, a nun; (3) Kikuta Koichi, professor of law; and (4) Dando Shigemitsu, professor of law and former Supreme Court judge.

The group started to hold meetings periodically in Hibiya in Tokyo in order to raise public awareness, and a meeting on 1 December 1990 attracted 1400 people. The numbers of those who showed sympathy for their activities rose to 5500 shortly after the group's foundation, including Diet members, attorneys, academics and local assembly members.[11] Regional branches were established in Nagoya, Osaka, Hiroshima, Shikoku and Sendai in the following years. Besides holding meetings, members approached Ministers of Justice in person and tried to convince them not to authorise executions. They attended the inauguration party of each Minister of Justice with bouquets, visited the home towns of Ministers in order to hold meetings and protests, and even placed advertisements in local newspapers in order to raise public awareness.[12]

Whilst anti-death-penalty NGO activities were taking place at the beginning of the 1990s, which covers the *de facto* moratorium from 1989 to 1993, most of the NGO members whom I interviewed were reluctant to claim that they had an impact. This is because they are fully aware that human rights NGOs have not been integrated into the governmental decision-making process in Japan, and it is inappropriate to claim that they have any impact on governmental policy. Indeed, when I asked interviewees how they assessed the 'influence' that the anti-death-penalty NGOs had possibly exerted during the *de facto* moratorium, some of them replied by asking me how I defined the term 'influence'.[13] This is because they felt that it was inappropriate to describe the effect they could have on the Japanese government in this way. Other interviewees, such as attorneys and academics, agreed with a majority of NGO workers on their limited contribution to this *de facto* moratorium. In particular, denials by governmental officials were strikingly strong. They tended not to admit that any policy changes were due to NGO pressures; and such a tendency was also observed in postal correspondence with a former Minister of Justice, Sato Megumu. Regarding the question about whether or not there was any interaction with anti-death-penalty NGOs during his term, Sato responded that: (1) there was no such thing, except that he received letters petitioning him not to authorise executions;[14] and (2) 'anti-death-penalty NGOs were not so active during his term'.[15]

Thus, this clarifies that no significant public protest was observed over the absence of executions for three year and four months. The following factors may appear at first sight to have contributed to a 'softening' of the public pro-death-penalty sentiment: (1) increased media coverage of the issue of capital punishment; (2) decreased media coverage of serious murder cases; and (3) novelists' protest against the literary world regarding the discrimination against death row inmates. However, it is also possible that public opinion of capital punishment was already more neutral than it appeared to be based upon the results of governmental opinion polls. After this brief examination of the social climate during this *de facto* moratorium period, the next section investigates how the Japanese government sought to justify capital punishment.

5.3 Governmental Justification for Capital Punishment (1989–1993)

The central reason for executions being put on hold during this period is that Ministers of Justice did not authorise executions. Having said that, it is not necessarily right to attach much weight to the individual behaviour of a single Minister of Justice, for two main reasons: (1) this issue was handled within the tightly knit institutional dynamics where selected elites in the Ministry of Justice and the Public Prosecutor's Office have a near monopoly; and (2) not all the Ministers of Justice refused to authorise executions because of their personal convictions. For example, Hasegawa Shin (28 February–13 September 1990), the first Minister of Justice during this term, stayed in office for less than one year because of his health, and did not have any opportunities to authorise executions. Similarly, the next Minister of Justice, Kajiyama Seiroku (13 September–29 December 1990), served for an even shorter period and was also not given opportunities to authorise executions. By contrast, Sato Megumu (29 December 1990–5 November 1991), who took over from Kajiyama, is known as the Minister of Justice who did not authorise executions because of his religious beliefs. However, it should be noted that Sato did not clearly express his personal opinion on the issue of capital punishment during his term: it was only after he resigned that he disclosed the fact that he had refused to authorise executions.

In fact, Sato's remarks on various human rights issues in the Diet meetings indicate that he did not seek to actively engage in the discussion. Rather, he stressed that it was important to prioritise law and order over human rights. For example, the continuation of the *daiyō kangoku* (police detention) system was questioned in the Legal Affairs Committee on 20 February and 25 April 1991. Since confession is often extracted by torture in *daiyō kangoku*, which can lead to miscarriages of justice, the abolition of the system was frequently discussed in the Diet meetings. However, Sato rejected the possibility that *daiyō kangoku* would be abolished immediately. He demonstrated a reluctance to have the issue dealt with by the Ministry of Justice, and stressed on 20 February 1991 that it was the police and the Public Prosecutor's Office that were in charge of maintaining legal order in Japan,[16] avoiding accusations that the Ministry of Justice was not taking the initiative in abolishing *daiyō kangoku*. On 25 April 1991 he commented that: 'Although I am aware of the reports by Amnesty International on this system and international movements to uplift human rights of prisoners, it is currently challenging to abolish the *daiyō kangoku* system with a limited budget (within the Ministry of Justice).'[17] Sato's response implied that the *daiyō kangoku* issue could be dealt with in the Public Prosecutor's Office, and that the Ministry's own concerns overrode the issue of preventing wrongful convictions.

Moreover, in the Legal Affairs Committee on 20 February 1991 on human rights, when he discussed the issue of foreigners' human rights in Japan,[18] Sato stressed the superiority of law and order to human rights: 'individual's human rights must be protected under legal order (and not the other way around)'.[19] Significantly, Sato appears to have applied double standards to the human rights policy in Japan. He stated that the law is situated above human rights regarding the treatment of defendants in *daiyō kangoku* and of foreigners in Japan. On the other hand, he appears to have placed individual human rights above the law on the issue of capital punishment. In other words, believing that every single person has the right to live, he appears to have chosen not to be bound by Article 475 of the Code of Criminal Procedures that specifies the duty of Ministers of Justice: Sato did not authorise executions in line with the 'expected' procedure during his term.

Of course, he tried to achieve a balance between his personal conviction and his responsibility as the Minister of Justice on the issue of capital punishment. Sato asked the Director-General of the Criminal Affairs Bureau to bring him documents that he was supposed to sign to authorise executions.[20] However, after reading the documents for two death row inmates, taking two weeks to do so, he refused to authorise the executions.[21] His official claim about legal provisions and human rights issues thus differed strikingly from what he disclosed after he resigned. This may have been because he was reflecting the policy of the Ministry of Justice, which endeavours to act on precedents.

Currently, anti-death-penalty advocates treat Sato as a heroic figure who directly contributed to maintaining the *de facto* moratorium. However, it is not well known that Sato did not assert human rights concerns, either directly or indirectly related to capital punishment. The reason why he did not take initiatives concerned with improving domestic human rights issues during his term appears to be that he chose to act on precedents in keeping with his role as a government member. Of course, he may not have been aware that neglecting these issues—abolishing the *daiyō kangoku* system and tackling foreigners' human rights—could be linked to an increase in death sentences, contrary to his personal conviction. For example, a confession can be extracted in *daiyō kangoku* through torture, and foreign residents in Japan subjected to this treatment can also be victims of the capital punishment system. Given that the issue of capital punishment has been treated by the Japanese government solely as a criminal justice matter, and a distinct one that in their view does not deserve attention from the perspective of human rights, Sato may not have been aware of this dynamic. However, he may have tried to stress the superiority of law and order over human rights as a Minister of Justice only in the official setting. In reality, he appears to have chosen not to authorise executions in line with the relevant legal provisions and the expectations of his official office.

When Tawara Takashi (5 November 1991–12 December 1992) succeeded Sato, he did not have any opportunities to authorise executions. Since Sato stated after his resignation that he did not authorise executions owing to his personal convictions,[22] Tawara was constantly questioned in the Diet meetings about his position on capital punishment and whether or not he would authorise executions. However, he confined himself to giving general comments. For example, when he was questioned in the Legal Affairs Committee on 12 March 1992 on the French experience of the abolition of capital punishment, and Sato's non-authorisation of executions, Tawara responded in only one sentence: that the Ministry of Justice respected the current law, and that it had not been taking any particular measures towards change in the current criminal justice system.[23]

Furthermore, the submissive attitude of the Ministry of Justice to the Public Prosecutor's Office on the issue of Japanese criminal justice—the issue of wrongful conviction cases specifically—was highlighted in the Legal Affairs Committee on 4 and 17 December 1991. Article 14 of the Public Prosecutor's Office Act specifies the relationship between the Ministry of Justice and the Public Prosecutor's Office as follows: 'The Minister of Justice may control and supervise public prosecutors generally in regard to their functions. However, in regard to the investigation and disposition of individual cases, he/she may control only the Prosecutor-General.' Although this indicates that Ministers of Justice are not responsible for supervising an individual public prosecutor, a Diet member, Seya Hideyuki, claimed that Ministers of Justice should not simply await the outcome of prosecutors' work, since wrongful conviction cases could be avoided if Ministers of Justice kept an eye on their investigation activities.[24] However, Tawara proclaimed that the Public Prosecutor's Office was in charge of maintaining legal order in Japan, and it was highly important for Ministers of Justice to trust it to be rigorous and fair.[25]

Tawara thus endeavoured to act on precedents, and did not take any initiatives regarding capital punishment or wrongful convictions. Equally importantly, the anti-death-penalty politicians of the time were not competent in capitalising upon the emerging international and domestic anti-death-penalty trend to stimulate debate and change at the governmental level. To judge from parliamentary proceedings, all that was achieved with Tawara was questioning him about whether or not he would authorise executions. The issue was not fundamentally discussed from the perspective of: (1) why the state neglects to protect the basic rights of the Japanese citizens once they are on death row; (2) by what measures wrongful conviction cases could be prevented; or (3) what the government could offer for victim satisfaction without the use of capital punishment. A simplistic 'abolition or retention' discussion did not help ministry bureaucrats face the fact that Japanese society at that time had been keeping order without the use of capital punishment. As a result, Ministry officials appear to have continued to show reserved attitudes towards the existing Japanese criminal justice system.

To sum up, four Ministers of Justice stayed in office for a year or less during this *de facto* moratorium period, and it is difficult to analyse the governmental discourse on capital punishment. In particular, the first two, Hasegawa and Kajiyama, did not have opportunities to discuss the issue of capital punishment or to authorise executions. Sato chose not to authorise executions on account of his religious beliefs. However, since the issue of capital punishment was not brought up during his term, Sato neither disclosed his anti-death-penalty sentiment nor proclaimed retention of the system, thereby potentially separating his personal view from his official duty. Instead, he appears to have chosen to act on precedents as the Minister of Justice, and proclaimed the superiority of law and order over human rights during his term. It was only Tawara during this period who was asked his opinion on the capital punishment system, after it was revealed that Sato did not authorise executions on the grounds of personal beliefs. Although it is risky to analyse governmental discourse on the capital punishment system during this period simply through several statements by a single Minister of Justice, Tawara's comments suggest that the system existed since it was still on the statute as an available criminal justice sentence.

5.4 Conclusion

This chapter has examined social climate during the *de facto* moratorium period from 1989 to 1993, and how the Japanese government continued to maintain the dominant governmental discourse on capital punishment. It merits some attention that overt protests against the execution-free period did not take place, contrary to the general understanding that the majority of the Japanese public supported the system. The central reason for this may appear to relate to media coverage of the issue of capital punishment, limited media coverage of serious murder cases and some novelists' support for Nagayama regarding his status in the literary world. 'Public opinion' appears to vary depending on when the opinion polls are conducted and how questions are phrased, and 'strong' or 'persistent' public support for capital punishment may not have existed in the first place. Indeed, the foundation of Forum 90 in 1990 attracted public attention to this issue, as shown in the number of participants at one of their meetings.

However, whilst these events appear to have contributed to increased public awareness about the issue of capital punishment to some extent, it does not necessarily mean that abolitionism surged rapidly amongst the general public. For example, as the case of Nagayama shows, those who called for death row inmates' rights as writers appeared to have considered this as a distinct issue, separate from the rights and wrongs of capital punishment. Moreover, abolitionists' voices were not counted as a crucial factor in governmental decision-making; they were seen as a small fraction of public opinion. As Sato Megumu recalls, their activities were not treated as a collective voice of Japanese society by government.[26]

Whilst the existing literature overestimates the personal convictions of the Ministers of Justice in examination of this period, an in-depth analysis of parliamentary proceedings reveals that not all the Ministers endeavoured to halt executions or advance abolitionism. Rather, most of them stayed in their office for a short period and did not have opportunities to authorise executions. Exceptionally, Sato Megumu disclosed that he had refused to authorise orders because of his personal beliefs. However, his discourse in the Legal Committee meetings indicates that he did not clearly express his views on capital punishment or tackle relevant human rights issues during his term. Instead, he focused on presenting official views, such as that the law is situated above human rights. The only Minister of Justice who had an opportunity to discuss the issue of capital punishment was Tawara, and his statement illuminates the dutiful approach that the Ministry of Justice takes. In other words, the Ministry of Justice justifies and uses the capital punishment system since the law provides for it. Given that abolishing this system requires repealing or amending all the relevant legal provisions, it is not likely that the Ministry of Justice will take such an initiative.

Consequently, whilst some people amongst scholars, anti-death-penalty NGOs and the media tend to treat this period as worthy of close attention (see Chap. 3), it appears that this *de facto* moratorium period was caused simply by a high turnover of Ministers of Justice. Frequent changes of personnel did not provide the Ministers with opportunities to authorise executions, and created a 'gap' in capital punishment policy, which appeared as a *de facto* moratorium period. Although Sato's decision not to authorise executions is not unimportant, as Chap. 2 clarified, important decisions are made within the tightly knit institutional framework, and the role that Ministers of Justice can play is limited. Therefore, it is not helpful to try to specify the domestic or international factors that led decisively to the *de facto* moratorium periods. Rather, it is important to focus on how the Ministry of Justice tries to justify capital punishment policy even during the absence of executions. The following chapter examines governmental narratives on capital punishment after this *de facto* moratorium period.

Notes

1. Johnson, D.T. (2006) 'Japan's Secretive Death Penalty Policy: Contours, Origins, Justifications, and Meanings', *Asian-Pacific Law & Policy Journal*, 7, pp. 62–124, p. 113.
2. The International Federation for Human Rights (2008) 'The Death Penalty in Japan: The Law of Silence—Going against the International Trend', October 2008, p. 16. Available at: http://www.fidh.org/IMG/pdf/japon505a2008.pdf [Accessed 17 March 2016]; Another leading newspaper company, publishers of *Sankei*, is not included in the data by the International Federation for Human Rights. *Sankei* conducted opinion polls on capital punishment in 1972 and 1977, but not in the 1980s or 1990s.
3. Interview with two NGO workers, Tokyo, 17 May 2011.
4. Métraux, D.A. (2009) 'The Nagayama Criteria for Assessing the Death Penalty in Japan: Reflections of a Case Suspect', *Southeast Review of Asian Studies*, 31, pp. 282–289, p. 285.
5. Mori, T. (2008) *Shikei: Hito wa Hito wo Koroseru, Demo Hito wa Hito wo Sukuitai tomo Omou*, Tokyo: Asahi Shuppan Sha, p. 88.
6. *Ibid.*
7. Yasuda, Y., Kikuta, S. and Tsushima, S. (1996) '*Shikei Haishi e Mukete Dōsuruka: Kono 5 Nen no Ayumi to Tenbō*' (What We should do towards the Abolition of Death Penalty: Paths over the Five Years and Prospect), Tokyo: Impact Shuppan, pp. 106–143, pp. 123, 125.
8. Interview with two NGO members, Tokyo, 17 May 2011.
9. *Ibid.*
10. *Ibid.*
11. *Ibid.*
12. *Ibid.*; Forum 90 placed an opinion advertisement in the *Ōita Gōdō* newspaper in the home town of the former Minister of Justice Tahara, for example.
13. Postal correspondence with an NGO worker, 28 February 2011, and interview with an NGO worker, Tokyo, 12 April 2011.
14. The anti-death-penalty *Jōdo Shinshū* sect and Forum 90 sent him a letter on 17 April 1991 urging him not to authorise executions.
15. Postal correspondence with a former Minister of Justice, Sato Megumu, 8 February 2011.

16. Sato, M. (1991) *The 120th Legal Affairs Committee of the House of Representatives*, 20 February 1991, p. 16.
17. *Ibid*, p. 2.
    Sato did not clarify how abolition of the *daiyō kangoku* system could cause a financial problem.
18. According to Article 62 (1) of Immigration Control and Refugee Recognition Act, 'Any person may, if he/she has knowledge of a foreign national whom he/she believes to fall under any of the items of Article 24, report such information', and the person who reports the illegal immigrant can receive a reward up to ¥50,000 if that report is correct. Regarding this provision, a Diet member, Okazaki Hiromi, claimed that this can bias Japanese citizens against foreign residents in Japan in general.
19. Sato (1991) *op. cit.* p. 11.
20. Postal correspondence with Sato Megumu, 8 February 2011.
21. *Ibid.*
22. Sato also developed his personal opinion on the issue of capital punishment on an Asahi TV programme on 28 January 1992.
23. Tawara T. (1992) *The 123rd Legal Affairs Committee of the House of Councillors*, 12 March 1992, p. 11.
24. Seya, H. (1991) *The 122nd Legal Affairs Committee of the House of Councillors*, 17 December 1991, p. 9.
25. Tawara, T. (1991) *The 122nd Legal Affairs Committee of the House of Councillors*, 17 December 1991, pp. 8–9.
26. Postal correspondence with a former Minister of Justice, 8 February 2011.

CHAPTER 6

By Popular Demand: Governmental Justification for Capital Punishment 1993–2009

6.1 Introduction

This chapter investigates how the Ministry of Justice defended the capital punishment system between 1993 and 2009, the 16 years between the *de facto* moratorium periods. The first section explores the prevailing social climate on capital punishment. According to governmental opinion polls, 73.8 per cent of the Japanese public supported capital punishment in 1994, 79.3 per cent in 1999, 81.4 per cent in 2004 and 85.6 per cent in 2009 (see Appendix B). These results may at first sight indicate increased public support for capital punishment. However, this section clarifies that such a public mood was very much related to how the media and the government dealt with the prevailing crime situation. The second section investigates how the Ministry of Justice resumed the capital punishment system for the first time in three years and four months. Whilst the numbers of annual executions were no more than two from 1980 to 1989, and none from 1989 to 1993, they ranged from two to 15 per calendar year during this period (1993–2009). This section investigates how the government tried to maintain the dominant discourse on crime and punishment for the justification of capital punishment during this period.

M. Obara-Minnitt, *Japanese Moratorium on the Death Penalty*,
DOI 10.1057/978-1-137-55822-0_6

6.2 A Reawakened Pro-Death-Penalty Mood Among the Public?

The governmental opinion polls indicate that a majority of the Japanese public supported capital punishment during this period. However, leaving aside the methodological issues regarding the governmental surveys, the prime reason why the public may have looked punitive or pro-death penalty during this period appears to relate to: (1) the sensational media coverage of indiscriminate murder cases; (2) governmental response to these crimes; and (3) media reporting of the results of the governmental opinion polls regarding the public image of Japanese society. The following section examines how public pro-death-penalty sentiment was created by the media agencies, and how it was used strategically by the Japanese government as justification for the capital punishment system.

6.2.1 Media Coverage of Serious Murder Cases

Whilst media agencies appeared very active in calling for a national debate on the issue of capital punishment in the early 1990s,[1] this lost significant momentum following a number of high-profile serious crimes. The first case was the Aum gas attack, which was committed by the Aum sect in the Tokyo underground on 23 March 1995. As already discussed in Chap. 3, it was featured by the media as the biggest security threat in Japan in decades.

There then followed four juvenile crimes which the media sensationalised, heightening public anxiety about both the prevalence and seriousness of juvenile offending. For example, in the Sakakibara case a 14-year-old high school boy committed murders between 16 March and 27 May 1997, culminating in the strangling of an 11-year-old primary school boy in Kobe and cutting off his head, which he left at the school gate with a taunting note stuck in the victim's mouth.[2] Names of juvenile offenders are usually withheld in media reports for the purpose of protecting their privacy. However, as had happened in the Ayase murder case in 1988–1989, a weekly magazine, *Focus*, declared that this case should not be handled like other, less serious, juvenile crimes, and it disclosed the criminal's full name and picture in the issue of 9 July 1997.[3]

In addition to the Hikari case of a murder committed on 14 April 1999 by an 18-year-old boy (see Chap. 3), there were the Aichi murder case and the Saga bus hijack case, both involving murders committed in

2000 by 17-year-old boys. In the first of these cases, on 1 May 2000, a juvenile offender murdered a 64-year-old housewife by stabbing her 40 times, and also injured her 67-year-old husband seriously.[4] On 3 May 2000, influenced by the media coverage of the Aichi murder case, another 17-year-old high school boy hijacked a bus in Saga prefecture with a knife: a 68-year-old woman died and three others were seriously injured.

Indiscriminate murders were also committed by adults during this period, and as with the cases outlined above they were widely featured by the media. In the Wakayama curry poisoning case, four people were killed and 63 others badly affected at a community summer festival in Wakayama prefecture on 25 July 1998. Hayashi Masumi, a 42-year-old insurance salesperson, was arrested and sentenced to death for the murders and attempted murders in the Wakayama District Court on 18 May 2009.[5]

Another example was the Osaka school massacre case, in which a 37-year-old man, Takuma Mamoru, stabbed primary school children at Osaka Kyōiku University Ikeda Elementary School on 8 June 2001, killing eight children and injuring 13 more, as well as two teachers. The motive was found to be retaliation against Japanese society from which Takuma felt excluded, and a desire to be executed through capital punishment since he could not commit suicide by himself.[6] Therefore, anti-death-penalty activists proclaimed that Takuma would not have committed this indiscriminate crime if the capital punishment system did not exist in Japan.[7]

What is noteworthy in this case is that although Takuma was executed within a year after the final sentence was given,[8] no major public concern was aroused when he was singled out from other death row inmates, who had been imprisoned for decades. It may have been a strategic bureaucratic decision to execute Takuma within this short period in order to justify capital punishment, exploiting public fear aroused by serious murder cases. However, since Takuma did not apologise to the bereaved families even once, some in the victim lobby doubted whether swift punishment brought any sense of closure to this incident or eased the bereaved families' feelings.[9]

A later high-profile case was the Akihabara Murder Rampage, which was committed on 8 June 2008 by a 25-year-old man, Kato Tomohiro. He not only deliberately drove into people with his rental truck in a crowded intersection in Akihabara electronics district, which attracts anime/manga fans from across the world, but also stabbed others indiscriminately with his survival knife. The motive of this case, which killed seven and injured ten, was that he was tired of the world and wanted to kill someone at random.[10] The death sentence was handed down to him on 2 February 2015, for his 'meticulous preparation' and 'determined intent of murder'.[11]

6.2.2 *Governmental Response to Serious Murder Cases by Juvenile Offenders*

In reaction to the sequence of indiscriminate murder cases, particularly by juvenile offenders, the Japanese government changed its approach to dealing with juveniles, and sought to strengthen its pro-death-penalty stance. More precisely, the Ministry of Justice: (1) claimed the necessity to impose harsher punishments for juvenile offenders, (2) amended several legal provisions on the initiatives of the Public Prosecutor's Office, and (3) demonstrated through opinion polls that public fear had increased over a number of years. On 1 July 1997, three days after the offender in the Sakakibara case was arrested, Kajiyama Seiroku, then Chief Cabinet Secretary and former Minister of Justice, stressed that it was doubtful that social justice could be maintained when offenders did not receive appropriate punishment because of their ages.[12]

The Ministry of Justice also made a partial amendment to the prison system for juveniles on 9 September 1997. Whilst the maximum imprisonment for juvenile offenders used to be two years, this change made it possible to extend the period in increments of two years. This change also led to an increased use of these extended sentences. Following the Osaka school massacre, the Japanese government demonstrated a more punitive attitude towards criminals who were mentally ill. The Prime Minister, Koizumi Jun-ichiro, stated on 9 June 2001 that those individuals who were mentally ill tended to continue to repeatedly commit similar serious crimes, and that it was therefore necessary to revise Article 39 of the Penal Code which provides that 'an act of insanity is not punishable'.[13]

The results of the opinion poll on the issue of the death penalty conducted by the Prime Minister's Office were used for justification of several amendments of the legal procedures and retention of capital punishment. As already discussed in Chap. 2, a change was made in police policy on counting crimes after the Okegawa case,[14] and this generated a sudden and drastic increase in overall recorded crime and a decreased clearance rate compared to statistics gathered before the introduction of the changed rules.[15] However, the media only highlighted the new statistics, and consequently it appeared that public anxiety about the state of society surged from 10 per cent in 1990 to 47.9 per cent in 2005 (see Chap. 2). Media reports of these figures without contextual information to highlight the changed methodological approach may have influenced the subsequent opinion poll results.

Indeed, the reason for increased fearfulness amongst the Japanese public can be found in the other governmental poll, *Chian ni Kansuru Yoron Chōsa* (the Opinion Poll on Public Order and Safety). Although the questions were slightly different from 2004 to 2006, both results showed that the Japanese public tend to take in what the media report uncritically. The question was 'What made you become concerned about the current public order and safety?' in 2004 and 'Where do you acquire information about the current public order and safety?' in 2006. In 2004, 83.9 per cent of respondents answered that it was newspapers and television programmes that made them concerned about the current state of public order and safety; and in 2006, 95.5 per cent answered that these were the sources from which the public received up-to-date news on the criminal situation.[16] Whilst emerging public fearfulness as measured by the opinion polls had been heavily influenced by the high-profile coverage of murder cases, these same results were cited by the media and governmental officials alike to 'prove' that Japanese society was becoming more dangerous, and that harsher punishment and the retention of capital punishment were therefore an inevitable necessity.

The following section investigates exactly how governmental officials justified the capital punishment system during this period.

6.3 Governmental Justification for Capital Punishment

Similarly to the other case study periods, as a result of political corruption scandals or cabinet reshuffles 25 Ministers of Justice served within 19 years from 1993 to 2009. Although not all the Ministers, for this reason, had opportunities to clearly demonstrate the government's approach to capital punishment, this section highlights the key discussions in the Legal Affairs Committees, dividing this period into four phases: (1) 1993–1996, when executions were resumed and justified by Ministers of Justice on the basis of law; (2) 1996–2000, when the Ministry of Justice justified capital punishment, citing the climate of public opinion as a prime driver; (3) 2000–2002, when the Ministry of Justice justified executions, disregarding the anti-death-penalty victim lobby's protest; and (4) 2002–2009, when pro-death-penalty Ministers of Justice authorised a larger number of executions swiftly in order to maintain 'legal order'.

6.3.1 Governmental Justification on the Basis of Law (1993–1996)

Executions were resumed following authorisation by the Minister of Justice, Gotoda Masaharu (12 December 1992–9 August 1993). Given that Gotoda was consistent with his pro-death-penalty attitude throughout his term, his personal characteristics and leadership may appear as a crucial factor in this. However, a majority of the anti-death-penalty advocates whom I interviewed mentioned that more attention must be paid to the intentions of Ministry bureaucrats, who (they claimed) were instrumental in the nomination of Gotoda for this post, expecting him to resume executions.[17] By examining Gotoda's narratives on the issue of capital punishment in depth, the following section examines: (1) how the Ministry of Justice tried to maintain the dominant discourse on crime and punishment; and (2) how subsequent Ministers of Justice continued to justify capital punishment in order to keep Japan *hōchi kokka* (a law-abiding country).

Gotoda stressed his personal position in the Legal Affairs Committee on 23 February 1993, outlining the responsibility of Ministers of Justice regarding the capital punishment system. He argued that 'as long as capital punishment exists as a legal system and is sentenced to criminals under fair trials, I believe that it is *hōmu daijin no shokuseki* [a duty of Ministers of Justice] to authorise it. Otherwise, it will ruin *hō chitsujo* [legal order]'.[18] However, during the same meeting Gotoda also showed an open mind towards discussing the issue of capital punishment:

> Whilst opinion polls show that the vast majority of the Japanese citizens support retaining capital punishment, most of the Western countries have abolished the system. Although the USA is exceptional in this case, I am aware that there exists an international anti-death-penalty trend. Also, I have heard that a public survey was conducted on the street in Shikoku area a year ago or so, and anti-death-penalty sentiment appeared to be increasing amongst young generation in particular. Whilst opinion polls conducted by the Prime Minister's Office have revealed that there are more retentionists in Japan,

> we need to handle this issue very carefully keeping young generation's trend in mind.[19]

Members of Shikoku Forum, a regional NGO of Forum 90, conducted an opinion poll on the issue of capital punishment in the Shikoku area in October and November 1992. Out of 1955 people surveyed, 35 per cent (687 people) answered that the capital punishment system was necessary in Japan, 39 per cent (759 people) answered that it was not necessary and 26 per cent (509 people) answered that they did not know.[20] It deserves some attention that Gotoda had been informed about the NGO-led survey and that he referred to the results when answering questions in the Legal Affairs Committee.[21]

Whilst Gotoda thus appeared to have shown some understanding of an opinion poll result other than the governmental one, he authorised three executions on 26 March 1993 in order to stick to his principles and to keep Japan *hōchi kokka*. Although it was the first time in more than three years that executions took place in Japan, the Ministry of Justice did not make any official statement regarding this decision. For example, in the Legal Affairs Committee on 29 March 1993 Hama Kunihisa, head of the Criminal Affairs Bureau, refused to discuss the issue. According to him, the Ministry of Justice could not disclose information about the executions since it could hurt the feelings of the bereaved families of those executed, and could disturb the peace of mind of other inmates.[22] Gotoda showed a similar attitude and tried to legitimise his political decision, criticising the previous Ministers of Justice who had been putting executions on hold:

> When serious crimes occur, judges sentence criminals to capital punishment: executions then require authorisation of Ministers of Justice. Despite this, some Ministers do not authorise executions based on *kojinteki na shisō shinjō* [personal convictions] or *shūkyō kan* [religious views]. In my opinion, they should not be appointed in this post if they do not agree with such responsibility in the first place. If they were not aware of such issue, it is reasonable that they resign the job as soon as they realise it. [...] Otherwise, I doubt if one nation's *hō chitsujo* [legal order] can be maintained.[23]

In response to an accusation against his dutiful attitude by an anti-death-penalty Diet member, Takemura Yasuko, Gotoda tried to make his point clear as follows:

> What I am trying to say is that once you are assigned to a job, you are required to carry it out. Of course, it is possible to leave certain jobs to successors if you do not want to complete the duty, since one Minister's job can only last for approximately one year. However, how can you maintain *chitsujo* [order] like that? I believe that you should resign and contribute all of your efforts to anti-death-penalty activities if you are not happy with your responsibility.[24]

In the Legal Affairs Committee on 2 April 1993, another abolitionist Diet member, Suzuki Kikuko, criticised Gotoda's execution orders upon the basis of law: 'Although the *de facto* moratorium period was a kind of "sustainable legal order" that former Ministers of Justice and anti-death-penalty lobby had built up, Gotoda overturned it under the name of maintaining legal order.'[25] In response, Gotoda explained that he did not think there had been a certain legal order during the *de facto* moratorium period: those who had been sentenced to death must be executed, as this was how legal order was maintained.[26] Admitting that there were various opinions on this issue, Gotoda said there existed a sort of retributive sentiment amongst the Japanese public: the vast majority supported the idea of retaining capital punishment, putting themselves in the victims' and their families' shoes.[27] Consequently, Gotoda tried to demonstrate the government's responsibility regarding executions to the Ministers of Justice who came after him, and to demonstrate to the public the Japanese state's approach to crime and punishment.

6.3.2 Strategies Behind the Appointment of Gotoda?

Since Gotoda thus showed a consistent pro-death-penalty attitude, large numbers of the anti-death-penalty advocates whom I interviewed argued that the bureaucrats of the time in the Ministry of Justice must have acted strategically to ensure he was chosen in order to resume executions.[28] In the meantime, Gotoda states in his memoir *Jō to Ri* (Mercy and Rationality) that it was he himself who chose the post for his own reasons. According to him, the Prime Minister, Miyazawa Kiichi, asked Gotoda to join his administration in any post. Gotoda chose the Ministry of Justice since he considered that he could start his job without requiring much expertise.[29] The anti-death-penalty lobby's theory appears to stem from Gotoda's career background. Since Gotoda had first-hand experience of dealing with serious murderers in the National Police Agency, according to this theory the Ministry of Justice must have known that he would not fail to show a severe attitude towards criminals and would authorise executions in a business-like manner.[30]

Of course, it is not necessarily true that those in the National Police Agency always show a severe attitude towards criminals. For example, drawing on an experience when he was the Director-General of the National Police Agency and played a leading role in the *Asama Sansō* (Asama Lodge) incident on 19 February 1972, Gotoda recalls in his memoir a concern for the importance of human life:

> The primary purpose of the Japanese police is nothing but to secure the safety of citizens. In this incident, the first priority was given to save a hostage, Muta Yasuko. [...Moreover,] no matter who they are—even if they are rioters or criminals—they are still Japanese citizens. In order not to deprive them of life or human rights, the police owed responsibility to assure criminals' lives as well.[31]

However, an alternative view is that priority was not necessarily given to respecting the life of criminals but to arresting the criminals 'alive' in order to punish them with the appropriate penalty. As Johnson argues, the Japanese police and prosecutors are evaluated for their high efficiency in 'solving' crimes: shooting criminals as self-defence is usually avoided, and it is important for them to have criminals convicted and sentenced to appropriate punishment.[32] Whilst anti-death-penalty activists criticised the political decision to nominate Gotoda and his authorisation of executions, it merits some attention that two of those whom I interviewed showed some understanding of Gotoda's political actions. According to them, 'as it is clear from the fact that he consistently claimed the importance of maintaining legal order, Gotoda must have been the only Minister of Justice who sincerely cared about what is best for Japanese citizens: "capital punishment should be used for social justice"'.[33]

Gotoda's successor, Mikazuki Akira (9 August 1993–28 April 1994), an attorney and law professor, showed a great deal of sympathy towards Gotoda, and acted on precedents. Regarding the authorisation of executions, Mikazuki had already made up his mind before he took his office as the Minister of Justice. Mikazuki clearly states in his book *Hōgaku Nyūmon* (Introduction to Studies of Law) (1982) that capital punishment can be used once illegal acts are observed and the judge sentences a convicted person to death.[34] Moreover, it has been revealed that Mikazuki had told an abolitionist Diet member, Futami Nobuaki, about his decision to authorise executions in advance. Futami visited Mikazuki on 9 August 1993, when Mikazuki took office, and Mikazuki told Futami the following: after debating with himself in a hotel room for a few days, he finally decided to accept the job offer, which included the 'responsibility' of authorising executions when required.[35] Mikazuki did not try to engage in the debate on the propriety of Article 475 of the Code of Criminal Procedure, which specifies the duty of the Minister of Justice to authorise executions, and he authorised executions in a bureaucratic manner.

In the meantime, Mikazuki's successors did not make official statements on their justification. This was partly because most of them stayed in office as Ministers of Justice for short periods (see Appendix C) but partly because anti-death-penalty Diet members stopped bringing the issue to the Legal Affairs Committees shortly after the Aum gas attack on 20 March 1995. Special Committees on Religious Groups took place repeatedly, even several days in a row during the term of Miyazawa Hiroshi (9 October 1995–11 January 1996). Attention had been paid to investigating the possibility that similar crimes would be committed by other similar religious groups, and on how to prevent this. Unlike Ministry bureaucrats who do not pay an electoral price for being non-responsive, Diet members are sensitive to public opinion. Therefore, a lack of discussion on the abolition of capital punishment in the Committee meetings may imply that anti-death-penalty Diet members found it risky to bring up the issue against the background of growing public outcry over the Aum attack. This case shows that there exists a boundary dividing anti- and pro-death-penalty lobbies in Japan. The results of the opinion polls by non-governmental bodies indicate that the public show some understanding of the issues and an interest in suspending executions to allow the opportunity to discuss the fundamental issue of capital punishment, and in exploring the introduction of an alternative penalty such as life imprisonment without parole (see Chap. 3). However, most anti- and pro-death-penalty groups tend to consider that they are at different ends of the spectrum, and that it is a challenging task to overturn a trend when it is in fashion in society.

6.3.3 Governmental Justification Using Social Climate (1996–2000)

6.3.3.1 Executions of High-Profile Death Row Inmates

Regarding the four executions authorised by Matsuura Isao (7 November 1996–11 September 1997) on 1 August 1997, it appears that the Ministry of Justice used the growing public fear aroused by serious murder cases as justification for capital punishment. As mentioned earlier, in light of the Sakakibara murder case in March–May 1997, Kajiyama Seiroku, then Chief Cabinet Secretary and former Minister of Justice, stressed on 1 July 1997 that it was doubtful that social justice could be maintained when offenders did not receive appropriate punishment because of their ages.[36] It was on 1 August 1997 that the four death row inmates were executed: (1) Nagayama Norio; (2) Hidaka Yasumasa and Hidaka Nobuko, who had given up their rights of submitting pleas for retrials, expecting reprieves; and (3) Kanda Hideki, who murdered his father, father's partner and father's partner's granddaughter on 8 March 1985.

Since Nagayama and the Hidakas were particularly well known to the public, questions arose amongst the anti-death-penalty lobby on how these inmates were chosen out of dozens of other inmates.[37] What the abolitionist lobby presumed was that singling out Nagayama in particular, who was 19 years old at the time of the crime, must have been a temporary measure to relieve the public fear aroused by serious murder cases perpetrated by juveniles.[38] In other words, Ministry bureaucrats presumably sought to demonstrate to the public that the Japanese government would not hesitate to punish offenders through capital punishment regardless of an offender's age.[39]

As the executions strategically took place in the middle of the summer holiday, the Legal Affairs Committee did not sit again before Matsuura resigned. Therefore, his successor, Shimoinaba Kokichi (11 September 1997–30 July 1998), and ministry bureaucrats were urged to comment on behalf of Matsuura in the Legal Affairs Committee on 13 November 1997. However, Harada Akio, head of the Criminal Affairs Bureau, confined himself to mentioning that he could not comment on an individual execution since the Ministry of Justice had not officially been disclosing relevant information. He stressed that Ministry bureaucrats selected death row inmates to be executed after careful investigations, such as whether or not a reprieve could be granted.[40] Shimoinaba also discussed the retention of capital punishment in general terms:

> Given that it is less than one per cent of all the criminals that are sentenced to death, it is certain that the Supreme Court judges have been extremely careful with the decision of sentencing such penalty to offenders. Capital punishment has an aspect of bringing justice to the society, and I believe that retention of the current system is inevitable.[41]

Thus, Harada's and Shimoinaba's defence of the use of capital punishment made it appear that if the public wondered why particular inmates were executed, regardless of the length of time they had spent on death row, it was a trivial matter. Their argument also sounded like a justification of the Minister's responsibility to sign the document for execution as a matter of expected routine: since criminals are sentenced to death in the trustworthy judicial system and singled out for executions after careful investigations, it was, they suggested, natural that Ministers of Justice should sign execution orders that their underlings bring to them. Having said that, Shimoinaba's remarks merit some attention because he fulfilled his official duty on the basis of his personal conviction regarding social justice. As with a former Minister of Justice, Gotoda, Shimoinaba had experience as a chief in the homicide division in Osaka and in the National Police Agency. He claimed that his professional career led him to realise that the use of capital punishment can bring social justice to the public.[42] Whereas anti-death-penalty Ministers are often accused of mixing private and public matters, proponents of capital punishment appear to be allowed to follow their personal convictions in conducting official duty as long as they are in line with the official responsibilities provided for by the law.

6.3.3.2 Amendment of the Ministry's Secretive Policy

Finally, what was significant during the term of Nakamura Shozaburo (30 July 1998–8 March 1999) was that from 19 November 1998 the number and date of executions started to be announced officially. This may at first sight have appeared to be a firm step towards making capital punishment policy more open, and encouraging public debate regarding abolition or retention. However, the real intention of the Ministry of Justice appears to have been the opposite. In response to questions regarding this sudden change in policy in the Legal Affairs Committee on 3 December 1998, Matsuo Kunihiro, head of the Criminal Affairs Bureau, stated that the Ministry of Justice aimed to receive public support and understanding through demonstrating that fair punishment was taking place under fair judgement.[43] Therefore, as a response to the growing public fear aroused by the excessive media coverage of serious crimes, the policy change appears to have been aimed at showing the public that capital punishment was being used in order to bring social justice, and that the Ministry did not intend to alter the system.

6.3.4 Governmental Justification in Disregarding the Feelings of Victims' Bereaved Families (2000–2002)

Although executions did not take place during the period when Komura Masahiko was Minister (5 December 2000–26 April 2001), it was not because he did not have the opportunity to authorise executions. As discussed in Chap. 3, since Komura received pleas from the victim's bereaved family, namely Harada Masaharu, on 18 April 2001, he promised not to authorise the execution of Hasegawa Toshihiko, who killed Harada's brother in an insurance-related murder committed in 1983.[44] However, despite Harada's pleas, Hasegawa was executed on 27 December 2001 under the authorisation of the subsequent Minister of Justice, Moriyama Mayumi (26 April 2001–22 September 2003). When criticised for her political decision in the Legal Affairs Committee on 3 April 2002, Moriyama defended herself by stating that it was not appropriate for the final decision made by the Supreme Court judge to be overturned by the victims' bereaved families.[45] Although the Ministry of Justice often cites the feelings of the victims' bereaved families as justification of capital punishment, her remarks appear to have implied the Ministry's actual approach to the system: executions are merely conducted as a part of judicial procedures stipulated by the law.

In fact, Moriyama had already demonstrated an assertive attitude regarding the issue of capital punishment when she took office as the Minister of Justice. When offered the option of ordering an official moratorium period in order to enable fundamental discussion of the capital punishment system, Moriyama disagreed with the idea in the Legal Affairs Committee on 28 June 2001, stating that it could upset the feelings of death row inmates if executions were first put on hold and later resumed.[46] Although introduction of life imprisonment without parole was also proposed as an alternative to the death penalty in the Legal Affairs Committee on 11 April 2002, Moriyama voiced her concern that imprisoning offenders until their natural death could destroy their personality.[47] Moreover, in the Legal Affairs Committee on 19 October 2001, she stressed that the issue of retaining or abolishing capital punishment should be solely left to domestic decision-making based on domestic factors such as criminal situations, public opinion and the criminal justice system.[48]

Finally, what seems to have prompted Moriyama to treat the issue of capital punishment merely as an issue of law and order, not as an issue of human rights, was her lack of knowledge about miscarriage of justice cases in the 1980s. For example, when the issue of a pension for Menda Sakae, a former death row inmate, was briefly discussed in the Legal Affairs Committee on 2 July 2003,[49] Moriyama commented that 'his name rings the bell but I do not know much about his details'.[50] It is possible to suspect that she tried to disengage herself from the discussion through pretending insufficient awareness of the case. However, Menda is not the kind of figure who only the anti-death-penalty lobby knows about; he is widely known for having been detained on death row for 34 years for a wrongful conviction. Since this event happened under the responsibility of the Ministry of Justice and the Public Prosecutors' Office, such a remark by Moriyama was particularly inappropriate, as she was an outspoken pro-death-penalty Minister of Justice.

6.3.5 Governmental Justification on the Basis of Law (2002–2009)

What characterises this period is a huge increase in the number of executions: 13 authorised by Hatoyama Kunio (27 August 2007–26 September 2008) within less than a year. This section examines the discourse of Ministers of Justice, including Hatoyama, whom *Asahi* condemned as Shinigami, or the Grim Reaper, and who tried to discuss a way in which executions could be authorised automatically and objectively regardless of the personal convictions or religious views of Ministers of Justice.

The first two Ministers of Justice stayed in office for approximately a year each. Nozawa Taizo (22 September 2003–27 September 2004) authorised two executions and Nono Chieko (27 September 2004–31 October 2005) authorised one. As briefly discussed, one of the two death row inmates whose execution Nozawa authorised was Takuma Mamoru from the Osaka school massacre case on 8 June 2001. Given that his death sentence was only finalised on 26 September 2003 and he was executed on 14 September 2004, it was a speedy execution, as if to show a tough stance on the series of indiscriminate murder cases.

Meanwhile, Sugiura Seiken (31 October 2005–26 September 2006) declared in his inauguration speech that he would not authorise executions because of his religious and philosophical views, and avoided authorisation during his term. When he was asked his views on the system, he stated that it was natural that the death penalty system would be abolished in the long run from the perspective of civilisation theory.[51] Like Sato Megumu, who managed to avoid authorisations during the *de facto* moratorium period from 1989 to 1993, Sugiura is a former attorney and respects the teachings of *Jōdo Shinshū* Buddhism. However, what merits attention is that he retracted his statement within one hour, stating that it was merely his personal view on the issue and not that of the Minister of Justice.[52] On 24 February 2006 a Diet member, Ishizeki Takashi, compared Sugiura's stance on the death penalty with that of Gotoda, who maintained a strong pro-death-penalty view during his term. Ishizeki mentioned that Sugiura's refusal to authorise executions was unreasonable, given that the quasi-jury system was due to be introduced in 2009 and would give ordinary citizens a heavy duty of imposing the death penalty when appropriate. In response, Sugiura stated that he would handle the issue very carefully, and clarified that he was not an anti-death-penalty figure.[53]

As if it was necessary to resume executions to avoid another *de facto* moratorium period, Nagase Jin-en (26 September 200627 August 2007) was subsequently appointed. In his inauguration speech and parliamentary meetings, Nagase stated that executions had to be conducted according to what the law provides,[54] and authorised ten executions in total, for the first time in 466 days since 16 September 2005. He authorised three to four executions every three months; of these, the first execution was conducted on Christmas Day in 2006 and the third was on 23 August 2007, only four days before he resigned. It is worth highlighting that executions were conducted during parliamentary sessions, whereas previously this was usually avoided under the Ministry's secretive policy in order to distract the Japanese public and deter the anti-death-penalty lobby from voicing dissent (see Chap. 2). Although this was the largest number of executions per Minister in decades, and the schedule of the executions spurred an outcry from the anti-death-penalty lobby, the next Minister of Justice, Hatoyama, demonstrated a tougher stance, with 13 executions in less than a year.

What characterised Hatoyama's term was another amendment to the Ministry's secretive policy, the largest number of executions per Minister in decades and his business-like approach to implementing the death penalty policy. Names of those executed started to be announced officially by the Ministry of Justice from Hatoyama's term onwards. This is similar to the amendment made during Nakamura's term in 1998—disclosure of the fact of executions—and it aimed to gain further public support by demonstrating that those guilty of serious murder are executed, which serves as social justice. Indeed, one of the death row inmates executed during Hatoyama's period was Miyazaki Tsutomu, who molested and strangled four primary school girls in Tokyo and Saitama prefectures between 1988 and 1989 (see Chap. 4). Given that his death sentence was finalised on 17 January 2006 and he was executed on 17 June 2008, it was another swift execution.

In addition, three to four executions each were conducted every other month during Hatoyama's term. As with Nagase, Hatoyama was determined to authorise executions during his term, and in the press conference on 25 September 2007 he denounced the fact that Article 475 (2) of the Code of Criminal Procedure which requires the Minister to authorise executions 'within six months from the date when the judgment becomes final and binding' had been neglected.[55] What is more, he stated that he wondered if there was any way to conduct executions within half a year automatically and objectively without involving the Ministers of Justice.[56] According to him, the current system required debate about who was to be executed next and about the fact that personal views of Ministers of Justice could override legal provisions of executions. Hatoyama's remarks soon invited criticisms by the media, who referred to his view on the death penalty as *belt conveyer no shikei* (executions on a conveyer belt).

Two subsequent Ministers, Yasuoka Okiharu (2 August 2008–24 September 2008) and Mori Eisuke (24 September 2008–16 September 2009), followed suit and authorised swift executions. Yasuoka deserves attention because he authorised three executions during his extremely short term of less than two months. Given that he had authorised three executions within five months during his previous term (4 July 2000–5 December 2000), Yasuoka appears to have been strategically chosen in order to maintain the government's pro-death-penalty stance. Mori authorised nine executions in total, two of them, on 28 October 2008, within a month of being appointed. Although Hatoyama was criticised by the media as the Grim Reaper, because of the 13 executions that he authorised during his term, it appears from the two subsequent Ministers and their swift executions that Hatoyama was not an eccentric figure but a model Minister of Justice, who was determined to 'abide by law' and complete his responsibility.

6.3.6 *Governmental Justification for Capital Punishment (1993–2009)*

This section investigates the resumption of executions from 1993 to 2009. Although 25 Ministers of Justice served within 16 years, the Ministry of Justice made sure that one or more executions took place each calendar year. Firstly, Gotoda and Mikazuki not only resumed executions but also tried to maintain the principle that it was a responsibility of Ministers of Justice to authorise executions in order to maintain legal order. Although the provisions of Article 475 and 476 of the Code of Criminal Procedure, which specifies the duty of the Minister of Justice regarding the authorisation of executions, have been interpreted in various ways by different scholars, Gotoda, in particular, denounced non-authorisation as a neglect of duty.[57] With the exception of Sugiura, subsequent Ministers uncritically authorised executions simply to act on precedent, and did not seek to encourage domestic debate on the ethical concerns of capital punishment.

Secondly, through analysis of the timing of executions, it was evident that the Ministry of Justice had been conducting executions in order to give a political signal that legitimated state killing.[58] Examples of this include the execution of Nagayama Norio, who was 19 at the time of his crime, in response to the public outcry against the successive indiscriminate murder cases by juvenile offenders; and the execution of Takuma Mamoru, who had stabbed primary school children indiscriminately, within a year of the final sentence being given. Annual executions also took place to show that the system continued. The Ministry started to disclose executions officially in 1998 in order to garner more public support for the capital punishment system. Furthermore, execution of one inmate was authorised on legal grounds regardless of the protest of the victim's bereaved family. Although victims' feelings are often cited by the government as the justification of capital punishment, this appears only to refer to the pro-death-penalty victim lobby, which is in favour of the government's policy.

6.4 Conclusion

This chapter has investigated how executions were resumed, and how the Ministry of Justice as a pro-death-penalty actor tried to maintain the dominant discourse on crime and punishment for the justification of capital punishment. The first section studied the social climate around capital punishment through examining the excessive media coverage of domestic terrorism, juvenile crimes and the increase in the reported crime rate. It argued that these factors appeared to have divided the public into two extremes, for and against the death penalty, without allowing debates on alternatives.

The second section examined how the Ministry of Justice tried to justify the capital punishment system on the basis of law and by strategic use of the prevailing social climate. Multiple executions began to take place from March 1993, and some key Ministers of Justice such as Gotoda and Mikazuki appear to have re-established a principle for the succeeding Ministers to follow, referring to Article 475 of the Code of Criminal Procedure: that it is required for Ministers of Justice to authorise executions in order to fulfil their duty and to maintain legal order for the public. Similarly, Moriyama proclaimed that Japan retained capital punishment since it was deeply embedded in Japanese culture. However, the real key drivers of this policy were still bureaucrats in the Ministry of Justice. They appear to have managed to use Gotoda and Mikazuki's legal approach, and Moriyama's cultural approach, as useful political signals to legitimise state killing in Japan.

An amendment was made to the Ministry's secretive policy and executions started to be announced by the Ministry of Justice during Nakamura's term. Some anti-death-penalty advocates perceived that this was a definite step towards spurring public debate on the rights and wrongs of capital punishment. However, the Ministry's aim was apparently to gain further public support through a demonstration that the capital punishment system had been in use for social justice.

Moreover, in addition to the 'institutional ambivalence' represented by the *de facto* moratorium period from 1989 to 1993, another ambiguity was observed during this period. Whilst the Ministry of Justice usually cites public opinion and the feelings of bereaved families as justification for capital punishment, Moriyama authorised an execution primarily on the basis of the law, ignoring the bereaved family's plea. This illuminated the fact that the Ministry of Justice tends to change its priority or its justification of capital punishment depending on the situation.

The following chapter examines the next two *de facto* moratorium periods, or the lapse of time where executions did not take place mainly because of a frequent change of Ministers of Justice.

Notes

1. The International Federation for Human Rights (2008) 'The Death Penalty in Japan: The Law of Silence—Going against the International Trend', October 2008, pp. 1–68, p. 16. Available at: http://www.fidh.org/IMG/pdf/japon505a2008.pdf. [Accessed 19 March 2016]
2. Asahi Newspaper Agency (2000) *Kurai Mori: Kōbe Renzoku Jidō Sasshō Jiken* (Dark Forest: Repetitive Child Murder Case in Kobe), Osaka: Asahi Shinbun Sha, pp. 56–57.
3. Asahi Newspaper Agency (2000) *op. cit.* pp. 167–169.
4. Machizawa, S. (2000) *Saga Bus Jack Jiken no Keikoku: Koritsu Suru Kazoku, Kowareta 17 Sai* (Alert from the Saga Bus Jack Case: Isolating Family, Broken 17-year-old), Tokyo: Magazine House, p. 122.
5. Regarding this case, there remained a possibility that the crime was set up by someone else (*Japan Times* (2004) 'Hayashi Breaks Silence over Wakayama Curry Poisoning', 19 June 2004. Available at: http://search.japantimes.co.jp/cgi-bin/nn20040619a1.html [Accessed 19 March 2016]). However, since she had a previous criminal record of conspiring with her husband in an insurance-related murder attempt, she was convicted without any definite evidence against her or confession from her.
6. Shinoda, H. (2008) *Document Sikeishū* (Documentary of Death Row Inmate), Tokyo: Chikuma Shinsho, p. 9.
7. Mori, T. (2008) *Shikei: Hito wa Hito wo Koroseru, Demo Hito wa Hito wo Sukuitai tomo Omou* (Death Penalty: People Could Kill People, but People Also Feel Like Saving People), Tokyo: Asahi Shuppan Sha, p. 121.
8. The death sentence on Takuma was finalised on 26 September 2003, and he was executed on 14 September 2004.
9. *Japan Times* (2004) 'Takuma Hangs for Massacre of Eight Kids at Osaka School', 15 September 2004. Available at: http://www.japantimes.co.jp/text/nn20040915a1.html [Accessed 19 March 2016].
10. *Kyōdō News* (2008) '7 Killed, 10 Injured in Akihabara Stabbing Spree', 9 June 2008, http://www.japantimes.co.jp/news/2008/06/09/national/7-killed-10-injured-in-akihabara-stabbing-spree/#.VfgNdxF_Okr [Accessed 19 March 2016].

11. *Japan Times* (2015), 'Death Sentence Upheld for Akihabara Rampage Killer', 2 February 2015. http://www.japantimes.co.jp/news/2015/02/02/national/crime-legal/death-sentence-confirmed-akihabara-rampage-killer/#.VfgNWBF_Okr [Accessed 19 March 2016].
12. Asahi Newspaper Agency (2000) *op. cit.* pp. 205–208.
13. 'The Act on Medical Care and Treatment for Persons Who Have Caused Serious Cases Under the Condition of Insanity' was adopted in 2003 and came into force in 2005.
14. Hamai, K. and Ellis, T. (2008) 'Japanese Criminal Justice: Was Reintegrative Shaming a Chimera?', *Punishment & Society*, 10(1), pp. 25–46, p. 26. Available at: http://www.port.ac.uk/departments/academic/icjs/staff/documentation/filetodownload,73687,en.pdf [Accessed 19 March 2016].
15. Kawai, M. (2004) *Anzen Shinwa Hōkai no Paradox: Chian no Hōshakaigaku* (The Paradox of Destruction of Security Myth: Sociology of Law in Security), Tokyo: Iwanami Shoten, p. 39.
16. Prime Minister's Office (2004) *Chian ni Kansuru Yoron Chōsa (Opinion Poll on Public Order and Safety)*. Available at: http://www8.cao.go.jp/survey/h16/h16-chian/2-1.html [Accessed 19 March 2016]; (2006) *Chian ni Kansuru Yoron Chōsa (Opinion Poll on Public Order and Safety)*. Available at: http://www8.cao.go.jp/survey/h18/h18-chian/2-3.html [Accessed 19 March 2016].
17. Interview with an NGO worker, Tokyo, 12 April 2011; with a MOFA official, Tokyo, 9 May 2011; and with two NGO workers, Tokyo, 17 May 2011. Although interviewees hypothesised that it was a decision made amongst the bureaucrats in the Ministry of Justice strategically, it is the Prime Minister who nominates the Ministers (see Chap. 2).
18. Gotoda, M. (1993a) *The 126th Legal Affairs Committee of the House of Representatives*, 23 February 1993, p. 17.
19. Gotoda (1993a) *Ibid.*
20. Shimaya, N. (2005) '*Gotoda Soshō: Tokyō Chisai ga Futō Hanketsu*' (Gotoda Litigation: Tokyo District Court Rejects Appeal), p. 1. Available at: http://www.jca.apc.org/stop-shikei/news/82/4.html [Accessed 19 March 2016].
21. However, Shikoku Forum members were upset, five years after this Committee meeting, because Gotoda misused the information in his memoir, stating that the Shikoku Forum survey showed the

same result as the one conducted by the Prime Minister's Office. Although 74 members of Shikoku Forum who were involved in conducting this survey sued Gotoda and a publisher of his book in Matsuyama prefecture on 20 May 1999, they lost in all the trials in Matsuyama, Takamatsu, and Tokyo District Court and the Supreme Court (Sakuma, T. (2004) '*Nippon Report: Hō Chitsujo Iji*' (Japan Report: Maintenance of Legal Order), 8 May 2004, p. 5. Available at: http://homepage3.nifty.com/tetuh/105.html [Accessed 19 March 2016]).

22. Hama, K. (1993) *The 126th Legal Affairs Committee of the House of Councillors*, 29 March 1993, p. 3.
23. Gotoda, M. (1993b) *The 126th Legal Affairs Committee of the House of Councillors*, 29 March 1993, p. 2.
24. Gotoda (1993b) *op. cit.* p. 3.
25. Suzuki, K. (1993) *The 126th Legal Affairs Committee of the House of Representatives*, 2 April 1993, p. 12.
26. Gotoda, M. (1993c) *The 126th Legal Affairs Committee of the House of Representatives*, 2 April 1993, p. 12.
27. Gotoda (1993c) *op. cit.* p. 13.
28. Interview with an NGO worker, Tokyo, 12 April 2011; with a MOFA official, Tokyo, 9 May 2011; and with two NGO workers, Tokyo, 17 May 2011.
29. Gotoda, M. (1998) *Jō to Ri: Gotoda Masaharu Kaikoroku (Ge)* (Mercy and Rationality: Gotoda Masaharu's Memoir (Part 1)), Tokyo: Kōdansha, p. 266.
30. *Ibid.*
31. Gotoda, M. (1994) *Sei to Kan* (Politics and Government), Tokyo: Kōdansha, p. 26.
32. Johnson, D.T. (2002) *The Japanese Way of Justice: Prosecuting Crime in Japan*, Oxford University Press, USA, pp. 243–244.
33. Interview with two NGO workers, Tokyo, 17 May 2011.
34. Mikazuki, A. (1982) *Hōgaku Nyūmon* (Introduction to Studies of Law), Tokyo: Kōbundō.
35. Cited in Sakuma (2004) *Ibid.*
36. Asahi Newspaper Agency (2000) *op. cit.* pp. 205–208.
37. Yasuda, Y. (1998) '*Uchitsuzuku Tairyō Shikei Shikkō: 12 Gatsu Shikkō Soshi wo*' (Mass Executions: Calling for Blocking Executions in December), *Nenpō Shikei Haishi* (Annual Report: Abolishing Capital Punishment), Tokyo: Impact Shuppan, p. 103.

38. Yasuda (1998) *Ibid.*
39. Yasuda (1998) *Ibid.*
40. Harada, A. (1997) *The 141st Legal Affairs Committee of the House of Councillors*, 13 November 1997, p. 7.
41. Shimoinaba, K. (1997) *The 141st Legal Affairs Committee of the House of Councillors*, 13 November 1997, p. 9.
42. Shimoinaba, K. (1998) *The 142nd Legal Affairs Committee of the House of Representatives*, 13 May 1998, p. 15.
43. Matsuo, K. (1998) *The 144th Legal Affairs Committee of the House of Councillors*, 3 December 1998, p. 6.
44. Harada, M. (2004) *Otōto wo Koroshita Kare to Boku* (He who Killed My Brother and I), Tokyo: Popura, pp. 108–109.
45. Moriyama, M. (2002a) *The 154th Legal Affairs Committee of the House of Representatives*, 3 April 2002, p. 8.
46. Moriyama, M. (2001a) *The 151st Legal Affairs Committee of the House of Councillors*, 28 June 2001, p. 17.
47. Moriyama, M. (2002b) *The 154th Legal Affairs Committee of the House of Councillors*, 11 April 2002, p. 9.
48. Moriyama, M. (2001b) *The 153rd Legal Affairs Committee of the House of Representatives*, 19 October 2001, p. 8.
49. Menda could not have pension rights after he was exonerated and freed. This was because the Ministry of Justice had not supposed that death row inmates would be freed after proof of innocence, and had not informed them about joining the pension system when it was introduced in 1961. Therefore, Menda had not paid his insurance premiums while he was on death row (*Japan Times* (2009) 'Man off Death Row Wants Pension', 4 June 2009. Available at: http://search.japantimes.co.jp/cgi-bin/nn20090604b2.html [Accessed 19 March 2016]).
50. Moriyama, M. (2003) *The 156th Legal Affairs Committee of the House of Representatives*, 2 July 2003, p. 11.
51. Sugiura, S. (2006) *The 164th Legal Affairs Committee of the House of Representatives*, 24 February 2006.
52. *Ibid.*
53. *Ibid.*
54. Nagase, J. (2006) *The 165th Legal Affairs Committee of the House of Representatives*, 20 October 2006.

55. Cited in Hiroshima Bar Association (2007) '*Shikei Shikkō ni Kansuru Hatoyama Hōshō Hatsugen ni Kōgi suru Kaichō Seimei*' (Statement by the Chair to Protest Against Justice Minister Hatoyama's Remarks on Executions), 17 October 2007. Available at: https://www.hiroben.or.jp/iken_info.php?ikenid=12 [Accessed 19 March 2016].
56. *Ibid.*
57. Gotoda (1993a) *Ibid.*; (1993b) *op. cit.* pp. 2–3.
58. Yasuda (1998) *Ibid.*

CHAPTER 7

Democracy Inaction: Governmental Justification for Capital Punishment During the *De Facto* Moratorium Periods (2009–2010 and 2010–2012)

7.1 Introduction

This chapter analyses the Ministry of Justice's justification of the capital punishment system between 2009 and 2012, which includes two *de facto* moratorium periods (one year from 28 July 2009 to 28 July 2010, and one year and eight months from 28 July 2010 to 29 March 2012). It investigates the extent to which the newly introduced *saiban-in seido* (quasi-jury system) was strategically used to underscore the government's position on capital punishment.[1] For approximately 54 years from 1955 to 2009,[2] Japan was governed by the pro-death-penalty Liberal Democratic Party. Following its replacement in government by the Democratic Party of Japan in September 2009, the issue of capital punishment was 're-discovered' by Ministers of Justice, a few of whom were outspoken anti-death-penalty advocates. However, in the light of *saiban-in seido*, which was introduced in May 2009, the Ministry of Justice started to give weight to the feelings of lay assessors who supported death sentences. The Supreme Court reported that 41,834 people (54.9 per cent male and 43.3 per cent female) were chosen as lay assessors between May 2009 and December 2014, and they handed down sentences to 7262 convicts, including 21 death sentences in the First Court.[3] This chapter critically investigates whether or not the introduction of *saiban-in seido* has had an impact on the government's justification of the capital punishment policy.

M. Obara-Minnitt, *Japanese Moratorium on the Death Penalty*,
DOI 10.1057/978-1-137-55822-0_7

7.2 Persisting Pro-Death-Penalty Mood and Full Public Support of *Saiban-In Seido*?

According to the government's opinion polls in 2014, 80.3 per cent (85.6 per cent in 2009) of the public supported capital punishment (see Chap. 6) and the Supreme Court reported in 2015 that 95.5 per cent of lay assessors supported *saiban-in seido* both in 2012 and 2014.[4] Whilst this data appears to underscore governmental justification for capital punishment and *saiban-in seido*, methodological issues can be observed in in-depth examination of the survey. The first part of this section critically examines the results of the surveys conducted by the Supreme Court and newspapers and discusses the gap in governmental and social attitudes. The second part focuses on the lack of rights of lay assessors not to participate in *saiban-in seido* where they are required not only to determine both guilt (or innocence) but also the sentence to be imposed; and emerging mental health problems encountered by lay assessors.

7.2.1 'Public Opinion' of **Saiban-In Seido**

Prior to the introduction of *saiban-in seido* in Japan, it was debated amongst scholars that the Japanese public would be reluctant to serve as lay assessors because of a lack of confidence in giving sentences to criminals without sufficient knowledge of the law.[5] As discussed in Chap. 3, the Japanese public tends to prefer legal incidents to be dealt with by legal professionals,[6] since they appear to 'regard law like an heirloom samurai sword, something to be treasured but not used'.[7] In contrast and seeming to overturn such a hypothesis, the Supreme Court, using opinion poll results, reported in 2012 and 2014 that the vast majority supported the system.

According to the opinion polls conducted by the Supreme Court with lay assessors in 2012, 95.5 per cent found the experience either great or good despite 52.8 per cent reporting they were initially unwilling to participate (Fig. 7.1). The results in 2014 were very similar, with 95.5 per cent support whilst 51.1 per cent were initially unwilling to participate. This could at first sight illuminate the fact that the vast majority of lay assessors enjoyed participating in the system where they were given responsibility of determining whether to hand down death sentences. Nonetheless, examining the breakdown of percentages can provide us with alternative views: 95.5 per cent (2012) is a totalled percentage combining (1) 55.5 per cent who answered 'it was a great experience' and 40.0 per cent who answered

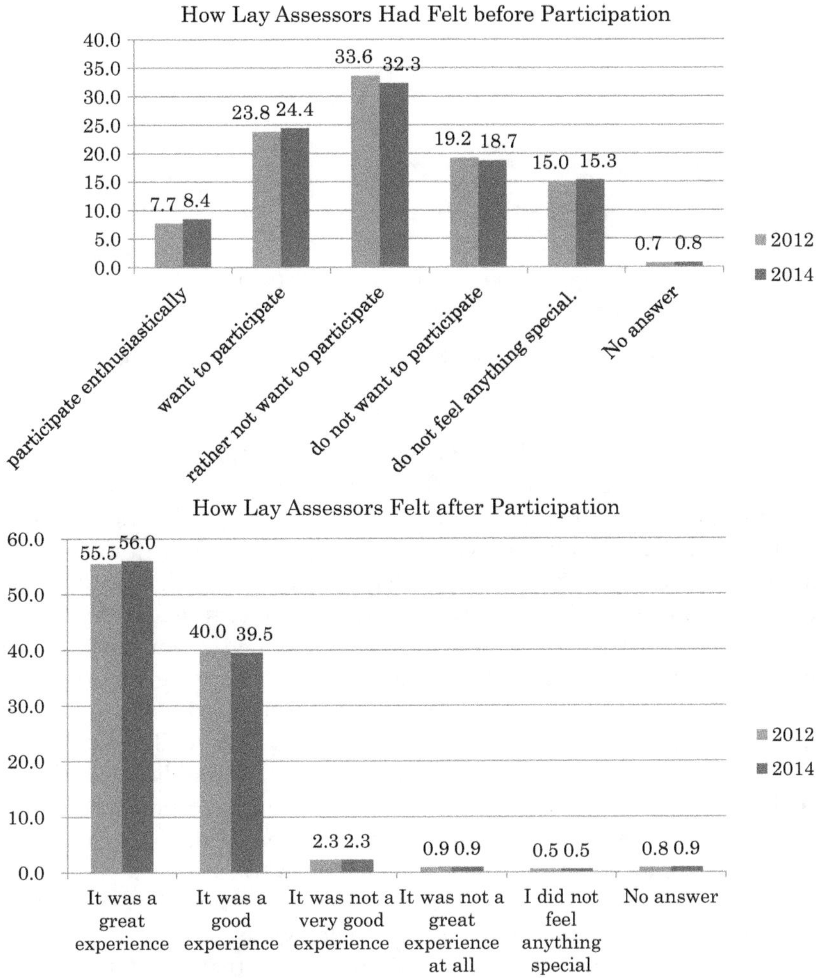

Fig. 7.1 Opinion Poll on Lay Assessors by the Supreme Court

'it was a good experience'; and (2) 52.8 per cent is composed of 33.6 per cent who answered 'I would prefer not to participate' and 19.2 per cent who answered 'I do not want to participate'.

What merits attention is that the survey does not inform us about the views of a key subset of lay assessors, those involved in passing death sentences. As Fig. 7.2 shows, numbers of death sentences issued by lay

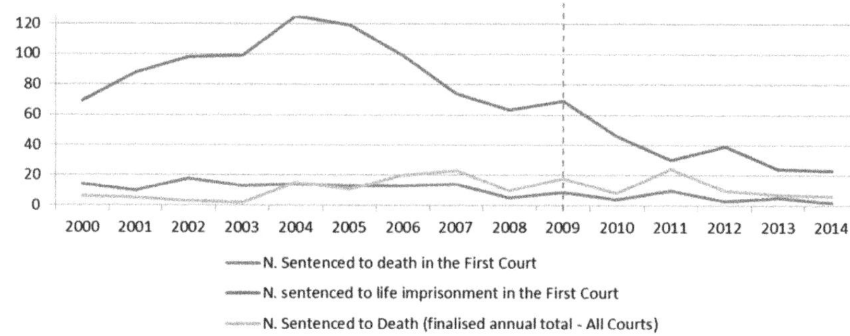

Fig. 7.2 Numbers Sentenced to Death and Life Imprisonment in the First Court

assessors in the First Court have stayed low in both numerical and percentage terms, with a peak of ten in 2011. From the survey data we have no way of knowing how many lay assessors involved in passing death penalties undertook the survey and what percentage they represent of the total number surveyed. It is therefore conceivable to have a high positive satisfaction result overall in percentage terms even if all those surveyed who were involved in passing death sentences responded negatively, because they represent such a small percentage of the total survey group. In addition respondents may have answered that it was a 'good' experience simply because serving as a lay assessor was out of their daily routine and they found it interesting. As discussed in Chap. 3, public opinion can also be influenced by governmental behaviour and the poll results that the government publishes. The pro-*saiban-in-seido* mood expressed in the 2012 survey may have influenced the public who answered the survey conducted in 2014, which resulted in a similar outcome. It appears that the numbers of those who felt the experience great and good were strategically totalled in order to draw the conclusion that the vast majority support the system uncritically.

The *Yomiuri* newspaper opinion polls conducted on 28–29 June 2014 also provide us with interesting data. According to the results, 74 per cent of the Japanese public supports the retention of *saiban-in seido*. However, the same technique appears to have been adopted to generate a positive mood towards the new system: only 18 per cent answered that 'we should keep *saiban-in seido* as it is'; 56 per cent answered 'we should keep it upon reviewing the system'; 17 per cent answered 'we should abolish the system'; and 8 per cent answered 'I would rather not respond'.[8] In other words, although *Yomiuri* reported that the majority of the Japanese public felt positive about the retention of *saiban-in seido*, 56 per cent of the public felt that the system needed to be first reviewed, whereas 18 per cent supported the system uncritically. The actual social climate around this system can be observed from the unwillingness by members of the public to participate as lay assessors. According to the same opinion poll, 79 per cent responded that they would not like to participate in the system as lay assessors, because of a lack of confidence in handing down an appropriate sentence (58 per cent). This is a similar result to the 76 per cent polled in March 2013, which supports the hypothesis made by law scholars before the introduction of the system; and it is in sharp contrast to the positive results reported by the Supreme Court.

Another opinion poll specifically dealt with the (un)willingness of lay assessors to be involved in the decision of whether or not to sentence to a death penalty. The *Mainichi* newspaper conducted an opinion poll in May 2012 in order to evaluate what lay assessors felt about the idea of imposing the death sentence. Surveys were sent to the 467 lay assessors who responded to the initial contact. Of the male respondents, 55 per cent said that it was better that lay assessors should get involved in death penalty cases, in contrast to 41 per cent of female respondents.[9] Although *Mainichi* presented this as a gender distinction and implied lay assessors' support for the capital punishment system, the mental care of lay assessors after handing down death sentences started to arise as a very important issue following the introduction of the system. The *Japan Times* (30 May 2012) portrayed the lay assessors as experiencing adverse mental and physical symptoms arising from these duties, as they 'hav[e] to commit to long court proceedings, as well as the difficulty in deciding whether a defendant should live or die'.[10] The article quotes the views of one of the lay assessors who had imposed a death sentence: 'The defendant did not appear to be an evil man, and I felt as if I could have become friends with him under different circumstances.'

The next section discusses the anti-*saiban-in-seido* movement, the lack of lay assessors' rights not to participate in *saiban-in seido* and how the government has been dealing with lay assessors who developed post-traumatic stress disorder after the trials.

7.2.2 *Lay Assessors' Rights not to Participate in* Saiban-In Seido?

For the publicity of *saiban-in seido*, the Supreme Court introduced a parrot mascot character in 2008: *Saiban-inko*, *inko* being a parrot in Japanese. Whilst the Minister of Justice at the time, Hatoyama Kunio, wore the mascot costume himself and tried to engage with the public, a protest group made an anti-*saiban-in-seido* mascot character called *Saiban-in-wa-irana-inko* ('we don't need a *saiban-in-seido*' parrot) and held meetings and parades, which spread across the nation. One of the largest was held in Hibiya, Tokyo on 21 April 2009, approximately one month before the introduction of the system. One of the speakers included a professor in law, Adachi Masakatsu, and he highlighted that it is extremely problematic that out of all the countries which have jury systems it is only Japan that makes lay assessors determine both guilt (or innocence) and the sentence to be imposed.[11] Following this meeting, 2000 people held an anti-saiban-in-*seido* parade that marched towards Ginza, Tokyo, and influenced other like-minded groups across the nation.

Despite this protest, the system was introduced in 2009 as scheduled. However, lay assessors' post-traumatic stress disorder became an important issue and started to be addressed by scholars, solicitors and medical doctors. *Mainichi* reports that from December 2014, *Saiban-in Keikensha Network* (Lay Assessors' Network), which is mainly composed of lay assessors and solicitors, started investigations into whether or not lay assessors had felt a psychological burden as a consequence of their role.[12] According to the questionnaire, over 70 per cent of the respondents (30 out of 42) answered yes, and stated that they would need continuous support for their mental health after the trials in which they had participated. All of them raised issues about the negative impact of the ongoing sense of responsibility after making a decision about the fate of the convicts. In addition, 22 raised the required level of secrecy surrounding their duty as lay assessors; and 18 raised the brutal photographs from the crime scenes and testimony which describes them.[13] The Lay Assessors Act provides that 'lay judges are subject to a life time secrecy obligations [...and those] who leak trial-related information will be punished'.[14] An additional burden is the fact that not only do they feel that the pressures are significantly magnified by deciding whether or not the convicts should live or die, but they are also not allowed to talk to their family, friends or colleagues about what was discussed in the courts.[15]

One of the most recent studies of lay assessors' stress disorder was conducted by a Doctor of Medicine, Nanbu Saori. Nanbu focused on a trial case on 30 September 2014 after which a female lay assessor in her 60s sued the Japanese government for state compensation for ¥2million ($17,796.25).[16] The lay assessor claimed that she developed Acute Stress Disorder as she: (1) felt obliged to participate in the system; (2) was shown photographs of crime scenes during the trial; and (3) was involved in sentencing the convicted person to the death penalty—all against her will.[17]

Once members of the public are chosen as lay assessors from the electoral registers, it is required for them to participate in the system with limited circumstantial exceptions, including that the lay assessor is aged 70 or over or pregnant, as specified in the Lay Assessor Act Article 16 'Reasons to Decline'. In this case, however, her reason for not wanting to judge or impose a sentence was not on the list, and she felt obliged to participate against her will; otherwise she would have had to pay a penalty of ¥100,000 ($889.81) for neglecting the duty.[18] This means that less financially able members of society will have no choice but to participate, regardless of their views on *saiban-in seido* or the death penalty system.

As part of the procedure, the lay assessor was shown photographs of the victims (husband and wife) covered with blood and a voice recording of the wife up to the point that she was stabbed. This not only made the lay assessor physically sick both during and after trials, but also left her unable to cook or eat meats which reminded her of the victims' flesh.[19] What is worse, the feeling of guilt after being involved in sentencing the convicted person to death made her develop deep depression and insomnia, which led her to lose her job after taking extended sick leave.[20] The lay assessor's family tried to seek help and contacted the court, but was told that lay assessors were allowed to receive counselling services in Tokyo up to five times free of charge, but had to pay travel expenses themselves.[21]

Following this, her solicitor argued that *saiban-in seido* violates the lay assessors' human rights, which are protected in the Japanese constitution. Article 18 of the Japanese constitution provides that: 'No person shall be held in bondage of any kind. Involuntary servitude, except as punishment for crime, is prohibited.' The Supreme Court previously declared on 16 November 2011 that *saiban-in seido* was not against Article 18 of the Japanese constitution. However, the solicitor argued that her client's responsibility as a lay assessor, with the requirement to get involved in the decision whether the convict should live or die, would apply as 'involuntary servitude', which is prohibited in Article 18.[22] In other words, lay assessors' freedom and rights not to kill people are neglected in *saiban-in seido*. The solicitor also argued that this conflicts with Article 13, which stipulates that 'All of the people shall be respected as individuals. Their right to life, liberty, and the pursuit of happiness shall, to the extent that it does not interfere with the public welfare, be the supreme consideration in legislation and in other governmental affairs.'

Although the lay assessor lost in this case, it is important to acknowledge that despite the 'wide support of *saiban-in system*' reported by the Supreme Court, she is not the only assessor who is suffering from the feelings of guilt that she was by association involved in state killing through acting as a lay assessor. The NHK reported on 21 May 2014 about the agony of two other lay assessors after handing down death sentences.[23] Yonezawa Toshiyasu, 22 at the time, participated in *saiban-in seido* and sentenced the convicted person to the death penalty. When Yonezawa later had an opportunity to talk about this experience to his friend, he was asked: 'Does that mean you killed a person?'. As the convicted person in this case withdrew from his right to appeal, his death penalty was finalised, meaning he could be executed at any time without any notification. Yonezawa reported that he remained consistently anxious and alert to potential news about the person he was involved in convicting and sentencing, and only felt briefly relieved when there was no news on TV about the execution.

A series of experiences following Yonezawa's involvement in sentencing the convicted person to the death penalty and being questioned about his decision by his friend made him take action. Yonezawa became one of 20 people who have participated in the system as lay assessors and signed a petition and submitted it to the Ministry of Justice.[24] The petition calls upon the Ministry to disclose further information regarding the procedure and the mental and physical conditions of the death row inmates between sentence and execution, prior to placing the responsibility upon lay assessors to judge whether a person should live or die. Furthermore, the petition calls on the Ministry not to go ahead with executions while disclosure of information is insufficient. In response, Tanigaki Sadakazu, Minister of Justice at the time, maintained that it was not possible to suspend executions without legal backing or to disclose information on the death row inmates, as this could upset the *shinjō no antei* (stability of emotions) of those to be executed, their family and other inmates waiting for executions.[25] Although *Saiban-in Seido ni Kansuru Kentōkai* (Review Meetings on *Saiban-In Seido*) have been held since 2009 by the Ministry of Justice, to which experts have been invited, the abovementioned issues are still outstanding.

The NHK also reports on another female lay assessor, who, since being involved in a decision to convict and sentence to death the accused, has debated every day whether or not her decision to pass the death sentence was right. It was three years after she participated in the system that the Shizuoka District Court ordered a retrial of Hakamada Iwao, claiming that fabricated evidence had been used by prosecutors (see Chap. 2). The lay assessor argues that she made a decision to pass a death sentence based on the evidence that was presented to her and other lay assessors; and if the evidence was incorrect or fabricated, there was nothing they could have done. Consequently she remains fearful and anxious that the death sentence that she and her colleagues imposed may have been a miscarriage of justice.

The results of the opinion poll conducted by the Supreme Court suggests almost full support of the lay assessors who are involved in *saiban-in seido* and their right to impose death sentences, and their 'support' inadvertently gives succour to governmental retention of the capital punishment policy. However, in-depth investigation of this support illuminates different perspectives, including lay assessors: (1) developing stress disorder after involvement in sentencing to the death penalty; (2) protesting against the system and calling for a moratorium of executions until there has been full disclosure of information on death row inmates; and (3) fearing miscarriages of justice, which result in death sentences being passed on innocent people.

Finally, it is important to recognise that opponents of *saiban-in-seido* are not necessarily opponents of the death penalty. The former group focuses on the unconstitutionality of *saiban-in seido*. Their argument is that the responsibility placed upon lay assessors, requiring them to determine both guilt (or innocence) and the sentence to be imposed, compromises their human rights. They propose that the responsibility of both findings of guilt and sentencing should rest with judges with sufficient legal knowledge to bear the legal burden, not necessarily to abolish the death penalty. This is similar to the phenomenon discussed in Chap. 4: it is a separate issue from abolishing the death penalty to call for the human rights of novelists on death row or to fight for those who are on death row for decades on false charges. Having said that, the anti-*saiban-in-seido* movement and the abolitionist movement are not automatically diametrically opposed, given that more lay assessors are likely to emerge in the future who have suffered from the guilty responsibility of involvement in state killing; and this is likely to contribute to re-evaluation of the capital punishment system in Japan.

The following section examines the governmental justification for capital punishment during this period, a justification that used the decisions of lay assessors as a 'legitimate' source.

7.3 Governmental Justification for Capital Punishment

Because of political corruption scandals or cabinet reshuffles, ten Ministers of Justice served in the four years from 2009 to 2012. This section examines how the Ministry of Justice justified capital punishment during two execution-free periods.

7.3.1 Governmental Justification During the De Facto *Moratorium Period (2009–2010)*

Chiba Keiko (16 September 2009–17 September 2010) was the first Minister of Justice under the Democratic Party of Japan, which replaced the Liberal Democratic Party in September 2009 after 54 years in office. As discussed in Chap. 2, Chiba had a long history as an outspoken anti-death-penalty advocate and member of the Parliamentary League for the Abolition of the Death Penalty. However, once she was appointed as the Minister of Justice under the administration of Hatoyama Yukio, she resigned from the Parliamentary League for the Abolition of the Death Penalty. Since she appeared to have chosen to separate her personal view and official responsibility as the Minister of Justice, the sudden change in her attitude attracted criticisms from several Diet members. For example, in the Legal Affairs Committee on 13 April 2010, Maruyama Kazuya referred to Chiba's remarks regarding capital punishment as 'model answers' for a governmental official;[26] and Shimomura Hirobumi said on 16 April 2010 that Chiba's way of speech was strikingly different from when she was a Diet member, as she was extremely careful on the issue of capital punishment.[27]

In the Legal Affairs Committee on 16 March 2010, Chiba offered several explanations of why she took a cautious approach to the public pro-death-penalty sentiment, the ethical issue of 'state killing' and her responsibility as the Minister of Justice to authorise executions.[28] Her remarks about lay assessors in *saiban-in seido* in the Legal Affairs Committee on 24 February 2010 deserve special attention. In explaining lay assessors' reluctance to participate in *saiban-in seido* and the agony of sentencing those convicted to death, Chiba clarified that capital punishment exists as a legal penalty in Japan and that the Minister of Justice is required to authorise execution orders when necessary.[29] Although she did not say directly that she felt responsible for authorising executions based on the decisions made by lay assessors, her remarks sound as if she had started to attach some weight to the role that lay assessors play in the capital punishment system.

Although Chiba managed to avoid giving her authorisation for the execution of convicted criminals for nearly a year, on 28 July 2010 two death row inmates were executed without prior notice, much to the chagrin of anti-death-penalty activists (see Chap. 2). Newspaper and television coverage, on the other hand, shed light on positive aspects of the event: Chiba became the very first Minister of Justice actually to witness a hanging, and indicated that she was keen to set up an internal study group to look at the issue within the Ministry of Justice and to allow the media access to the execution sites in order to spur domestic debate.[30]

7.3.2 *Governmental Justification During the* De Facto *Moratorium Period (2010–2012)*

The next Minister of Justice, Yanagida Minoru (17 September 2010–22 November 2010), resigned within a short period over remarks that made light of his position as the Minister of Justice,[31] and did not make any official statement on the issue of capital punishment. The then vice-Minister of Justice, and later Minister of Justice, Ogawa Toshio, tried to justify the capital punishment system during Yanagida's term consistently. In the Legal Affairs Committee on 26 October 2010, a Diet member, Tashiro Kaoru, questioned Ogawa about how the Ministry of Justice had been dealing with the examination of possible miscarriages of justice in order to prevent the detention and execution of the innocent. In response, proclaiming that Japan already had a three-tiered judicial and appeal system in order to avoid false charge cases, Ogawa noted that the appeal process was *ikaga na monoka* (questionable), since retrials could ignore the previous rulings from the first to third trials, and function as the fourth or fifth trial.[32] Despite the fact that the right to a retrial is specified in Article 435 of the Code of Criminal Procedure, Ogawa doubted the necessity of this system by implication, suggesting that human errors are never made in the current criminal justice system. Subsequently, in the Legal Affairs Committee on 28 October 2010, Ogawa stressed that it was challenging to advance abolitionism in Japan, given the 'wide public support' for the death penalty.[33]

The third Minister of Justice, Sengoku Yoshito (22 November 2010–14 January 2011), did not actively deal with the issue of capital punishment, but his successor Eda Satsuki (14 January 2011–2 September 2011) was outspoken and showed his anti-death-penalty sentiment. As with the former Minister of Justice Chiba, Eda resigned from the Parliamentary League for the Abolition of the Death Penalty once he was appointed to the Ministry. However, he still endeavoured to discuss the issue of capital punishment during his term. As already discussed in Chap. 2, he: (1) described capital punishment as a ***kekkan no aru*** (defective) penalty, raising the possibility of erroneous executions; (2) claimed that the death penalty must be authorised by the Minister of Justice so that domestic and international trends could be studied comprehensively, and executions were not authorised mechanically; and (3) described the responsibility of Ministers of Justice regarding the authorisation of executions as a mere ***kunji kitei*** (advisory provision). With regard to the internal study group that former Minister Chiba established, Eda stated that the Ministry did not have a particular schedule when the enquiry would be published.[34] In response, Kawai accused Eda of 'running away' from his responsibility by using the ongoing discussion in the study group as an excuse.[35] Kawai continued by saying that it was not appropriate that Ministers of Justice should struggle between their personal beliefs and an official duty to authorise executions: rather, it was prison guards, who hang death row inmates upon order, who struggle between these two viewpoints.[36]

The fifth Justice Minister, Hiraoka Hideo (2 September 2011–13 January 2012), showed a similarly critical attitude towards the issue of capital punishment in the Diet meetings. Although he also refrained from giving a date for the publication of the internal study group at the Legal Affairs Committee on 25 October 2011, he stressed the importance for Ministers of Justice to consider various factors regarding capital punishment, and stated that it was not appropriate to authorise execution orders in a dutiful manner.[37] In his argument, he noted the international trend that: (1) only three out of 34 Organisation for Economic Co-operation and Development (OECD) countries retain capital punishment; (2) one of them, South Korea, is *de facto* abolitionist; and (3) 17 [now 19] out of 50 US states have abolished capital punishment.[38] With regard to the interpretation of Article 475, Hiraoka expressed the same view as Eda, and implied that Ministers' non-compliance with this provision did not necessarily generate legal problems, such as neglect of an official governmental duty.[39] However, a Diet member, Uozumi Yuichio,[40] commented that despite the fact that the Ministry of Justice had given important responsibilities to lay assessors in *saiban-in seido*, Ministers of Justice had failed to fulfil their duty to authorise executions, thus upsetting legal order in Japan.

7.3.3 Governmental Justification on the Basis of Law (2012)

It was the sixth Minister, Ogawa Toshio (13 January 2012–4 June 2012), who authorised the execution of three death row inmates on 29 March 2012, bringing to an end the *de facto* moratorium, which lasted for approximately 20 months from 28 July 2010. As already discussed in Chap. 2, as the vice-Minister of Justice during the term of Hiraoka, Ogawa had justified capital punishment on legal grounds consistently, and in his inauguration speech he clarified that it was the duty of the Minister of Justice to authorise executions. This was because the number of death row inmates in Japan had risen to approximately 130, the largest number since the end of the Second World War (see Chap. 2). Eda also denied the possibility that discussion in the study group would result in changes to the death penalty system. He emphasised that the purpose of the study group was not to achieve the establishment of an alternative system but merely to study the discussion around retention and abolition of the death penalty system: this issue primarily depends on the opinion of the public or sovereign members of Japanese society.[41] A former Minister of Justice, Chiba, had initiated a new role for lay assessors in the capital process during her term, and Ogawa tried to stress this in the Legal Affairs Committee on 28 March 2012. Namely, he emphasised that governmental opinion polls indicate wide public support for capital punishment; and that death sentences which have been imposed by *saiban-in seido* demonstrate that citizen jurors have been supporting the death penalty.[42] Since the introduction of *saiban-in seido*, nine people had been sentenced to death in 2009, four in 2010 and nine in 2011. Therefore, Ogawa tried to justify capital punishment as if Ministers' refusal to authorise executions would go against 'the conclusion that ordinary citizens drew after going through the agony (of judging whether a person should live or die)'.[43]

The seventh Minister of Justice, Taki Minoru (4 June 2012–1 October 2012), took a similar approach to Ogawa, and tried to justify capital punishment on legal grounds. He stressed in the Legal Affairs Committee on 15 June 2012 that capital punishment was a fair system equipped with the retrial system, and amnesty could also be granted when appropriate.[44] Then on 28 August 2012, he emphasised the legal responsibility of Ministers of Justice regarding executions as follows:

> It is not in line with the legal provisions that Ministers of Justice neglect the duty of authorising executions due to personal convictions. Once the Supreme Court handed down a death sentence after going through the agony of judging whether a person should live or die, the Ministry of Justice should respect the decision.[45]

What needs to be noted about Taki is the timing of the executions he authorised. Although he stayed in office for only approximately four months, he authorised executions of two inmates each on 3 August and 27 September 2012. Regarding the latter in particular, he was heavily accused by the anti-death-penalty lobby for his timing. Taki had already implied at the press conference on 25 September 2012 that he would refrain from being re-appointed as the Minister of Justice after the Cabinet shuffle on 1 October 2012, considering his age, 74. Therefore, the anti-death-penalty advocates argued that Taki may have authorised executions of two more death row inmates as a 'rush job' before he resigned from his post.[46] Both Ogawa and Taki also authorised executions during parliamentary sessions. As discussed in Chaps. 2 and 3, Japan does not usually conduct executions during parliamentary sessions or public and political holidays in order to distract the public or hinder the abolitionist lobby from voicing dissent. Although it is hazardous to conclude from these events that the Ministry of Justice altered its secretive policy, it is interesting that executions were conducted, despite risking more criticisms from the abolitionist lobby than usual.

Tanaka Keishu was subsequently appointed (1 October 2012–23 October 2012) until he resigned after a scandal regarding his personal connection with gangsters. In contrast to his two predecessors, he showed a cautious stance on the issue of capital punishment: 'I think rigorously of the execution of death sentences because it is stipulated in law, but I will thoroughly examine cases, rather than take the execution as a foregone conclusion.'[47] Given that Tanaka appeared reluctant to authorise executions in a business-like manner as a mere official duty of the Minister of Justice, it is likely that he would not have authorised executions even if he had stayed in office longer.

After Taki had temporarily served as the Minister of Justice for two months (24 October 2012–26 December 2012), Tanigaki Sadakazu was appointed (26 December 2012–3 September 2014). Following Nagase and Hatoyama, Tanigaki authorised 11 executions. One to three executions on each occasion were conducted six times, the first execution during his term including a high-profile death row inmate: Kobayashi Kaoru. Kobayashi, 36 at the time, kidnapped, sexually assaulted and murdered a seven-year-old girl in Nara prefecture on 17 November 2004 (see Chap. 2). This was one of the few cases which involved a sole victim yet a death sentence was handed down in light of the nature of the crime. The choice of this particular inmate may have been a signal from the Ministry of Justice to demonstrate that it takes a tough attitude even on crimes with a solo victim, and that this is 'social justice'.

7.4 Governmental Justification for Capital Punishment (2009–2012)

From an analysis of the governmental discourse on capital punishment between 2009 and 2012, it can be observed that there was an 'institutional ambivalence' represented by two *de facto* moratorium periods. As already discussed, the central reason that executions were put on hold is that Ministers of Justice did not authorise executions during this period. However, whilst it is important to explore why execution-free periods were achieved contrary to legal obligations, it is more important to investigate how the Ministry of Justice was still justifying capital punishment during these periods. Most Ministers of Justice held office for only a few months because of the frequent changes in the cabinet, with Chiba (approximately one year) and Eda (nine months) being exceptions. Furthermore, whilst four Ministers of Justice served during the *de facto* moratorium period, not all of them were opponents of the capital punishment system or refused to authorise executions because of their personal beliefs. Yanagida did not stay in office long enough to be given opportunities to authorise executions during his term, and neither did Sengoku.

Of course, it is remarkable that both Eda and Hiraoka demonstrated initiatives to re-interpret Article 475 of the Code of Criminal Procedure, which specifies the responsibility of Ministers of Justice regarding authorisations of executions. Eda referred to this legal provision as *kunji kitei* (advisory provision). Hiraoka agreed to this, and also spoke about the worldwide trend to abolish the death penalty. It may appear from this that personal convictions of Ministers of Justice do matter, and influence capital punishment decision-making. However, the role they played in achieving the execution-free period should not be exaggerated. As the example of Chiba shows, even an outspoken anti-death-penalty advocate ended up authorising executions after facing internal pressures within the Ministry of Justice. Given that the issue of capital punishment has been handled within tightly knit institutional dynamics, where certain elites in the Ministry of Justice and the Public Prosecutor's Office have near monopoly power, it is important to understand the stance of the Ministry of Justice in justifying capital punishment on legal grounds.

In addition, it should be noted that some Ministers of Justice, including Chiba and Ogawa, uncritically incorporated the duty of lay assessors as a legitimate source for justifying capital punishment. They sounded as if they were sympathetic towards lay assessors, who have to go through the agony of determining guilt or innocence and imposing a sentence. However, the underlying motive would appear to be the justification of state killing on the grounds of respecting the decisions made by lay assessors.

7.5 Conclusion

This chapter has examined the social climate regarding the issue of the death penalty and *saiban-in seido*, and the government's consistent pro-death-penalty attitude despite the existence of two *de facto* moratorium periods.

The first part investigated how the pro-*saiban-in-seido* mood can be shaped by the Supreme Court and is used to legitimise the retention and use of the death penalty. Whilst the Supreme Court reports that the vast majority of lay assessors support *saiban-in seido*, examination of the results of the survey conducted by the Supreme Court and a newspaper revealed different perspectives. In fact, whilst the Supreme Court tries to demonstrate lay assessors' strong support of the system, the other survey illuminated the contradictory fact that the vast majority of the general public does not want to participate in the system because of a lack of sufficient knowledge in order to determine whether a person should live or die. In addition, there is an emerging issue of post-traumatic stress disorder amongst lay assessors, who suffer from guilt after handing down death sentences; and a group of lay assessors has demanded that the Ministry of Justice should break the secretive policy on the death penalty and disclose full information, and is calling for a moratorium until this is achieved. This suggests that there appears to exist a legitimacy issue in the governmental claim that: (1) *saiban-in-seido* has been strongly supported by lay assessors, and that (2) Ministers' refusal to authorise executions would go against the decisions made by lay assessors. What is more, whilst anti-*saiban-in-seido* and anti-death-penalty campaigns are currently seen as two separate movements, it is possible to hypothesise that the more lay assessors express their feeling of guilt in lending a hand to state killing, the more chances will emerge for the former group to be integrated in the latter for a more comprehensive and effective public movement.

The second section examined the government's consistent pro-death-penalty attitude despite the existence of two *de facto* moratorium periods. As in the other *de facto* moratorium periods, some Ministers of Justice were outspoken abolitionists and contributed to prolonging the execution-free periods. However, the moratorium period was also caused by a frequent change of Ministers who did not have opportunities to authorise executions. Given that Chiba, who was previously an outspoken anti-death-penalty advocate, ended up separating her personal opinion from governmental responsibility and authorised executions, it is difficult to put too much weight on the role that anti-death-penalty Justice Ministers can play in the running of the capital punishment policy.

The constitutionality of *saiban-in seido* is still a controversial issue amongst scholars, and lay assessors' 'rights' to impose death sentences are inadvertently giving succour to the government's justification of capital punishment. The voice of the 'minority'—lay assessors who claim the right not to judge or impose death sentences and call for a moratorium on executions—appears to be strategically ignored in order to maintain the government's pro-death-penalty stance.

Notes

1. In Japan, a jury system was in use from 1928 to 1943. Under that system, jurors used to determine guilt or innocence but not the sentence, which was the responsibility of judges. As will be discussed in later, under the quasi-jury system, which was introduced in 2009, lay assessors determine both guilt (or innocence) and the sentence

to be imposed. In order to distinguish from the jury system, this chapter uses the term quasi-jury system as found in the extant literature such as Anderson, K. and Ambler, L. (2006) 'The Slow Birth of Japan's Quasi-Jury System (*Saiban-in Seido*): Interim Report on the Road to Commencement', *Journal of Japanese Law*, 11(21), pp. 55–80; and Fukurai, H. (2011) 'Japan's Quasi-Jury and Grand Jury Systems as Deliberative Agents of Social Change: De-Colonial Strategies and Deliberative Participatory Democracy', *Chicago-Kent Law Review*, 86, pp. 789–987.

2. Although the LDP was ousted from power in 1993, it re-emerged as the ruling party from 1994.
3. Supreme Court (2015) '*Saiban-In Seido no Jisshi Jōkyō ni tsuite*' (Interim Report on the Quasi-Jury System), Available at: http://www.saibanin.courts.go.jp/vcms_lf/27.4jissi.pdf [Accessed 19 March 2016].
4. *Ibid.*
5. Fukurai (2011) *op. cit.* p. 818.
6. Kawashima, T. (1967) *Nihonjin no Hōishiki* (Japanese Legal Consciousness), Tokyo: Iwanami Shoten.
7. Dean, M. (2002) *Japanese Legal Syst*em 2nd ed., Abingdon: Routledge-Cavendish, p. 4.
8. *Yomiuri* (2014) '*Saiban-in Seido "Keizoku wo" 74 %—Yomiuri Yoron Chōsa*' (74 % of the Public Supports the Retention of the Quasi-Jury System—Opinion Poll by Yomiuri Newspaper), 11 July 2014.
9. *Mainichi* (2012) *Saiban-in Keiken sha ni taisuru Anketo* (Questionnaire to Those who have Served as Lay Assessors in Quasi-Jury System), 18 May 2012.
10. *Japan Times* (2012) 'Lay Judges Torn by Death Penalty: Citizens Find Deeming Who Lives, Dies Tests their Moral Fiber', 30 May 2012. Available at: http://www.japantimes.co.jp/text/nn20120530f1.html [Accessed 19 March 2016].
11. *Saiban-in Seido wa iranai Inko no Web Daiundō* (Big Online Movement by a Parrot which does not Want a Quasi-Jury System), '*Inko no Album Nikki*' (Parrot's Video Diary), Available at http://saibanin-iranainko.com/inkoalbum.html [Accessed 19 March 2016].
12. *Mainichi* (2015) '*Saiban-In 'Kokoro ni Futan' Zutto Keikensha 42 nin chū 7 Wari 'Atta' 'Shinri go Shibaraku Shitekara' 14 nin/Hikoku ga Jyōkoku 'Kei Tadashikatta ka"* (70 Per Cent of 42 Lay Assessors

Felt Psychological Burden, 14 Felt This Shortly after Trials, Convict Made an Appeal, 'Was My Judgement Right?'), 18 April 2015.

13. *Ibid.*
14. Yamamura, E. (2009) 'What Discourages Participation in the Lay Judge System (Saiban'in Seido) of Japan?: An Interaction Effect between the Secrecy Requirement and Social Network', Munich Personal RePEc Archive, No. 15920, p. 3. Available at: https://mpra.ub.uni-muenchen.de/15920/1/MPRA_paper_15920.pdf [Accessed 19 March 2016].
15. Yamamura (2009) *op. cit.* pp. 4, 7.
16. Nanbu S. (2015) '*Saiban-in no Stress to "Kueki" ni Kansuru Kōsatsu*' (Study on Lay Assessors's Stress and 'Involuntary Servitude'), *Yokohama Daigaku Ronsō Jinbun Kagaku Keirestu*, Vol, 66, No 2.
17. Nanbu (2015) *op. cit.* p. 37.
18. Nanbu (2015) *op. cit.* p. 41.
19. Nanbu (2015) *op. cit.* p. 47.
20. Nanbu (2015) *op. cit.* pp. 46–7.
21. Nanbu (2015) *op. cit.* p. 46.
22. Nanbu (2015) *op. cit.* pp. 47–50.
23. *NHK* (2014) '*Saiban-in Seido 5 nen: Inochi wo Sabaku Omomi*' (5 Years since the Introduction of the Quasi-Jury System—Weight of Judging People's Lives), 21 May 2014.
24. *Ibid.*
25. *Mainichi* (2015) '*Shikei Shikkō, Saiban In no Kunō Genjitsu ni*' (Execution of the Death Penalty: Agony of Lay Assessors Turns into Reality), 18 December 2015. Available at: http://mainichi.jp/articles/20151218/k00/00e/040/220000c [Accessed 19 March 2016].
26. Maruyama, K. (2010) *The 174th Legal Affairs Committee of the House of Councillors*, 13 April 2010, p. 6.
27. Shimomura, H. (2010) *The 174th Legal Affairs Committee of the House of Representatives*, 16 April 2010, p. 14.
28. Chiba, K. (2010) *The 174th Legal Affairs Committee of the House of Representatives*, 24 February 2010, p. 10.
29. Chiba, K. (2010) *The 174th Legal Affairs Committee of the House of Councillors*, 16 March 2010, p. 9.
30. *Asahi* (2010) *Shikei Shikkō ni Tachiai Chiba Hōshō: 'Konpon kara no Giron ga Hitsuyō'* (Justice Minister Chiba who Witnessed a Hanging: 'Fundamental Discussion is Needed on the Death Penalty'), 28 July

2010. Available at: http://www.asahi.com/national/update/0728/TKY201007280290.html [Accessed 19 March 20165].

31. Yanagida stated in an activity report meeting in Hiroshima on 14 November 2010 that what Ministers of Justice should give two main statements in the Diet meetings: (1) I have to refrain from commenting on the individual case; and (2) the Ministry of Justice has been handling this issue upon the basis of the law and evidence.
32. Ogawa, T. (2010) *The 176th Legal Committee of the House of Councillors*, 26 October 2010, p. 6.
33. Ogawa, T. (2010) *The 176th Legal Committee of the House of Councillors*, 28 October 2010.
34. Eda (2011a) *op. cit.* p. 7.
35. Kawai, K. (2011) *The 177th Legal Affairs Committee of the House of Representatives*, 9 August 2011, p. 7.
36. *Ibid.*
37. Hiraoka, H. (2011) *The 179th Legal Affairs Committee of the House of Representatives*, 25 October 2011, p. 13.
38. *Ibid.*
39. *Ibid.*
40. Uozumi, Y. (2011) *The 179th Legal Affairs Committee of the House of Councillors*, 27 October 2011, p. 29.
41. Ogawa (2012) *op. cit.* p. 32.
42. Ogawa, T. (2012) *The 180th Legal Affairs Committee of the House of Councillors*, 28 March 2012, pp. 8–9.
43. Wakasa quoted in *Japan Times* (2012) *Ogawa Has No Qualms about Executions Justice Minister Says Lay Judges, Public Call Shots on Inmates' Fate*, 6 April 2012, Available at: http://www.japantimes.co.jp/text/nn20120406b5.html [Accessed 19 March 2016].
44. Taki, M. (2012) *The 180th Legal Affairs Committee of the House of Representatives*, 15 June 2012, p. 44.
45. Taki, M. (2012) *The 180th Legal Affairs Committee of the House of Councillors*, 28 August 2012, p. 5.
46. *Asahi* (2012) *Tainin Shisa no Taki Hōshō, Futari no Shikei Shikkō, 'Kakekomi' wa Hitei* (Justice Minister Taki Implies Resignation, Denying Two Executions as a Rushed Job), 28 September 2012.
47. *Japan Times* (2012) Caution on Hangings Pledged, 3 October 2012, Available at: http://www.japantimes.co.jp/text/nn20121003a6.html [Accessed 19 March 2016].

CHAPTER 8

Conclusions: New Light in Old Rooms. Governmental Justification for Capital Punishment in Japan Reconsidered

8.1 Introduction

This volume has examined how the Ministry of Justice justified capital punishment between 1980 and 2015 and in particular during the *de facto* moratorium periods, through case studies of the years 1989–1993, 2009–2010 and 2010–2012. Its primary goal has been to investigate the closed institutional dynamic where capital punishment is justified on legal and cultural grounds.

The aim of Chap. 2 was to present an analytical framework to understand capital punishment policy in Japan. The first section illuminated the elite-driven nature of the policy and re-investigated the existing rationale that the Japanese government retains capital punishment after considering historical, external and internal factors. Examining the highly interdependent relationships within the government, it explained that with the exception of the information selectively collected and presented as part of government opinion polls, public opinion or anti-death-penalty NGOs do not play significant roles in this policy. The second section threw light on the fact that this policy has been dealt with by the government as an issue of criminal justice upon the basis of law, and not as an issue of human rights.

Chapter 3 critically examined the validity of governmental justification for capital punishment on domestic and cultural grounds. Firstly, comparison of the opinion polls conducted by the government and non-governmental bodies indicated that 'wide public support' for the capital

M. Obara-Minnitt, *Japanese Moratorium on the Death Penalty*,
DOI 10.1057/978-1-137-55822-0_8

punishment system stems from strategically phrased questions in the government opinion polls and selective interpretation of the results. Secondly, reviewing Japanese culture or concepts represented by the act of ***shinde wabiru*** and human rights and legal consciousness, it was stressed that Japanese culture appears to have been strategically cited by the government in order to legitimise state killing. Thirdly, it clarified that: (1) the Japanese view on the capital punishment system appears to have been heavily influenced by the media coverage of serious murder cases and a pro-death-penalty mood to be found in the results of opinion polls; and (2) the Japanese public's resistance to the abolition of capital punishment appears to stem from a lack of sympathy for the domestic anti-death-penalty campaigns. Finally, it presented the approach that is required to examine the *de facto* moratorium for a better understanding of the elite-driven nature of capital punishment policy in Japan.

Chapters 4, 5, 6 and 7 empirically examined how the Ministry of Justice justified the capital punishment system from 1980 to 2012. Chapter 4 focused on the period from 1980 to 1989, when the government legitimised the system despite the emergence of criminal justice issues, including the disclosure of successive miscarriages of justice. Chapter 5 examined the *de facto* moratorium period from 1989 to 1993, and investigated how consistently the Ministry of Justice justified the system even during the execution-free period. Chapter 6 focused on the period from 1993 to 2009, and examined how executions were resumed and how the government tried to maintain the dominant discourse on crime and punishment for the justification of capital punishment. Chapter 7 focused on the period from 2009 to 2012, including the two *de facto* moratorium periods. It investigated how the introduction of *saiban-in seido* since 2009 has been contributing to governmental justification for capital punishment.

Finally, this concluding chapter summarises the main findings of the book and reflects on several issues that should be tackled by international and domestic anti-death-penalty NGOs.

8.2 Institutional Dynamic: Pro-Death-Penalty Actors in Japan

One of the main claims of this volume is that the issue of capital punishment has been the province of a narrow elite in two government agencies, irrespective of public opinion or the views of party politicians. The

Ministry of Justice justifies capital punishment on the basis of the law, and personal convictions held by the Ministers of Justice do not necessarily challenge the retention of the system. Whilst non-authorisation of executions by anti-death-penalty Ministers of Justice may appear to create a 'gap' in capital punishment policy, it is wrong to consider that they play a crucial role in this policy. Rather, it is employed-for-life bureaucrats in the Ministry of Justice and the Public Prosecutor's Office who exert tremendous power in justifying and retaining the system in the long run. Indeed, the Public Prosecutor's Office is involved in the crucial parts of capital punishment policy. Public prosecutors generate confessions from offenders to produce sentences of capital punishment, and possess the right to immediately appeal against a retrial.

The Ministry of Justice tends to be submissive to the Public Prosecutor's Office on the issue of Japanese criminal justice. Article 14 of the Public Prosecutor's Office Act indicates that Ministers of Justice are not responsible for supervising an individual public prosecutor and it does not actively take measures to avoid miscarriages of justice (see Chap. 5).

Chapter 2 clarified that: (1) capital punishment has been dealt with as an issue of law and order, not as an issue of human rights in Japan; and (2) the Ministry of Justice tries to ensure annual executions take place in a business-like manner. As Kakusho argues, death row inmates have been considered by the government as those who are merely waiting for execution.[1] Moreover, the recent lawsuit regarding the Hikari murder case demonstrated that the fundamental rights of death row inmates tend to be neglected once a death sentence is finalised. These facts appear to explain why several rules regarding detention and execution either infringe Article 11 of the Constitution of Japan, which guarantees fundamental human rights, or Article 36, which forbids cruel punishments by public officers, or else are not specified in the Act on Penal Detention Facilities and Treatment of Inmates and Detainees. Keeping in mind Johnson's nine main hypotheses which encompass historical, external and internal factors comprehensively, Chap. 2 discussed that the actual reason why the government retains capital punishment mainly stems from the institutional framework where this policy is handled as an issue of law and order, not an issue of human rights.

Chapter 2 also clarified that since the issue of capital punishment is elite-driven and not dealt with as an issue of human rights, there is no room for anti-death-penalty NGOs or public opinion to play a crucial role. For example, human rights NGOs in Japan do not have official consultative status in drafting official reports on the human rights record in Japan, and the Japanese government does not usually make official comments on their recommendations. Therefore, anti-death-penalty NGOs cannot get involved in governmental decision-making regarding capital punishment policy.

Although public opinion appears at first sight to be the determining factor in Japan's retention of capital punishment, examination of the opinion polls conducted by the Prime Minister's Office and non-governmental bodies, together with an in-depth survey by a research group, provide alternative views (see Chap. 3). Public opinion on this issue can vary depending on: (1) the media coverage of crime; (2) the discussion about introducing life imprisonment without parole as an alternative penalty; and (3) the public level of understanding of the capital punishment system. More importantly, the issue of capital punishment primarily revolves around institutional decision-making, and public opinion plays a relatively passive role in Japan. It is bureaucrats in selected governmental agencies who produce the pro-death-penalty norm, and the Japanese public's pro-death-penalty actors sentiment appears to have been strategically built up in the media and via governmental opinion polls.

Finally, it is interesting to note that despite the Japanese government maintaining that this is an issue of law and order, not an issue of human rights, it appears to have a legitimacy problem about state killing (see Chap. 2). There exists: (1) an ambivalence in the borderline between capital punishment and life imprisonment and in the timeline between sentences and executions; (2) special consideration shown to prison guards who get involved in the actual hanging; (3) extreme secrecy surrounding the policy; and (4) small-scale executions compared to other retentionist countries.

8.3 Cultural Dynamic: Strategic Use of Culture in the Governmental Discourse

The second main claim in this volume is that Japanese culture has been over-represented by governmental officials and the existing literature as a determining factor for the retention of capital punishment (see Chap. 3). In fact, a strategic use of culture in the language used by the government appears to be encouraging pro-death-penalty advocates, in particular, to believe that Japan's retention of capital punishment has been culturally determined. A former Minister of Justice, Moriyama, put tremendous emphasis on the concept of ***shinde wabiru***, and claimed that capital punishment in Japan was deeply embedded in Japanese culture. However, in-depth investigation of this concept revealed that: (1) it is not necessarily a sentiment that contemporary Japanese appreciate; (2) this act is not essentially meaningful when spontaneity is lacking; and (3) a contrasting proverb has been ignored.

Despite the methodological issues regarding the governmental opinion polls, those conducted by non-governmental bodies also indicate public support for capital punishment to some extent (see Chap. 3). This may appear at first sight to relate to the Japanese view on criminals. Self-discipline is admired amongst the Japanese public, and those who do not comply with this principle tend to be excluded from society. As Komiya contends, the reintegrative function is limited in Japan, and once people become criminals, it is less likely for them and their families to be accommodated in society again.[2] Even so, it is hazardous to conclude that the Japanese public are 'punitive' towards offenders for cultural reasons. For example, with the emergence of a vocal victim lobby such as that surrounding Motomura on the Hikari case in 1999, the idea of capital punishment as social justice started to be reconsidered. What is more, an amendment was made to the Juvenile Law in 2000 in order to impose harsher punishment on youth offenders. In the meantime, the media showed a reserved attitude when the death sentence was finally upheld on the Hikari case offender in 2012. An *Asahi* newspaper editorial on 21 February 2012 generated a discussion of the rights and wrongs of punishing a young man who had committed the crime at the age of 18, without giving him a chance of correction or rehabilitation. Thus, whether or not the public show a 'punitive' attitude towards offenders or pro-death-penalty sentiment appears to depend on the climate of media coverage and the legal measures taken by the government.

Japan's retention of capital punishment also appears at first sight to stem from a lack of human rights consciousness among the Japanese public. However, this also relates to the way the Japanese government treats the legal status and rights of death row inmates. For example, Opinion Polls on Defense of Human Rights, conducted by the Prime Minister's Office, do not include the human rights of death row inmates in the list. Therefore, there is little chance for the public to perceive the capital punishment system as a domestic human rights concern. The general public's 'indifferent' attitude appears to stem from a low level of understanding of the capital punishment system and of the treatment of death row inmates,[3] and this closely relates to the secretive policy of the Ministry of Justice and biased opinion polls.

Japanese legal consciousness can also at first glance seem another important factor in evaluating public awareness regarding the capital punishment system. Kawashima discusses the fact that the Japanese public tend to prefer legal incidents to be dealt with by legal professionals,[4] since they appear to 'regard law like an heirloom samurai sword, something to be treasured but not used'.[5] Therefore, they tend not to show much sympathy with or give legitimacy to vocal anti-death-penalty campaigns which aim to challenge the existing Japanese legal system. However, besides that, attention must be paid not only to public resistance to the NGO activities that go against government policy, but also to the characteristics of the domestic anti-death-penalty NGOs. For example, activities of a core member of the largest anti-death-penalty NGO in Japan, Forum 90, have been playing a crucial key in mobilising public opinion. Yasuda Yoshihiro, founding member of Forum 90, is a defence attorney for defendants in high-profile cases. Since he proclaims the rights of criminals or death row inmates professionally, it appears difficult for him, Forum 90 and other domestic anti-death-penalty NGOs to enjoy sympathy from the public, whose discussion tends to revolve around victim satisfaction.

Consequently, there are problems in considering that the issue of capital punishment is culturally determined in Japan. Rather, a strategic use of language by governmental officials appears to be making the public and pro-death-penalty advocates believe that capital punishment is deeply embedded in Japanese culture. As long as the government creates the pro-death penalty norm and exports it to civil society using Japanese culture as its justification, the public are less likely to recognise that the existing capital punishment system sacrifices the human rights of death row inmates.

8.4 Governmental Justification for Capital Punishment During the *De Facto* Moratorium Periods (1989–1993, 2009–2010 and 2010–2012)

The final argument in this volume was highlighted from the case study of the *de facto* moratorium periods: it is not necessarily critical to investigate what led decisively to the *de facto* moratorium periods; rather, it is more important to investigate how consistently the Japanese government has been trying to justify capital punishment on the basis of the law. For example, although the personal convictions of Ministers of Justice appeared at first sight to have contributed to the three execution-free periods, in-depth investigation of this factor revealed alternative views.

Regarding the *de facto* moratorium period between 1989 and 1993, although Minister Sato refrained from authorising executions on account of his personal beliefs, not all the Ministers were opposed to the death penalty: rather, they did not stay in office long enough to authorise executions. Moreover, Sato was not necessarily keen on taking initiatives connected with the issue of human rights during his term. Instead, he proclaimed that the law is above human rights, and sought to act in line with the law-based policy of the Ministry of Justice.[6] It was only Tawara who represented the Ministry's official approach on capital punishment during this period, and his statement helped to illuminate the dutiful approach of the Ministry of Justice to this system. According to him, the Ministry of Justice: (1) retains capital punishment since the current law provides for it; and (2) continues to refer to the rigorous and fair activities of the Public Prosecutor's Office.[7] In fact, the capital punishment system has been justified as a legal penalty on the basis of various legal provisions.[8] Whether the Ministry of Justice holds executions officially, abolishes the capital punishment system or introduces an alternative penalty such as life imprisonment without parole, any of these courses would require the repealing or amending of existing legal provisions. It is unlikely that the Ministry of Justice, which tries to act on precedents on the basis of law, will agree to this. In fact, Tawara's statement illuminated the Ministry's view that the capital punishment system has been retained because the current law provides for it.

Besides the 'institutional ambivalence' represented by non-executions from 1989 to 1993, the Ministry of Justice also showed some contradictory or inconsistent attitudes in order to justify capital punishment policy from 1980 to 2002: (1) altering the criminal justice policy; (2) interpreting legal provisions in favour of governmental decisions; and (3) changing the prime source of justification of the policy. Firstly, the Ministry of Justice 'dealt with' the false charge cases in the 1980s by increasing the amount of financial compensation in cases where innocent people are detained or executed. Recalling the available measures, such as the three-tier judicial system and retrial system, it did not try to review the criminal justice system, where the Public Prosecutor's Office exerts tremendous power. Secondly, when the Ministry of Justice was accused of detaining a death row inmate, Hirasawa, until his natural death, it claimed that it was not necessarily required for Ministers of Justice to strictly comply with Article 475 of the Code of Criminal Procedure. Thirdly, although the Ministry of Justice often claims that capital punishment functions as social justice for the victims' bereaved families, Moriyama authorised executions against the will of an anti-death-penalty lobby, on the pretext of maintaining legal order. Thus, in order to justify capital punishment consistently, the Ministry of Justice tends to alter its claim or its policy depending on the situation.

With regard to the *de facto* moratorium periods of 2009–2010 and 2010–2012, as with the previous execution-free period, most Ministers of Justice did not stay in office long enough to be given opportunities to authorise executions. What differentiates the previous *de facto* moratorium period is that some Ministers such as Eda and Hiraoka were outspoken anti-death-penalty advocates and appeared to have given some meaning to this time lapse, to which the Japanese government has never added any political significance. Both Eda and Hiraoka challenged the interpretation of Article 475 of the Code of Criminal Procedure, which specifies the responsibility of Ministers of Justice regarding authorisations of executions, and tried to legitimate 'institutional ambivalence' because of the nature of the system, which concerns the life of the inmates. However, this issue has been handled by bureaucrats in the Ministry of Justice and the Public Prosecutor's Office, and these initiatives by anti-death-penalty Ministers did not contribute to establish official moratorium periods. On the contrary, besides the wide public support of capital punishment (which the Prime Minister's Office reports), lay assessors' participation in *saiban-in seido* has begun to be used as one of the primary sources of governmental justification of capital punishment. Despite the emerging issue of lay assessors' stress disorder and their call for full disclosure of the information relating to this policy, and moratorium on executions until this has been achieved, their voice does not appear to be reflected in the current situation.

Consequently, execution-free periods, which are mainly caused by a frequent change of Ministers of Justice and often labelled as *de facto* moratorium periods, are always followed by the appointment of pro-death-penalty Ministers of Justice and executions authorised by them on the basis of law. In fact, even if anti-death-penalty Ministers of Justice tried to fundamentally discuss the death penalty during their terms, subsequent pro-death-penalty Ministers of Justice endeavoured to maintain the governmental pro-death-penalty discourse and authorise executions, as if seeking to deal with the 'backlog'. This was particularly evident during the terms of Gotoda and Mikazuki after the *de facto* moratorium period of 1989–1993; and with Hatoyama and Tanigaki's large number of executions after more recent *de facto* moratorium periods.

8.5 Implications for International and Domestic Anti-Death-Penalty Advocates

Having examined both the institutional and cultural dynamics of the capital punishment system, I will suggest the implications for international and domestic anti-death-penalty advocates. As this book has evidenced, capital punishment policy is primarily elite-driven in Japan and anti-death-penalty activists are excluded from the decision-making process. However, it is still important for them to recognise why the Japanese government resists their campaigns and what strategy would raise public awareness of this issue despite the secretive governmental policy.

The primary task for international anti-death-penalty advocates is to acknowledge the tightly knit institutional framework that surrounds capital punishment policy. Those who face these foreign pressures in Japan tend to be Prime Ministers or Ministry of Foreign Affairs officials. However, they are not in a position to express an independent opinion on capital punishment and simply reproduce the policy of the Ministry of Justice. Moreover, international anti-death-penalty bodies need to start from the perspective that capital punishment is and has been dealt with solely as a criminal justice issue in Japan, not as an issue of human rights. Although on the basis of the evidence presented here it is clear that the Japanese government fails to comply with the internationally recognised anti-death-penalty norm, it is not necessarily the case that this is out of disagreement with the human rights norm. Rather, it appears that the overriding conservative nature and practice of the Ministry of Justice in routinely and unquestioningly acting on legal precedents, combined with its resistance to new ideas or opinions serves to stymie attempts to deal with capital punishment policy from a human rights perspective or to abolish this historically held governmental policy. For this reason, a blanket approach of seeking to impose an international or European anti-death-penalty norm from a human rights perspective is currently inappropriate and likely to be ineffective.

Having said that, the validity of the Japanese government's position, asserting that the death penalty is merely a matter of law and order, must be highlighted and scrutinised given the government's 'institutional ambivalence' and legitimacy issues surrounding the policy. Both international and domestic human rights NGOs could use this approach as a focal point to redefine the death penalty as a matter of illegitimate use of state power, and eventually as a matter of human rights violation.

With regard to the cultural restraints in Japan, it is important to understand that it is the political culture that has often hindered abolitionism from gaining ground. The Ministry of Justice's conceptual reframing of death row inmates as individuals who can only be released through death does not necessarily reflect the general public's views on life and death. Rather, it appears to arise as the illogical conclusion from the lack of legal status and rights of death row inmates in Japan. Therefore, it is important to consider and deconstruct the language the Japanese government has been using in its effort to make the issue appear culturally dependent.

To advance abolitionism in Japan it is crucial to effectively bridge the divide between the anti-death-penalty and the anti-*saiban-in-seido* movements. Although the media coverage of serious murder cases can contribute significantly to public attitudes on retentionism, the way the public construe the mainstream anti-death-penalty NGOs' activities also appears to be hindering the extraction of the retentionism root from Japanese civil society. Since key high-profile members of the anti-death-penalty NGOs tend to be defence attorneys, they are often perceived by the public as overemphasising the human rights of criminals and sidelining or disregarding those of victims and their bereaved families.

Anti-death-penalty NGOs provide a perfect platform for consciousness-raising amongst the general public and lay assessors by providing accurate information and research regarding Japan's capital punishment system. This is essential since the introduction of the *saiban-in seido*, which has elevated members of the general public without knowledge of the law to a key role as lay assessors in determining both guilt (or innocence) and the sentence to be imposed. It is therefore crucial for the public to gain sufficient information about the capital punishment system, and encourage them to take part in an informed discussion about the retention of the death penalty.

It is also beneficial for NGOs to try to stimulate public discussion around the alternative ways in which justice can be brought to victims, their bereaved families and the general public. In order to do this, they must convey messages from anti-death-penalty victim lobbyists as well as the experiences and views of lay assessors, who are not necessarily anti-death penalty but raise the issue of stress disorder and question the legitimacy and transparency of the capital punishment policy. The call by some of their number for the moratorium on executions until there is greater transparency, public scrutiny and understanding of the whole process would counterbalance the widespread viewpoint of the pro-death-penalty victim lobby. The more lay assessors express their feeling of guilt as an accessory to state killing, the more opportunities emerge for the convergence of the goals of the anti-*saiban-in-seido* movement and the anti-death-penalty movement, ensuring a more comprehensive and effective public movement.

Notes

1. Kakusho, T. (1991) *'Shikei Kakuteisha no Hōteki Chi-i to Jinken: Tsūtatsu "Shikei Kakuteisha no Sekken oyobi Shinsho no Hatsuju ni Tsuite" ni Kansuru Ichi Kōsatsu'* (The Legal Status and Rights of Prisoners Sentenced to Death), *Bulletin of Chiba and Keiai Junior College*, 13, pp. 13–30, p. 17.
2. Komiya, N. (1999) 'A Cultural Study of the Low Crime Rate in Japan', *British Journal of Criminology*, 39(3), pp. 369–390, p. 387.
3. Sato, M. (2009) 'Deliberative Survey on the Japanese Death Penalty System', *Institute for Contemporary Asian Studies, Temple University*, pp. 1–2, available at: http://www.tuj.ac.jp/icas/pdf/icjs_090616.pdf [Accessed 19 March 2016].
4. Kawashima, T. (1967) *Nihonjin no Hōishiki* (Japanese Legal Consciousness), Tokyo: Iwanami Shoten.
5. Dean, M. (2002) *Japanese Legal System* 2nd ed., Abingdon: Routledge-Cavendish, p. 4.
6. Sato, M. (1991) *The 120th Legal Affairs Committee of the House of Representatives*, 20 February 1991, p. 11.
7. Tawara, T. (1991) *The 122nd Legal Affairs Committee of the House of Councillors*, 17 December 1991, pp. 8–9; (1992) *The 123rd Legal Affairs Committee of the House of Councillors*, 12 March 1992, p. 11.
8. They include: (1) Article 31 of the Constitution of Japan, which allows a legal punishment to deprive a person of life or liberty excep-

tionally; (2) the Penal Code and the Nagayama Criteria, which specify crimes that are applicable to capital punishment under nine main criteria; (3) Articles 475 and 476 of the Code of Criminal Procedure, which stipulate the responsibility of Ministers of Justice regarding the timing of authorising and conducting executions; (4) Article 11 of the Penal Code, which specifies the execution method as hanging; (5) Article 472 of the Code of Criminal Procedure, which provides that execution is carried out on the initiative of the head of the Public Prosecutor's Office; and (6) Article 98 (1) of the National Civil Service Law, which specifies that civil servants have to carry out duties set by senior staff.

Appendices

Appendix A: Numbers Executed and Sentenced to Death 1945–2015

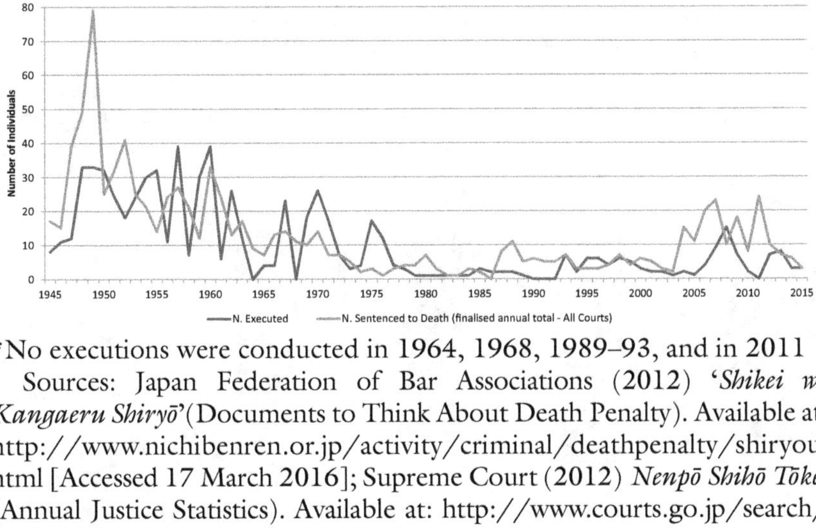

*No executions were conducted in 1964, 1968, 1989–93, and in 2011

Sources: Japan Federation of Bar Associations (2012) '*Shikei wo Kangaeru Shiryō*'(Documents to Think About Death Penalty). Available at: http://www.nichibenren.or.jp/activity/criminal/deathpenalty/shiryou.html [Accessed 17 March 2016]; Supreme Court (2012) *Nenpō Shihō Tōkei* (Annual Justice Statistics). Available at: http://www.courts.go.jp/search/jtsp0010 [Accessed 17 March 2016]

M. Obara-Minnitt, *Japanese Moratorium on the Death Penalty*,
DOI 10.1057/978-1-137-55822-0

Appendix B: Opinion Poll on Basic Legal System by the Prime Minister's Office

Q.1 Out of these opinions on the issue of capital punishment, which one do you agree with?:

(1) It is unavoidable *in certain circumstances*;
(2) It should be abolished *in all circumstances*;
and (3) I do not know.

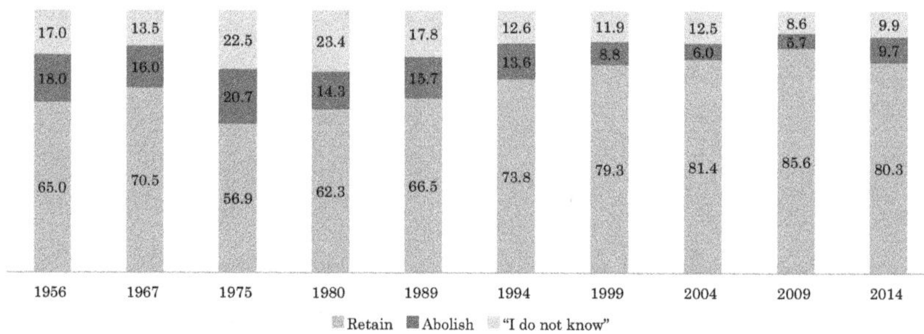

Q.2 In case of abolishing capital punishment, which do you think is better?: (1) abolish it straight away or (2) decrease the number of the use of capital punishment first?

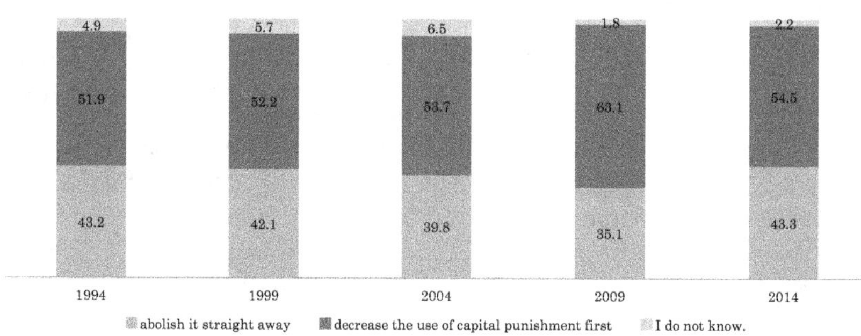

Q.3 Do you think Japan should not abolish capital punishment in the future; or can abolish the system when the situation changes?

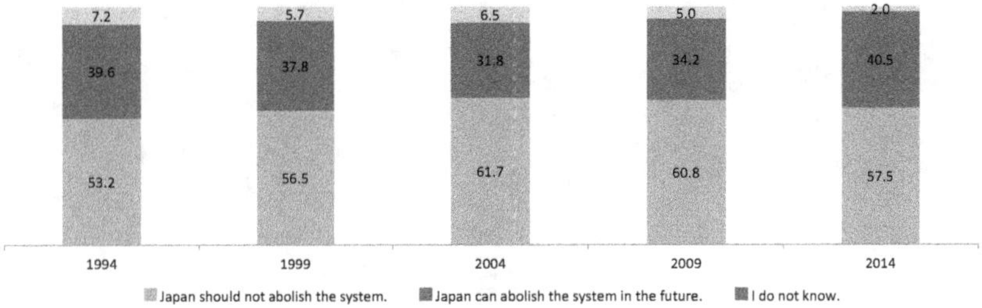

Q.4 What do you think about the argument that serious crimes would increase if capital punishment is abolished, or remain unchanged?

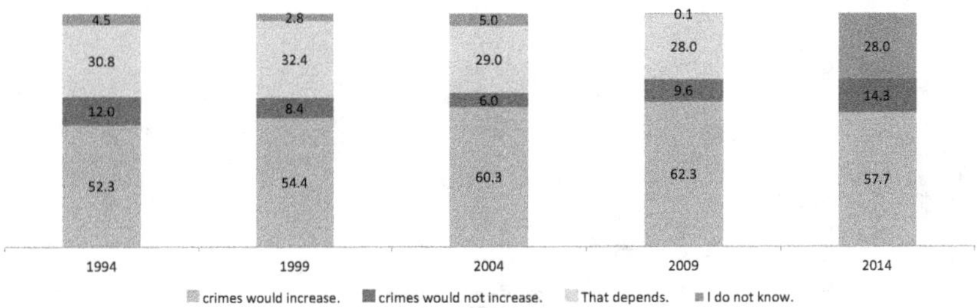

*There was no answer option 'That depends' in the questionnaire in 2014

Source: Prime Minister's Office (1994, 1999, 2004, 2009 and 2014) *Kihonteki Hōseido ni Kansuru Yoron Chōsa* (Opinion Poll on Basic Legal System)

Appendix C: Ministers of Justice 1980–2016

Name	*Sex*	*Year*	*Length of appointment (approximate)*	*Numbers of executions*	*View on capital punishment*	*Party*	*Cabinet*
Okuno Seisuke	Male	17 Jul. 1980 to 20 Nov. 1981	1 year and 4 months	1	Hawk	Liberal Demo-	Suzuki Zenko
Sakata Michita	Male	30 Nov. 1981 to 27 Nov. 1982	1 year	1		cratic Party (LDP)	
Hatano Akira	Male	27 Nov. 1982 to 27 Dec. 1983	1 year and 1 month	1			Nakasone Yasuhiro
Sumi Eisaku	Male	27 Dec. 1983 to 1 Nov. 1984	11 months	1			
Shimasaki Hitoshi	Male	1 Nov. 1984 to 28 Dec. 1985	1 year and 1 month	3			
Suzuki Seigo	Male	28 Dec. 1985 to 22 Jul. 1986	6 months	2			
Endo Kaname	Male	22 Jul. 1986 to 6 Nov. 1987	1 year and 4 months	2			
Hayashida Yukio	Male	6 Nov. 1987 to 27 Dec. 1988	1 year and 1 month	2			Noboru
Hasegawa Takashi	Male	27 Dec. 1988 to 30 Dec. 1988	4 days	0	Not known		Takeshita Noboru
Takatsuji Masami	Male	30 Dec. 1988 to 3 Jun. 1989	6 months	0		Public Sector	
Tanigawa Kazuo	Male	3 Jun. 1989 to 10 Aug. 1989	2 months	0		LDP	Uno Sosuke
Goto Masao	Male	10 Aug. 1989 to 28 Feb. 1990	6 months	1	Hawk		Kaifu Toshiki
Hasegawa Shin	Male	28 Feb. 1990 to 13 Sep. 1990	7 months	0	Not known		
Kajiyama Seiroku	Male	13 Sep. 1990 to 29 Dec. 1990	3 months	0			
Sato Megumu	Male	29 Dec. 1990 to 5 Nov. 1991	11 months	0	Dove		
Tawara Takashi	Male	5 Nov. 1991 to 12 Dec. 1992	1 year and 1 month	0	Hawk		Miyazawa Ki-ichi
Gotoda Masaharu	Male	12 Dec. 1992 to 9 Aug. 1993	8 months	3			
Mikazuki Akira	Male	9 Aug. 1993 to 28 Apr. 1994	8 months	4		Public Sector	Hosokawa Morihiro

Nagano Shigeto	Male	28 Apr. 1994 to 8 May 1994	11 days	0	Not known	Japan Renewal Party	Hata Tsutomu
Nakai Hiroshi	Male	8 May 1994 to 30 Jun. 1994	2 months	0		Democratic Socialist Party	
Maeda Isao	Male	30 Jun. 1994 to 8 Aug 1995	1 year and 2 months	5	Hawk	LDP	Murayama Tomi-ichi
Tazawa Tomoharu	Male	8 Aug. 1995 to 9 Oct. 1995	2 months	0	Not known		
Miyazawa Hiroshi	Male	9 Oct. 1995 to 11 Jan. 1996	3 months	3	Hawk		
Nagao Ritsuko	Female	11 Jan. 1996 to 7 Nov. 1996	10 months	3		Public Sector	Hashimoto Ryutaro
Matsu-ura Isao	Male	7 Nov. 1996 to 11 Sep. 1997	10 months	7		LDP	
Shimoinaba Kokichi	Male	11 Sep. 1997 to 30 Jul. 1998	10 months	3			
Nakamura Shoz-aburo	Male	30 Jul. 1998 to 8 Mar. 1999	8 months	3			Obuchi Keizo
Jin-nouchi Takao	Male	8 Mar. 1999 to 5 Oct. 1999	7 months	3			
Usui Hideo	Male	5 Oct. 1999 to 5 Apr. 2000	9 months	2			
		5 Apr. 2000 to 4 Jul. 2000					Mori Yoshiro
Yasuoka Okiharu	Male	4 Jul. 2000 to 5 Dec. 2000	5 months	3			
Komura Masa-hiko	Male	5 Dec. 2000 to 26 Apr. 2001	4 months	0	Dove		
Moriyama Mayumi	Female	26 Apr. 2001 to 22 Sep. 2003	2 years and 5 months	5	Hawk		Koizumi Jun-ichiro
Nozawa Daizo	Male	22 Sep. 2003 to 27 Sep. 2004	1 year	2			
No-ono Chieko	Female	27 Sep. 2004 to 31 Oct. 2005	1 year and 1 month	1			
Sugiura Seiken	Male	31 Oct. 2005 to 26 Sep. 2006	11 months	0	Dove		
Nagase Jin-en	Male	26 Sep. 2006 to 27 Aug. 2007	11 months	10	Hawk		Abe Shinzo
Hatoyama Kunio	Male	27 Aug. 2007 to 26 Sep. 2007	1 year	13			
		26 Sep. 2007 to 2 Aug. 2008					Fukuda Yasuo
Yasuoka Okiharu	Male	2 Aug. 2008 to 24 Sep 2008	1 month	3			
Mori Eisuke	Male	24 Sep. 2008 to 16 Sep. 2009	1 year	9			Aso Taro

(continued)

(continued)

Name	*Sex*	*Year*	*Length of appointment (approximate)*	*Numbers of executions*	*View on capital punishment*	*Party*	*Cabinet*
Chiba Keiko	Female	16 Sep. 2009 to 8 Jun. 2010 8 Jun. 2010 to 17 Sep. 2010	1 year	2	In-between	Democratic Party of Japan (DPJ)	Hatoyama Yukio Kan Naoto
Yanagida Minoru	Male	17 Sep. 2010 to 22 Nov. 2010	2 months	0	Hawk		
Sengoku Yoshito	Male	22 Nov. 2010 to 14 Jan. 2011	2 months	0	Dove		
Eda Satsuki	Male	14 Jan. 2011 to 2 Sep. 2011	8 months	0			
Hiraoka Hideo	Male	2 Sep. 2011 to 13 Jan. 2012	4 months	0			Noda Yoshihiko
Ogawa Toshio	Male	13 Jan. 2012 to 4 Jun. 2012	5 months	3	Hawk		
Taki Minoru	Male	4 Jun. 2012 to 1 Oct. 2012	4 months	4			
Tanaka Keishu	Male	1 Oct. 2012 to 23 Oct. 2012	23 days	0	Dove		
Taki Minoru	Male	24 Oct. 2012 to 26 Dec. 2012	2 months	0	Hawk		
Tanigaki Sad-akazu	Male	26 Dec. 2012 to 3 Sep. 2014	33 months	11		LDP	Abe Shinzo
Matsushima Midori	Female	3 Sep. 2014 to 21 Oct. 2014	2 months	0			
Uekawa Yoko	Female	21 Oct. 2014 to 7 Oct. 2015	1 year	1			
Iwaki Mitsuhide	Male	7 Oct. 2015 to 3 Aug. 2016	11 months	4			
Kaneda Katsutoshi	Male	3 Aug. 2016 to present	NA	0 (as of Sep. 2016)			

Appendix D: Opinion Poll by Yomiuri

Q. Do you think the capital punishment system should be retained, or abolished?

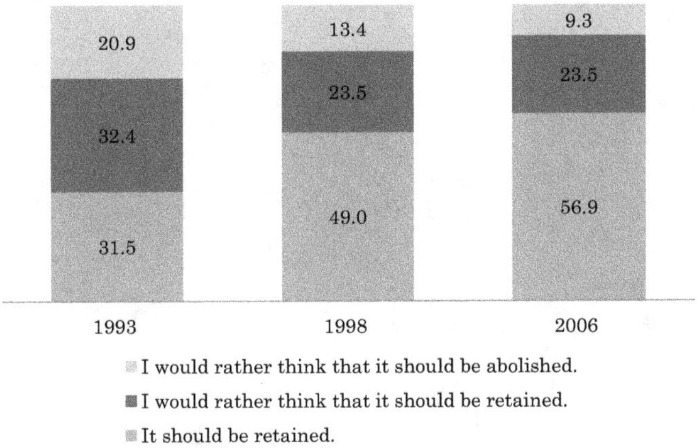

Source: House of Representatives (2008)

Appendix E: Opinion Poll by the Japan Broadcasting Corporation (NHK)

Q.1 Do you think the capital punishment system is necessary or should be abolished?

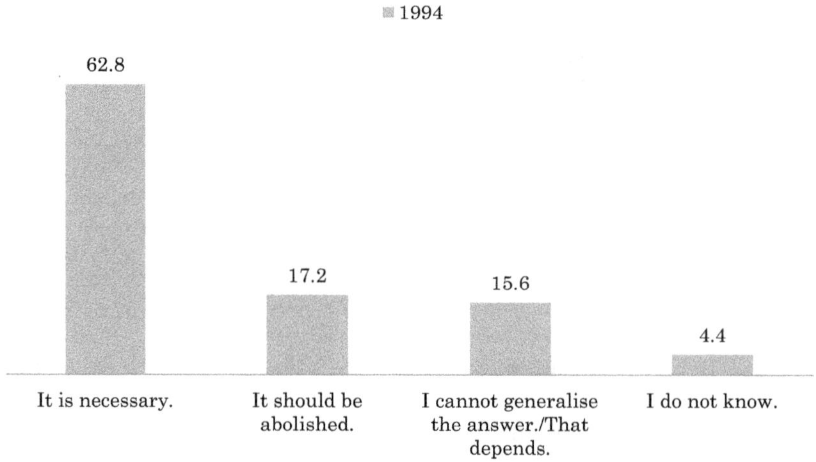

Q.2 What do you think about the plan for abolishing capital punishment if we place an alternative such as a life imprisonment without parole?

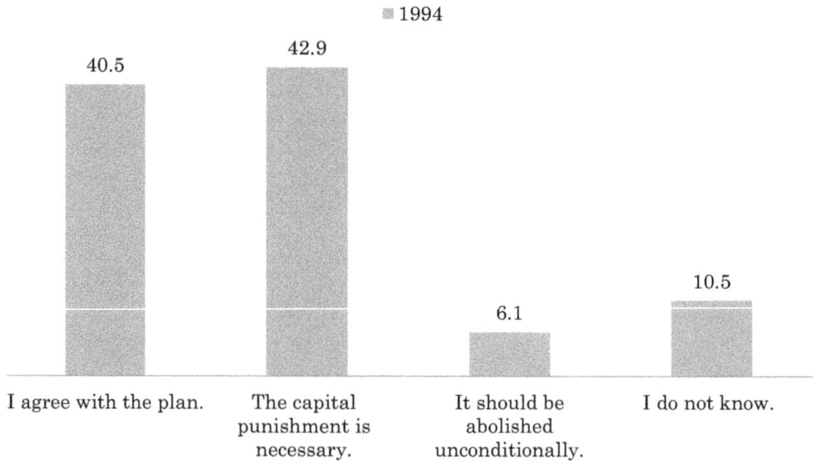

Q.3 Do you agree with the idea that we put executions on hold and discuss the issue of capital punishment fundamentally?

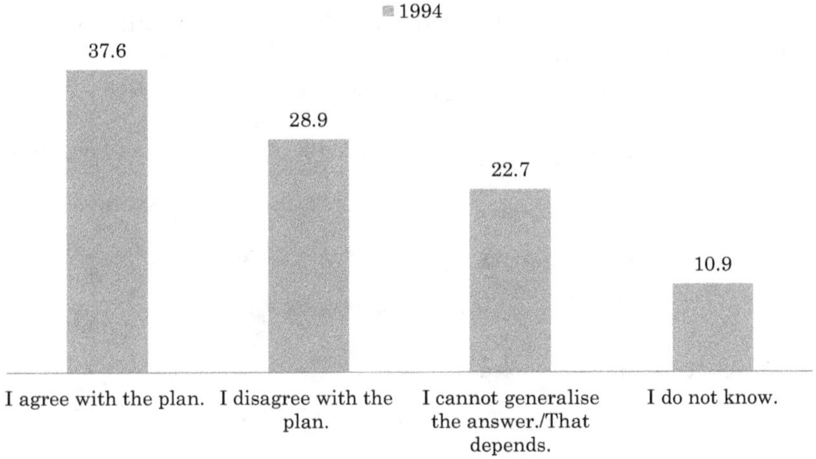

Appendix F: Opinion Poll by Asahi

Q.1 What do you think about capital punishment?

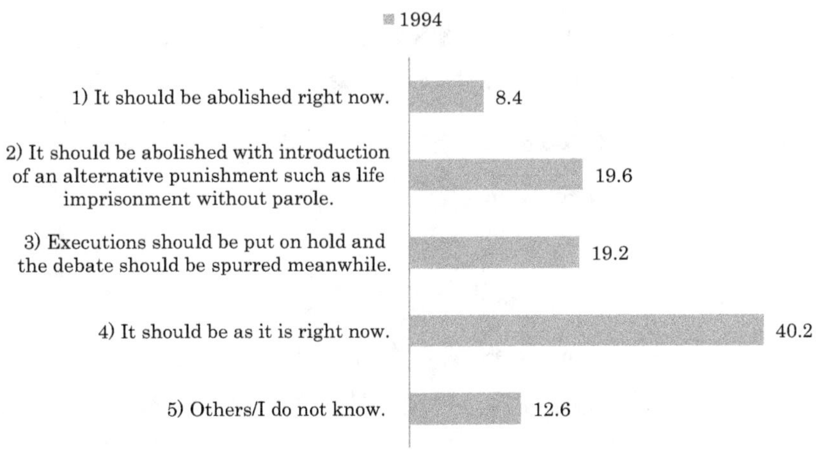

Source: House of Representatives (2008)

Appendix G: Japanese Human Rights Consciousness

Opinion Poll on Defence of Human Rights by the Prime Minister's Office 'Which of the Following Human Rights Issues are you Interested in?' (Multiple Choices)

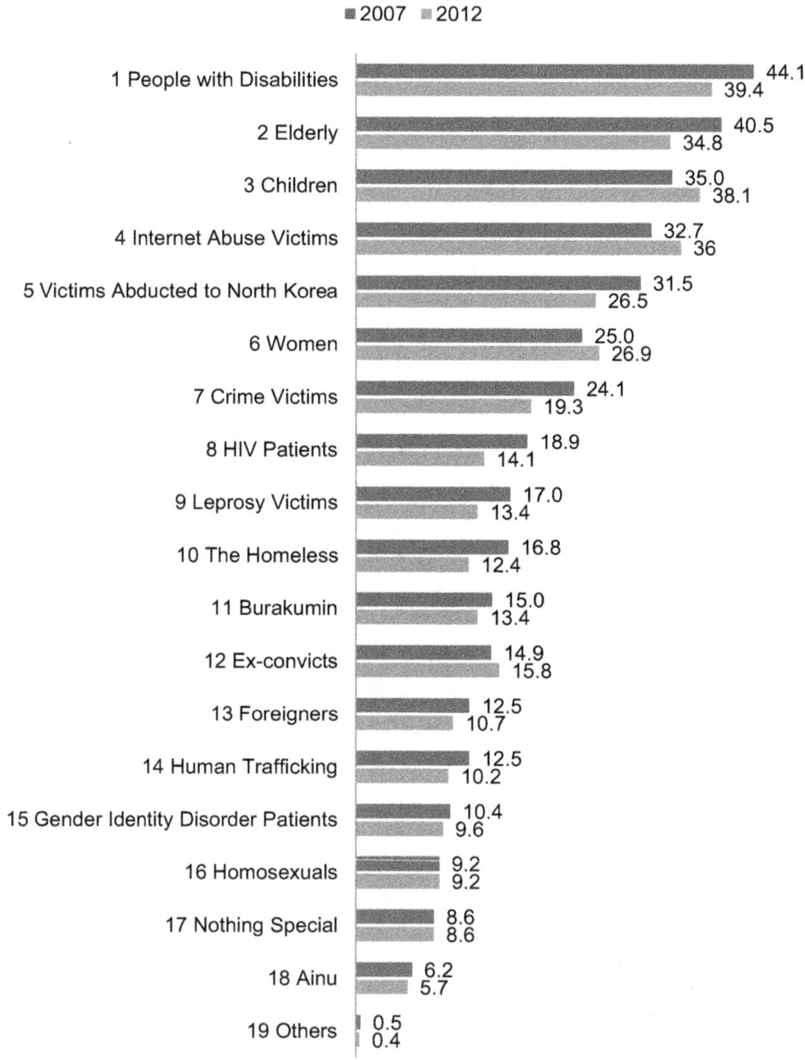

Bibliography

Advocates for Human Rights. (2012). JAPAN: Fourteenth Session of the Working Group on the Universal Periodic Review. Human Rights Council, 22 October–5 November 2012.

Ambler, L. (2008). The People Decide: The Effect of the Introduction of the Quasi-Jury System (Saiban-In Seido) on the Death Penalty in Japan, Article 1. *Northwestern Journal of International Human Rights, 6*(1), 1–23.

Amnesty International. (2008). Japan: Amnesty International Submission to the UN Human Rights Committee. 92nd session of the UN Human Rights Committee, 17 March – 4 April 2008, Pre-sessional Meeting of the Country Report Task Force on Japan. Accessed August 13, 2015, from http://www2.ohchr.org/english/bodies/hrc/docs/ngos/AIJapan92.pdf

Amnesty International. (2014). *Abolish the Death Penalty*. Accessed May 19, 2015, from http://www.amnesty.org/en/death-penalty

Anderson, K., & Ambler, L. (2006). The Slow Birth of Japan's Quasi-Jury System (*Saiban-in Seido*): Interim Report on the Road to Commencement. *Journal of Japanese Law, 11*(21), 55–80.

Aoyagi, F. (1986). *Nihonjin no Hanzai Ishiki (Japanese Consciousness on Crimes)*. Tokyo: Chūō Kōronsha.

Asahi. (2004, December 13). *Nara Slaying/Caught*. Accessed June 24, 2015, from http://www.asahi.com/english/nation/TKY200412310078.html

Asahi. (2010, July 28). *Shikei Shikkō ni Tachiai Chiba Hōshō: 'Konpon kara no Giron ga Hitsuyō'* (Justice Minister Chiba who Witnessed a Hanging: 'Fundamental Discussion is Needed on the Death Penalty'). Accessed August 19, 2015, from http://www.asahi.com/national/update/0728/TKY201007280290.html

M. Obara-Minnitt, *Japanese Moratorium on the Death Penalty*,
DOI 10.1057/978-1-137-55822-0

Asahi. (2011a, November 18). *Death Sentence Stands for Aum Cultist in Lawyer's Murder, 2011*. Accessed August 6, 2015, from http://ajw.asahi.com/article/behind_news/social_affairs/AJ201111180061

Asahi. (2011b, December 31). *19 nen buri Shikei Zero, Shinchō na Hōshō, Zehi no Giron wa Fukamarazu* (No Death Penalty for the First Time in 19 Years, Careful Minister of Justice, No Deep Discussion on the Rights and Wrong of the Penalty). Accessed August 16, 2015, from http://www.asahi.com/special/minshu/TKY201112280771.html

Asahi. (2012a, September 28). *Tainin Shisa no Taki Hōshō, Futari no Shikei Shikkō, 'Kakekomi' wa Hitei* (Justice Minister Taki Implies Resignation, Denying Two Executions as a Rushed Job).

Asahi (2012b, February 21). *Tensei Jingo* (The Voice of Heaven is the Voice of People).

Asahi. (2013, December 2). *"Shōko wa Netsuzō" Aratamete Shuchō: Hakamada Jiken Saishin Seikyū no Ikensho* ("Evidence Had been Fabricated": Written Opinion Calling for Hakamada Case Retrials).

Asahi. (2014a, March 28). *Hakamada Jiken no Kettei Yōshi: Saishin Kaishi Seikyū* (Summary of the Hakamada Case Rulings: Calling for Retrials). Accessed July 13, 2015, from http://www.asahi.com/articles/DA3S11053243.html

Asahi. (2014b, April 1). *Lawyers: Prosecutors' Appeal Exacerbates Hakamada's Suffering*. Accessed July 13, 2015, from http://ajw.asahi.com/article/behind_news/social_affairs/AJ201404010061

Asahi. (2014c, March 29). *48 nen me no "Mujitsu" Hakamada Jiken Saishin Kettei: Chōki Kōsoku Kokoro Mushibamu Shikei Shikkō no Kyōfu* ("Innocence" after 48years: Order of Commencement of Retrial for Hakamada Case, Heart Undermined by Long Imprisonment, Fear of Executions). Accessed July 13, 2015, from http://www.asahi.com/articles/DA3S11055388.html

Asahi Newspaper Agency. (2000). *Kurai Mori: Kōbe Renzoku Jidō Sasshō Jiken* (Dark Forest: Repetitive Child Murder Case in Kobe). Osaka: Asahi Shinbun Sha.

Axelrod, R. (1986). An Evolutionary Approach to Norms. *American Political Science Review, 80*(4), 1095–1111. Accessed August 13, 2015, from http://www-personal.umich.edu/~axe/Axelrod%20Norms%20APSR%201986%20%282%29.pdf

Badinter, R., Roth, K., & Mercer, J. (2008). *Abolition: One Man's Battle Against the Death Penalty*. Boston: Northeastern University Press.

Bae, S. (2008). *When the State No Longer Kills: International Human Rights Norms and Abolition of Capital Punishment*. Albany: State University of New York Press.

Boyd, R. (1987). Government-Industry Relations in Japan: Access, Communication, and Competitive Collaboration. *Comparative Government-Industry Relations: Western Europe, the United States, and Japan* (pp. 61–90).

Bring, O. (2009). The Death Penalty from a European View. In *EUIJ Conference 'Reflections on Life: European and Asian Perspectives on Capital Punishment'*. Tokyo: Waseda University. Accessed August 9, 2015, from http://www.euij-waseda.jp/common/pdf/Prof._Ove_Bring.pdf].

Brislin, T., & Inoue, Y. (2005). *Youth Crime Coverage in Japan and the U.S.: A Comparative Study of Naming Juveniles in Youth Crime Coverage*, presented at The Association for Education in Journalism and Mass Communication. *San Antonio, TX, August, 2005*, 1–15. Accessed August 18, 2015, from http://list.msu.edu/cgi-bin/wa?A3=ind0602a&L=AEJMC&E=8bit&P=4542176&B=--&T=text%2Fplain;%20charset=iso-8859-1

Buraku Liberation and Human Rights Research Institute (BLHRRI). (2005). '*Kigyō ni Okeru Jinken Sonchō no Torikumi no Genjyō: 70sha no Jirei Yori*' (Reality of the Enterprises' Efforts in Respecting Human Rights: Case Study of 70 Enterprises) (pp. i–26). Accessed July 21, 2015, from http://blhrri.org/kenkyu/bukai/jinken/kigyo/kigyo_survey_r/kigyo_survey_r.pdf

Buraku Liberation and Human Rights Research Institute (BLHRRI). (2012). What is Buraku Discrimination? Accessed July 21, 2015, from http://blhrri.org/blhrri_e/blhrri/buraku.htm

Burnham, P., Grant, W., & Layton-Henry, Z. (2004). *Research Methods in Politics.* London: Palgrave Macmillan.

Bye, R. T. (1919). *Capital Punishment in the United States.* Philadelphia: The Committee on Philanthropic Labor of Philadelphia Yearly Meeting of Friends.

Calnan, S. (2008). *The Effectiveness of Domestic Human Rights NGOs: A Comparative Study.* Boston: Martinus Nijhoff.

Campbell, J. C. (1989). Democracy and Bureaucracy in Japan. In E. S. Krauss & T. Ishida (Eds.), *Democracy in Japan* (pp. 113–137). Pittsburgh: University of Pittsburgh Press.

Centre for Prisoners' Rights. (2010, July 28). *Chiba Keiko Hōmu Daijin ni yoru Shikei Shikkō ni Kōgi Suru* (We Protest against Executions Authorised by Minister of Justice Chiba Keiko). Accessed July 13, 2015, from http://cpr.jca.apc.org/archive/statement#990

Checkel, J. T. (1999). Norms, Institutions, and National Identity in Contemporary Europe. *International Studies Quarterly, 43*(1), 84–114.

Checkel, J. T. (2012). Norm Entrepreneurship: Theoretical and Methodological Challenges, Workshop '*The Evolution of International Norms and "Norm Entrepreneurship": The Council of Europe in Comparative Perspective*', 11 January 2012, Wolfson College, University of Oxford.

Chiba, K. (1988). *The 112th Legal Affairs Committee of the House of Councillors*, 26 April 1988.

Chiba, K. (1989). *The 116th Legal Affairs Committee of the House of Councillors*, 5 December 1989.

Chiba, K. (2010a). *The 174th Legal Affairs Committee of the House of Representatives*, 24 February 2010, p. 10.

Chiba, K. (2010b). *The 174th Legal Affairs Committee of the House of Councillors*, 16 March 2010, p. 9.

Christian Science Monitor. (2010). *Japan Announces Death Penalty Review after Hanging Two Men*. Accessed July 13, 2015, from http://www.csmonitor.com/World/Asia-Pacific/2010/0729/Japan-announces-death-penalty-review-after-hanging-two-men

Chūnichi. (2012, April 16). *Hakamada Jiken: Kensatsu gawa no "Fuicchi"* (Hakamada Case: Mismatch on the Side of Public Prosecutors).

Clifford, W. (1976). *Crime Control in Japan*. Lenham: Lexington Books.

Cole, T. (2007). Commercial Arbitration in Japan: Contributions to the Debate on Japanese 'Non-Litigiousness'. *New York University Journal of International Law and Politics, 40*(1), 29–114.

Cortell, A. P., & Davis, J. W. (2005). When Norms Clash: International Norms, Domestic Practices, and Japan's Internalisation of the GATT/WTO. *Review of International Studies, 31*(01), 3–25.

De Mente, B. (1975). *Japanese Manners and Ethics in Business*. Phoenix: Phonenix Books.

Dean, M. (2002). *Japanese Legal System* (2nd ed.). Abingdon: Routledge-Cavendish.

Dezhbakhsh, H., Rubin, P. H., & Shepherd, J. M. (2003). Does Capital Punishment have a Deterrent Effect? New Evidence from Postmoratorium Panel Data. *American Law and Economics Review, 5*(2), 1–47.

Domoto, A. (1994). *The 131st Committee on Finance of the House of Councillors*, 18th November in 1994.

Eda, S. (2011a). *The 177th Legal Affairs Committee of the House of Representatives*, 9 March 2011.

Eda. S. (2011b). *The 177th Legal Affairs Committee of the House of Representatives*, 9 August 2011.

Ehrlich, I. (1973). Participation in Illegitimate Activities: A Theoretical and Empirical Investigation. *The Journal of Political Economy, 81*(3), 521–565.

Ehrlich, I. (1975). The Deterrent Effect of Capital Punishment: A Question of Life and Death. *American Economic Review, 63*(3), 397–417.

Ehrlich, I., & Becker, G. S. (1972). Market Insurance, Self-insurance, and Self-protection. *The Journal of Political Economy, 80*(4), 623–648.

Endo, K. (1987a). *The 108th Legal Affairs Committee of the House of Councillors*, 14 May 1987.

Endo, K. (1987b). *The 108th Legal Affairs Committee of the House of Representatives*, 15 May 1987.

Feldman, E. (2007). Law, Culture, and Conflict: Dispute Resolution in Postwar Japan, *Scholarship at Penn Law* (pp. 50–79). Accessed August 13, 2015, from http://lsr.nellco.org/cgi/viewcontent.cgi?article=1158&context=upenn_wps

Financial Times. (2011). *Japan to Consider Abolishing Death Penalty*, 21 January 2011.

Finnemore, M., & Sikkink, K. (1998). International Norm Dynamics and Political Change. *International Organization, 52*(04), 887–917.

Foote, D. H. (1992a). Benevolent Paternalism of Japanese Criminal Justice. *The California Law Review, 80*, 317–390.

Foote, D. H. (1992b). From Japan's Death Row to Freedom. *Pacific Rim Law & Policy Association, 1*, 11–103.

Fukurai, H. (2011). Japan's Quasi-Jury and Grand Jury Systems as Deliberative Agents of Social Change: De-Colonial Strategies and Deliberative Participatory Democracy. *Chicago-Kent Law Review, 86*, 789–987.

Fukushima, M. (2000). *The 149th Legal Affairs Committee of the House of Councillors*, 9 August 2000.

Fukushima, M. (2014). *The 186th Audit Committee of the House of Councillors*, 21 April 2014.

Fuse, Y. (2009). *Publicity and Secrecy Concerning Execution: Contrast between the U.S. and Japan*, in Annual Meeting of the American Society of Criminology, Marriott Downtown, Philadelphia, 4 November 2009.

Garland, D. (1993). *Punishment and Modern Society: A Study in Social Theory* (pp. 99–100). Chicago: University of Chicago Press.

George, B. J., Jr. (1984). Discretionary Authority of Public Prosecutors in Japan. *Law in Japan, 17*, 42–84.

Goto, M. (1989). *The 116th Legal Affairs Committee of the House of Councillors*, 5 December 1989.

Gotoda, M. (1993a). *The 126th Legal Affairs Committee of the House of Representatives*, 23 February 1993.

Gotoda, M. (1993b). *The 126th Legal Affairs Committee of the House of Councillors*, 29 March 1993.

Gotoda, M. (1993c). *The 126th Legal Affairs Committee of the House of Representatives*, 2 April 1993.

Gotoda, M. (1994). *Sei to Kan* (Politics and Government). Tokyo: Kōdansha.

Gotoda, M. (1998). *Jō to Ri: Gotoda Masaharu Kaikoroku (Ge)* (Mercy and Rationality: Gotoda Masaharu's Memoir (Part 1)). Tokyo: Kōdansha.

Guardian. (2011, July 4). *Japanese Man Admits Killing Lindsay Ann Hawker*. Last Accessed September 15, 2015, from http://www.guardian.co.uk/uk/2011/jul/04/japanese-man-lindsay-ann-hawker-murder

Hafner-Burton, E. M., & Tsutsui, K. (2005). Human Rights in a Globalizing World: The Paradox of Empty Promises. *American Journal of Sociology, 110*(5), 1373–1411. Accessed August 13, 2015, from https://umdrive.memphis.edu/rblanton/public/POLS_7508_Fall_2009/hafner_paradox.pdf.

Haley, J. O. (1992). Criminal Justice in Japan. *Journal of Japanese Studies, 18*(2), 553–556.

Hama, K. (1993). *The 126th Legal Affairs Committee of the House of Councillors*, 29 March 1993.

Hamai, K., & Ellis, T. (2006). Crime and Criminal Justice in Modern Japan: From Re-integrative Shaming to Popular Punitivism. *International Journal of the Sociology of Law, 34*(3), 157–178.

Hamai, K., & Ellis, T. (2008a). *Genbatsuka*: Growing Penal Populism and the Changing Role of Public Prosecutors in Japan? *Japanese Journal of Sociological Criminology, 33*, 67–92.

Hamai, K., & Ellis, T. (2008b). Japanese Criminal Justice: Was Reintegrative Shaming a Chimera? *Punishment & Society*, 10(1), 25–46. Accessed August 13, 2015, from http://www.port.ac.uk/departments/academic/icjs/staff/documentation/filetodownload,73687,en.pdf

Hara, Y. (2001). *Naze Shikei wa Kakusareru noka (Why Death Penalty is Hidden)*. Tokyo: Takarajimasha Shinsho.

Harada, A. (1997). *The 141st Legal Affairs Committee of the House of Councillors*, 13 November 1997.

Harada, M. (2004). *Otōto wo Koroshita Kare to Boku* (He, Who Killed My Brother, and I). Tokyo: Popura.

Hatano, A. (1983). *The 99th Legal Affairs Committee of the House of Representatives*, 10 August 1983.

Hatano, A. (1986). *The 104th Legal Affairs Committee of the House of Councillors*, 25 March 1986.

Hatoyama, Y. (1996). *Minshutō, Watashi no Seiken Kōsō, Bungei Shunjū*, November, pp. 112–130.

Hatoyama, K. (2008). *The 169th Legal Affairs Committee of the House of Representatives*, 11 April 2008.

Hawkins, D. G. (2001). The Domestic Impact of International Norms and Transnational Networks. The Annual Meeting of the American Political Science Association, San Francisco, 30 August–2 September 2001.

Hayashi, H. (1984). *The 101st Legal Affairs Committee of the House of Representatives*, March 1984.

Hayashi, M. (2014). *The 186th Legal Affairs Committee of the House of Councillors*, 24 April 2014.

Hayashida, Y. (1988a). *The 112th Legal Affairs Committee of the House of Representatives*, 25 March 1988.

Hayashida, Y. (1988b). *The 112th Legal Affairs Committee of the House of Councillors*, 26 April 1988.

Hiraoka, H. (2011). *The 179th Legal Affairs Committee of the House of Representatives*, 25 October 2011.

Hirata, K. (2002). *Civil Society in Japan: The Growing Role of NGOs in Tokyo's Aid and Development Policy*. New York: Palgrave MacMillan.

Hirata, K. (2004). Beached Whales: Examining Japan's Rejection of An International Norm. *Social Science Japan Journal*, 177–197, 188. Accessed August 13, 2015, from http://ssjj.oxfordjournals.org/cgi/reprint/7/2/177

Hiroshima Bar Association. (2007, October 17). '*Shikei Shikkō ni Kansuru Hatoyama Hōshō Hatsugen ni Kōgi suru Kaichō Seimei*' (Statement by the Chair to Protest Against Justice Minister Hatoyama's Remarks on Executions). Accessed September 30, 2015, from https://www.hiroben.or.jp/iken_info.php?ikenid=12

Holmén, H., & Jirström, M. (2009). Look Who's Talking!: Second Thoughts about NGOs as Representing Civil Society. *Journal of Asian and African Studies, 44*(4), 429–448.

Hook, G. D., Gilson, J., Hughes, C. W., & Dobson, H. (2001). *Japan's International Relations: Politics, Economics and Security*. London: Routledge.

Hough, M., Lewis, H., & Walker, N. (1988). Factors Associated with "Punitiveness" in England and Wales. In N. Walker & J. M. Hough (Eds.), *Public Attitudes to Sentencing: Surveys from Five Countries* (pp. 203–217). Aldershot: Gower Publishing.

House of Representatives. (2008). *Shikei Seido ni Kansuru Shiryō* (Documents to Think about the Death Penalty System). Accessed September 7, 2016, from http://www.shugiin.go.jp/internet/itdb_rchome.nsf/html/rchome/Shiryo/houmu_200806_shikeiseido.pdf/$File/houmu_200806_shi-keiseido.pdf

Inokuma, S. (1987). *The 108th Legal Affairs Committee of the House of Councillors*, 14 May 1987.

Ishigaki, Y. (1989). *The 116th Legal Affairs Committee of the House of Councillors*, 5 December 1989.

Japan Federation of Bar Associations. (2008, November 18). *Ryōkei Seido wo Kangaeru Chōtōha no Kai no Keihō nado no Ichibu wo Kaisei suru Hōritsuan (Shūshinkei Dōnyū Kankei) ni Taisuru Ikensho* (Written Opinion on the Legislative Bill which Nonpartisan Association Proposes the Partial Amendment of the Criminal Law (Introduction of Life Sentence without Parole). Accessed August 12, 2015, from http://www.nichibenren.or.jp/library/ja/opinion/report/data/081118.pdf

Japan Federation of Bar Associations. (2012). *Shikei wo Kangaeru Shiryō* (Documents to Discuss Death Penalty). Accessed August 9, 2015, from http://www.nichibenren.or.jp/activity/criminal/deathpenalty/shiryou.html

Japan Times. (2002, October 4). *Diet Group against Death Penalty to Make Its Move*. Accessed July 13, 2015, from http://www.japantimes.co.jp/text/nn20021004b1.html

Japan Times. (2004a, June 19). *Hayashi Breaks Silence over Wakayama Curry Poisoning*. Accessed August 16, 2015, from http://search.japantimes.co.jp/cgi-bin/nn20040619a1.html

Japan Times. (2004b, September 15). *Takuma Hangs for Massacre of Eight Kids at Osaka School*. Accessed August 16, 2015, from http://www.japantimes.co.jp/text/nn20040915a1.html

Japan Times. (2005, December 21). *Stalker-Killer's Life Term Upheld*.

Japan Times. (2006, September 27). *"Wanted to be Executed Quickly": Pedophile to Hang for Killing Nara Girl*. Accessed June 24, 2015, from http://www.japantimes.co.jp/news/2006/09/27/national/pedophile-to-hang-for-killing-nara-girl/#.VYsoufl_Okp

Japan Times. (2007a, August 27). *Three Men Who Met on Net Charged over Slaying*. Accessed June 24, 2015, from http://search.japantimes.co.jp/cgi-bin/nn20070827a1.html

Japan Times. (2007b, August 1). *10 Years after Hanging, Killer Still Offers Lessons to be Learned*.

Japan Times. (2007c, November 21). *Victims' Trial Role to be Avengers?* Accessed August 13, 2015, from http://www.japantimes.co.jp/text/nn20071121f3.html

Japan Times. (2008a, April 11). *Experts Doubt Wisdom of Proposal to Let Victims Attend Juvenile Trials*. Accessed August 13, 2015, from http://www.japantimes.co.jp/text/nn20080411f2.html

Japan Times. (2008b, June 18). *Lawmakers Slam Hatoyama over Executions*. Accessed August 18, 2015, from http://search.japantimes.co.jp/cgi-bin/nn20080618a6.html

Japan Times. (2009, June 4). *Man off Death Row Wants Pension*. Accessed August 16, 2015, from http://search.japantimes.co.jp/cgi-bin/nn20090604b2.html

Japan Times. (2010, January 6). *Writer: Juvenile Killer not a 'Devil' First Sentenced to Life, then Death, Accused was Abused, Name-Naming Book Says*. Accessed March 20, 2013, from http://www.japantimes.co.jp/text/nn20100106f2.html

Japan Times. (2012a, October 3). *Caution on Hangings Pledged*. Accessed August 19, 2015, from http://www.japantimes.co.jp/text/nn20121003a6.html

Japan Times. (2012b, May 30). *Lay Judges Torn by Death Penalty: Citizens Find Deeming Who Lives, Dies Tests their Moral Fiber*. Accessed August 19, 2015, from http://www.japantimes.co.jp/text/nn20120530f1.html

Japan Times. (2012c, January 15). *New Minister Won't Shirk from Hangings Inmates on Death Row at Postwar High; Hirata Arrest to Spare Cultists*.

Japan Times. (2012d, April 6). *Ogawa Has No Qualms about Executions Justice Minister Says Lay Judges, Public Call Shots on Inmates' Fate*. Accessed August 9, 2015, from http://www.japantimes.co.jp/text/nn20120406b5.html

Japan Times. (2013, February 21). *Opinion Divided on Life Term without Parole*. Accessed August 12, 2015, from http://www.japantimes.co.jp/news/2013/02/21/national/opinion-divided-on-life-term-without-parole/#.UU-ChRwZFBM

Japan Times. (2015a, October 5). *Death of Condemned Inmate who Died while Claiming Innocence Raises Questions over Retrial System*. Accessed October 15, 2015, from http://www.japantimes.co.jp/news/2015/10/05/national/social-issues/condemned-inmate-died-claiming-innocence-raises-questions-retrial-system/

Japan Times. (2015b, February 2). *Death Sentence Upheld for Akihabara Rampage Killer*. Accessed September 15, 2015, from http://www.japantimes.co.jp/news/2015/02/02/national/crime-legal/death-sentence-confirmed-akihabara-rampage-killer/#.VfgNWBF_Okr

Japan Times. (2015c, October 7). *'Retrial System Needs Revamping', Opinion*. Accessed October 15, 2015, from http://www.japantimes.co.jp/opinion/2015/10/07/editorials/retrial-system-needs-revamping/

Jiji Press. (2010, May 1). *Jiji.com: Torishirabe Kashika no Yukue* (Journey of Visualisation of Interrogation). Accessed June 29, 2015, from http://www.jiji.com/jc/v?p=new-special-investigation0001

Jiji Press. (2011, April 8). *Zenmen Kashika no Shikō Shiji, Tokusō Jiken de Kenji Sōchō ni: Eda Hōshō* (Minister of Justice Eda Instructs the Public Prosecutor General Visualisation of Interrogation: Special Investigation Case).

Johnson, C. (1972). *Conspiracy at Matsukawa*. Berkeley and Los Angeles: University of California Press.

Johnson, D. T. (2002). *The Japanese Way of Justice: Prosecuting Crime in Japan*. USA: Oxford University Press.

Johnson, D. T. (2005). The Death Penalty in Japan: Secrecy, Silence, and Salience. In A. Sarat & C. Boulanger (Eds.), *The Cultural Lives of Capital Punishment: Comparative Perspectives* (pp. 251–273). Stanford, CA: Stanford University Press.

Johnson, D. T. (2006). Japan's Secretive Death Penalty Policy: Contours, Origins, Justifications, and Meanings. *Asia-Pacific Law & Policy Journal, 7*, 62–124.

Johnson, D. T. (2011). *Nihon ga Shikei wo Sonchi suru Riyū: Kokonotsu no Kasetsu* (Why Japan Retains Capital Punishment: Nine Hypotheses). In A. Fukurai (ed.), *Shikei to Mukiau Saiban-in no Tame ni* (For Lay Judges who Handle Capital Punishment Sentencing). Tokyo: Gendai Jinbun Sha.

Johnson, D. T., & Zimring, F. E. (2009). *The Next Frontier: National Development, Political Change, and the Death Penalty in Asia*. Oxford: Oxford University Press.

Kaga, O. & Yasuda, Y. (2008). *Taidan: Shikei wa Shakai wo Yaban ni suru* (Dialogue: Capital Punishment Makes the Society Uncivilised), *Sekai*.

Kakei, E. (1984). *The 101st Legal Affairs Committee of the House of Representatives*, 2 March 1984.

Kakei, E. (1985). *The 103rd Legal Affairs Committee of the House of Representatives*, 11 December 1985.

Kakusho, T. (1991). *Shikei Kakuteisha no Hōteki Chi-i to Jinken: Tsūtatsu "Shikei Kakuteisha no Sekken oyobi Shinsho no Hatsuju ni Tsuite" ni Kansuru Ichi Kōsatsu* (The Legal Status and Rights of Prisoners Sentenced to Death). *Bulletin of Chiba and Keiai Junior College, 13*, 13–30.

Kato, K. (1995). *The 132nd Budget Committee of the House of Representatives*, 27th January 1995.

Katzenstein, P. J. (1996a). *Cultural Norms and National Security: Police and Military in Postwar Japan*. Ithaca: Cornell University Press.

Katzenstein, P. J. (1996b). *The Culture of National Security: Norms and Identity in World Politics*. New York: Columbia University Press.

Kawai, M. (2004). *Anzen Shinwa Hōkai no Paradox: Chian no Hōshakaigaku* (The Paradox of Destruction of Security Myth: Sociology of Law in Security). Tokyo: Iwanami Shoten.

Kawai, M. (2009). *Shūshinkei no Shikaku* (Blind Spot of Life Sentence without a Parole). Tokyo: Yōsensha.

Kawai, K. (2011). *The 177th Legal Affairs Committee of the House of Representatives*, 9 August 2011.

Kawashima, T. (1963). Dispute Resolution in Contemporary Japan. In A. T. Von Mehren (Ed.), *Law in Japan: The Legal Order in a Changing Society* (pp. 41–72). Cambridge, MA: Harvard University Press.

Kawashima, T. (1967). *Nihonjin no Hōishiki* (The Legal Consciousness of the Japanese). Tokyo: Iwanami Shoten.

Keidanren. (2004). *Charter of Corporate Behavior: Nippon Keidanren*. Accessed July 22, 2015, from http://www.csr-weltweit.de/uploads/tx_jpdownloads/csr_japan01_charter.pdf

Kikuta, K. (2002). *Nihon no Keimusho* (Japanese Prison). Tokyo: Iwanami Shoten.

Kiriyama, K. (2008). *Susumu Shūshinkeika: Mukichōeki no Genjitsu* (Growing Trend Towards Life Sentence Without Parole: Reality of Indefinite Imprisonment), *Sekai*. Tokyo: Iwanami Shoten.

Kirkpatrick, C. (1925). *Capital Punishment*. Philadelphia: Committee on Philanthropic Labor of Philadelphia Yearly Meeting of Friends.

Komiya, N. (1999). A Cultural Study of the Low Crime Rate in Japan. *British Journal of Criminology, 39*(3), 369–390.

Krauss, E. S. (1989). Politics and the Policymaking Process. In E. S. Krauss & T. Ishida (Eds.), *Democracy in Japan* (pp. 39–64). Pittsburgh: University of Pittsburgh Press.

Kyōdō. (2008, June 9). *7 Killed, 10 Injured in Akihabara Stabbing Spree*. Accessed September 15, 2015, from http://www.japantimes.co.jp/news/2008/06/09/national/7-killed-10-injured-in-akihabara-stabbing-spree/#.VfgNdxF_Okr

Kyōdō. (2012, February 24). *Jitsumei Hōdo 'Kiwamete Ikan' to Nichibenren: Hikarishi Jiken Hanketsu de Kaichō Seimei* (Media Coverage Disclosing Minor Offernder's Name: 'Extremely Regrettable' Says the Japan Federation of Bar Association: Chairman's Statement on the Hikari Case Ruling).

Lamperti, J. (2008). *Does Capital Punishment Deter Murder? A Brief Look at the Evidence. Retrieved October*, 8, pp. 1–10. Accessed August 16, 2015, from http://www.dartmouth.edu/~chance/teaching_aids/books_articles/JLpaper.pdf

Lee, S. J., & Arrington, C. (2008). The Politics of NGOs and Democratic Governance in South Korea and Japan. *Pacific Focus, 23*(1), 75–96.

Lifton, R. J. (1977). *Nihonjin no Shiseikan Jō* (Japanese View on Life and Death, Part 1). Tokyo: Iwanami Shoten.

Lippmann, W. (1997). *Public Opinion*. New Brunswick, NJ: Transaction Publishers.

Machizawa, S. (2000). *Saga Bus Jack Jiken no Keikoku: Koritsu Suru Kazoku, Kowareta 17 Sai* (Alert from the Saga Bus Jack Case: Isolating Family, Broken 17-year-old). Tokyo: Magazine House.

Mainichi. (2008, July 14). *High Court Upholds Lower Court Decision to Retry Two Men Convicted of 1967 Murder*.

Mainichi. (2010, August 28). *Keijō Hatsukōkai: Sei to Shi Wakeru Fumi-ita Shikkōshitsu 14 Jō* (First Public Exhbition of the Execution Ground: Square Plate which Divides Life and Death, 14-Tatami-Mat Death Chamber).

Mainichi. (2011, May 24). *Fukawa Jiken: Saishin Muzai, Mukikakutei kara 33 Nen, Kensatsu Shuchō Shirizokeru* (Fukawa Case: Proved Innocence after Retrial, 33 Years after Life Sentence was Confirmed, Rejecting Public Prosecutor's Office's Claim).

Mainichi. (2012a, February 20). *Death Penalty to Stand for Man over 1999 Murders of 2 as Minor*.

Mainichi. (2012b, February 4). *Hakamada Jiken: 3sha Kyōgi, DNA Kantei no Jiki Mitei, Shikeishū no Ane "Hayaku Shite"* (Hakamada Case: Three roundtable, Date of DNA Test Unscheduled, 'Hurry Up' Says His Sister).

Mainichi. (2012c, May 18). *Saiban-in Keiken sha ni taisuru Anketo* (Questionnaire to Those who have Served as Lay Assessors in Quasi-Jury System).

Mainichi. (2015a, April 18). *Saiban-In 'Kokoro ni Futan' Zutto Keikensha 42 nin chū 7 Wari 'Atta' 'Shinri go Shibaraku Shitekara' 14 nin / Hikoku ga Jyōkoku 'Kei Tadashikatta ka'* (70 Per Cent of 42 Lay Assessors Felt Psychological Burden, 14 Felt This Shortly after Trials, Convict Made an Appeal, 'Was My Judgement Right?').

Mainichi. (2015b, December 18). *Shikei Shikkō, Saiban In no Kunō* Genjitsu ni (Execution of the Death Penalty: Agony of Lay Assessors Turns into Reality). Accessed January 20, 2016, from http://mainichi.jp/articles/20151218/k00/00e/040/220000c

Maki, J. M. (1964). *Court and Constitution in Japan: Selected Supreme Court Decisions, 1948–60*. Seattle: University of Washington Press.

Maruyama, K. (2010). *The 174th Legal Affairs Committee of the House of Councillors*, 13 April 2010.

Masaki, A. (1964). *Shikei: Kieyuku Saigo no Yaban* (Death Penalty: Ultimate Barbarity Disappearing). Tokyo: Nihon Hyōron Sha.

Masaki, A. (1968). *Gendai no Chijoku: Watakushi no Shikei Haishi Ron* (Contemporary Shame: My Abolitionism). Tokyo: Kyōsei Kyōkai.

Mason, J. (1996). *Qualitative Researching*. London: Sage.

Masuda, M. (2009). *Fukuda kun wo Koroshite Nani ni Naru?* (What is the Point of Killing Mr. Fukuda?). Tokyo: Incidents.

Mathews, J. T. (1997). Power Shift. *Foreign Affairs, 76*(1), 50–66.

Matsui, S. (2010). *The Constitution of Japan: A Contextual Analysis*. Oxford: Hart Publishing.

Matsuo, K. (1998). *The 144th Legal Affairs Committee of the House of Councillors*, 3 December 1998.

McCargo, D. (2004). *Contemporary Japan* (2nd ed.). New York: Palgrave Macmillan.

McWilliams, A., Siegel, D. S., & Wright, P. M. (2006). Corporate Social Responsibility: Strategic Implications. *Journal of Management Studies, 43*(1), 1–18.

Menda S. (2004). *Menda Sakae Gokuchū Note: Watashi no Miokutta Shikeishū Tachi* (Menda Sakae's Notes on Death Row: Death Row Inmates Who I Saw Off). Tokyo: Impact Shuppan.

Métraux, D. A. (2009). The Nagayama Criteria for Assessing the Death Penalty in Japan: Reflections of a Case Suspect. *Southeast Review of Asian Studies, 31*, 282–289.

Mikazuki, A. (1982). *Hōgaku Nyūmon* (Introduction to Studies of Law). Tokyo: Kōbundō.

Ministry of Justice. (2007, May 25). *Keiji Shūyo Shisetsu oyobi Hishūyōsha no Shōgū ni Kansuru Hōritsu* (*Act on Penal Detention Facilities and Treatment of Inmates and Detainees*). Accessed August 16, 2015, from http://www.japaneselawtranslation.go.jp/law/detail/?ft=1&re=01&dn=1&x=42&y=5&co=01&ky=act+on+penal+detention+facilities+and+treatment+of+inmates+detainees&page=2

Ministry of Justice. (2013). *Shikei no Arikata ni Tsuite no Benkyō Kai* (Study Group on What Death Penalty Should be). Accessed August 16, 2015, from http://www.moj.go.jp/keiji1/keiji02_00005.html

Miura, T. (1985). *The 103rd Legal Affairs Committee of the House of Representatives*, 11 December 1985.

Mizutani, N. (2010). *Saiban no Shikkō* (Enforcement of Trials). In A. Goto & Yuji Shiratori (Eds.), *Shin Konmentar: Keiji Soshōhō* (New Konmentar: Code of Criminal Procedure). Tokyo: Nihon Hyōron Sha.

Moravcsik, A. (1997). Taking Preferences Seriously: A Liberal Theory of International Politics. *International Organization, 51*(04), 513–553.

Mori, T. (2008). *Shikei: Hito wa Hito wo Koroseru, Demo Hito wa Hito wo Sukuitai tomo Omou* (Death Penalty: People Could Kill People, but People Also Feel Like Saving People). Tokyo: Asahi Shuppan Sha.

Moriyama, M. (2001a). *The 151st Legal Affairs Committee of the House of Councillors*, 28 June 2001.

Moriyama, M. (2001b). *The 153rd Legal Affairs Committee of the House of Representatives*, 19 October 2001.

Moriyama, M. (2002a). *The 154th Legal Affairs Committee of the House of Representatives*, 3 April 2002.
Moriyama, M. (2002b). *The 154th Legal Affairs Committee of the House of Councillors*, 11 April 2002.
Moriyama, M. (2003). *The 156th Legal Affairs Committee of the House of Representatives*, 2 July 2003.
Motoji, S. (1939). *Nihon Keihō Ron: Gekan* (Theory of Japanese Criminal Law: Part 2). Tokyo: Yuhikaku.
Mukherjee, S. (1994). What is so Good about The Low Crime Rate in Japan. *Australian Rationalist, 37*, 7–19.
Nagase, J. (2006). *The 165th Legal Affairs Committee of the House of Representatives*, 20 October 2006.
Nakamura, J. (2006). The Present Situation of Aum Trials. *Zeitschrift für Internationale Strafrechtsdogmatik, 8*, 378–379. Accessed August 13, 2015, from http://www.zis-online.com/dat/artikel/2006_8_60.pdf.
Nanbu, S. (2015). *Saiban-in no Stress to "Kueki" ni Kansuru Kōsatsu* (Study on Lay Assessors's Stress and 'Involuntary Servitude'). *Yokohama Daigaku Ronsō Jinbun Kagaku Keirestu, 66*(2).
Neary, I. (2002a). *Human Rights in Japan, South Korea and Taiwan*. London: Psychology Press.
Neary, I. (2002b). *The State and Politics in Japan*. Oxford: Polity Press.
Neary, I. (2004). Parliamentary Democracy in Japan. *Parliamentary Affairs, 57*(3), 666–681.
Negoro, Y. (1987). *The 109th Legal Affairs Committee of the House of Councillors*, 27 August 1987.
New York Times. (1990, April 26). *Death Sentence Fuels Japan's Soul-Searching*.
New York Times. (2002, June 30). *Secrecy of Japan's Executions is Criticized as Unduly Cruel*. Accessed July 21, 2015, from http://www.nytimes.com/2002/06/30/world/secrecy-of-japan-s-executions-is-criticized-as-unduly-cruel.html?pagewanted=all&src=pm
New York Times. (2014, March 27). *Soul-Searching as Japan Ends a Man's Decades on Death Row*. Accessed July 13, 2015, from http://www.nytimes.com/2014/03/28/world/asia/freed-after-decades-on-death-row-man-indicts-justice-in-japan.html?_r=0
NHK. (2011). *Hōmu Daijin no Kunō* (Agony of Justice Ministers), broadcast on 27 February 2011.
NHK. (2014, May 21). *Saiban-in Seido 5 nen: Inochi wo Sabaku Omomi* (5 Years since the Introduction of the Quasi-Jury System—Weight of Judging People's Lives).
Nikkei. (2011a, October 31). *"Kōshukei wa Gōken": Pachinko Ten Hōka de Shikei Hanketsu, Osaka Chisai* (Hanging in Constitutional: Death Sentence for Setting Fire to the Pachinko Parlour, Osaka District Court).
Nikkei. (2011b, December 28). *Shikei Shikkō 19 nen buri ni Zero no Mitōshi, Kotoshi Ichinen kan no Saiban-in Saiban, Shikei 9 nin, Muzai 10 nin* (Zero

Execution for the First Time in 19 Years, Quasi-Jury Trials This Year, Death Penalty to Nine People, Innocence to 10 People).

Nikkei. (2012, May 23). *Moto Shōnen Jitsumei Bon no Shuppan Sashidome Mitomezu: Hikari shi Boshi Satsugai* (Publication Ban of the Book, with Juvenile Offender's Name Disclosed, Disapproved: Hikari Murder Case). Accessed July 22, 2015, from http://www.nikkei.com/article/DGXNASFK23013_T20C12A5000000/?uda=DGXZZO0207877015122009000000

North Carolina Department of Public Safety. (2012). *Offender Public Information.* Accessed December 31, 2015, from http://webapps6.doc.state.nc.us/opi/offendersearch.do?method=view

Ogawa, T. (2010a). *The 176th Legal Committee of the House of Councillors*, 26 October 2010.

Ogawa, T. (2010b). *The 176th Legal Committee of the House of Councillors*, 28 October 2010.

Ogawa, T. (2012a). *The 180th Legal Affairs Committee of the House of Representatives*, 16 March 2012.

Ogawa, T. (2012b). *The 180th Legal Affairs Committee of the House of Councillors*, 28 March 2012.

Okamura, Y. (1987). *The 108th Legal Affairs Committee of the House of Councillors*, 14 May 1987.

Okuno, S. (1980a). *The 92nd Legal Affairs Committee of the House of Councillors*, 27 August 1980.

Okuno, S. (1980b). *The 93rd Legal Affairs Committee of the House of Councillors*, 16 October 1980.

Okuno, S. (1980c). *The 93rd Legal Affairs Committee of the House of Councillors*, 18 December 1980.

Ono, S, (1950). *Keihō Kōgi Sōron* (Lectures on Criminal Law, General Part). Tokyo: Yuhikaku.

Osawa, M., & Mori, T. (2008). *Taidan: Wareware wa Tasha no Shi ni Mukiaeru ka: Akihabara Jiken to Shikei wo Megutte* (Dialogue: Whether or not We can Face Strangers' Death: Regarding Death Penalty for the Akihabara Case), *Sekai*. Tokyo: Iwanami Shoten.

Prime Minister's Office. (1990, 1995, 2000, 2005, 2009 and 2015). *Shakai Ishiki ni Kansuru Yoron Chōsa* (Opinion Poll on the Public Image of the Japanese Society).

Prime Minister's Office. (1994, 1999, 2004, 2009 and 2014). *Kihonteki Hōseido ni Kansuru Yoron Chōsa* (Opinion Poll on Basic Legal System).

Prime Minister's Office. (2004). *Chian ni Kansuru Yoron Chōsa* (Opinion Poll on Public Order and Safety). Accessed August 16, 2015, from http://www8.cao.go.jp/survey/h16/h16-chian/2-1.html

Prime Minister's Office. (2006). *Chian ni Kansuru Yoron Chōsa* (Opinion Poll on Public Order and Safety). Accessed August 16, 2015, from http://www8.cao.go.jp/survey/h18/h18-chian/2-3.html

Ramseyer, J. M., & Rosenbluth, F. M. (1998). *The Politics of Oligarchy: Institutional Choice in Imperial Japan*. New York: Cambridge University Press.

Richardson, B. (1998). *Japanese Democracy: Power, Coordination, and Performance*. New Haven: Yale University Press.

Risse, T., & Ropp, S. C. (1999). International Human Rights Norms and Domestic Change: Conclusions. In T. Risse, S. C. Ropp, & K. Sikkink (Eds.), *The Power of Human Rights, International Norms and Domestic Change* (pp. 234–278). Cambridge: Cambridge University Press.

Risse, T., & Sikkink, K. (1999). The Socialisation of International Human Rights Norms into Domestic Practices: Introduction. In T. Risse, S. C. Ropp, & K. Sikkink (Eds.), *The Power of Human Rights, International Norms and Domestic Change* (pp. 1–38). Cambridge: Cambridge University Press.

Roberts, J. V. (2002). Public Opinion and Sentencing Policy. In S. Rex & M. Tonry (Eds.), *Reform and Punishment: The Future of Sentencing* (pp. 18–39). Cullompton: Willan Publishing.

Robson, C. (2011). *Real World Research: A Resource for Users of Social Research Methods in Applied Settings* (3rd ed.). Chichester: Wiley.

Ruch, W. V. (1984). *Corporate Communications: A Comparison of Japanese and American Practices*. Westport, CT: Quorum Books.

Saiban-in Seido wa iranai Inko no Web Daiundō (Big Online Movement by a Parrot which does not Want a Quasi-Jury System), *Inko no Album Nikki* (Parrot's Video Diary). Accessed October 22, 2015, from http://saibanin-iranainko.com/inkoalbum.html

Sakata, M. (1982a). *The 96th Audit Committee of the House of Councillors*, 20 January 1982.

Sakata, M. (1982b). *The 96th Legal Affairs Committee of the House of Councillors*, 23 March 1982.

Sakuma, T. (2004, May 8). *Nippon Report: Hō Chitsujo Iji* (Japan Report: Maintenance of Legal Order). Accessed August 16, 2015, from http://homepage3.nifty.com/tetuh/105.html

Sankei. (2008, April 16). *Hikari shi Boshi Satsugai: TV Hōso wa Kanjōteki, BPO Kenshōi ga Ikensho* (Hikari Murder Case: TV Coverage is Emotional: Opinion Statement by the Broadcasting Ethics & Program Improvement Organisation).

Sankei. (2012, February 22). *13 Nen go no Shinpan: Keiji Bengo no Arikata Tou "Doraemon" no Shōgeki* (Trial after 13 Years: Shock of 'Doraemon' which Questions What Criminal Defence Should be).

Sarat, A. (2002). *When the State Kills: Capital Punishment and the American Condition*. Princeton: Princeton University Press.

Sato, M. (1991). *The 120th Legal Affairs Committee of the House of Representatives*, 20 February 1991.

Sato, M. (2008). Public Opinion and the Death Penalty in Japan. *Centre for Capital Punishment Studies, 4*, 1–39.

Sato, M. (2009). Deliberative Survey on the Japanese Death Penalty System. *Institute for Contemporary Asian Studies,* Temple University. Accessed May 19, 2015, from http://www.tuj.ac.jp/icas/pdf/icjs_090616.pdf

Schmidt, P. (2002). *Capital Punishment in Japan.* Leiden: Brill Academic Publishers.

Schwartz, F. (2002). Civil Society in Japan Reconsidered. *Japanese Journal of Political Science, 3*(02), 195–215.

Sellin, J. T. (1959). *The Death Penalty: A Report for the Model Penal Code Project of the American Law Institute.* American Law Institute.

Seya, H. (1991). *The 122nd Legal Affairs Committee of the House of Councillors,* 17 December 1991.

Shepherd, J. M. (2002). Fear of the First Strike: The Full Deterrent Effect of California's Two- and Three-Strikes Legislation. *Journal of Legal Studies, 31*(1), 159–201.

Shigitani, J. (2007). *Korekara no Enzai Hoshō wo Kangaeru* (Debating Future False Charge Trials), *Rippō to Chōsa*, 270 (pp. 64–75). Tokyo: The House of Councillors.

Shimasaki, H. (1985). *The 103rd Legal Affairs Committee of the House of Representatives,* 11 December 1985.

Shimaya, N. (2005). *Gotoda Soshō: Tokyō Chisai ga Futō Hanketsu* (Gotoda Litigation: Tokyo District Court Rejects Appeal). Accessed August 16, 2015, from http://www.jca.apc.org/stop-shikei/news/82/4.html

Shimoinaba, K. (1997). *The 141st Legal Affairs Committee of the House of Councillors,* 13 November 1997.

Shimoinaba, K. (1998). *The 142nd Legal Affairs Committee of the House of Representatives,* 13 May 1998.

Shimomura, H. (2010). *The 174th Legal Affairs Committee of the House of Representatives,* 16 April 2010.

Shinoda, H. (2008). *Document Sikeishū* (Documentary of Death Row Inmates). Tokyo: Chikuma Shinsho.

Shiotani, S. (1994). *Shikei Shū 34 Nen: Fukutsu no Otoko, Menda Sakae no Saigetsu* (Death Row Inmate for 34 Years: A Man with Great Fortitude, Years Menda Sakae Has Spent). Tokyo: East Press.

Sithole, K. (2012). *The Council of Europe and the Death Penalty: Intergovernmental Legitimation as Enabling and Constraining,* in Workshop 'The Evolution of International Norms and "Norm Entrepreneurship": The Council of Europe in Comparative Perspective', 11 January 2012, Wolfson College, University of Oxford.

Sky News. (2009). *Family Shaken by Arrest of Teacher's "Killer",* 10 November 2009'. Accessed September 15, 2015, from http://news.sky.com/home/world-news/article/15449184

Sugiura, S. (2006). *The 164th Legal Affairs Committee of the House of Representatives*, 24 February 2006.

Sumi, E. (1984). *The 101st Legal Affairs Committee of the House of Councillors*, 27 March 1984.

Supreme Court. (1983). *Saikō Saibansho Hanrei* (The Supreme Court Criminal Report), 37, No. 6, 8 July 1983.

Supreme Court. (2012a). *Nenpō Shihō Tōkei* (Annual Report of Justice Statistics). Accessed August 9, 2015, from http://www.courts.go.jp/search/jtsp0010

Supreme Court. (2012b). *Saiban-in Seido no Jisshi Jyōkyo ni tsuite* (Interim Report on the Quasi-Jury System). Accessed August 16, 2015, from http://www.saibanin.courts.go.jp/topics/pdf/saibanin_kekka.pdf

Supreme Court. (2015). *Saiban-In Seido no Jisshi Jōkyō ni tsuite* (Interim Report on the Quasi-Jury System). Accessed October 22, 2015, from http://www.saibanin.courts.go.jp/vcms_lf/27.4jissi.pdf

Sutherland, E. H. (1925). Murder and the Death Penalty. *Journal of the American Institute of Criminal Law and Criminology, 15*(4), 522–529.

Suzuki, S. (1986). *The 104th Legal Affairs Committee of the House of Councillors*, 25 March 1986.

Suzuki, K. (1993). *The 126th Legal Affairs Committee of the House of Representatives*, 2 April 1993.

Taki, M. (2012a). *The 180th Legal Affairs Committee of the House of Representatives*, 15 June 2012.

Taki, M. (2012b). *The 180th Legal Affairs Committee of the House of Councillors*, 28 August 2012.

Tamai S. (1953). *Shi to Kabe: Shikei wa Kakushite Shikkō Sareru* (Death and Wall: This is How Death Penalty is Executed), Yayoi Shobo.

Tamiya, Y. (2000). *Keijihō no Riron to Genjitsu (Theory and Reality of the Criminal Law)*. Tokyo: Iwanami Shoten.

Tanigaki, S. (2014). *The 186th Legal Affairs Committee of the House of Councillors*, 24 April 2014.

Tanihara, K., Kojima, S., Nakajima Y. and Mizuno, T. (2005). *Moto Shōnen' Satsujin Han no Saihan to Jitsumei Hōdō: Jyoshi Kōsei Konkurito Zume Satugai Jiken no Jun Shuhan Kaku wo Meguru Mass Media no Hōdō (Zenpen)* (The Media Naming of Adult Criminals with Juvenile Criminal Records: The 1989 Concrete-Packing Murder Case and 2004 Assault Case (Part 1)). *Jyōhō Kenkyū, 33*, 331–344. Accessed August 18, 2015, from http://www.bunkyo.ac.jp/faculty/lib/slib/kiyo/Inf/if33/if3311.pdf

Tanimoto, K. (2004). *Kigyō no Shakaiteki Sekinin (CSR) to Jinken* (Corporate Social Responsibility and Human Rights) (Vo. 158, pp. 10–21). Buraku Liberation and Human Rights Research Institute. Accessed July 21, 2015, from http://blhrri.org/info/book_guide/kiyou/ronbun/kiyou_0158-02.pdf

Tawara, T. (1991). *The 122nd Legal Affairs Committee of the House of Councillors*, 17 December 1991.

Tawara, T. (1992). *The 123rd Legal Affairs Committee of the House of Councillors*, 12 March 1992.

Telegraph. (2011a, July 7). *Lindsay Ann Hawker Flatmate Says Killer Should Get Death Penalty*. Accessed September 15, 2015, from http://www.telegraph.co.uk/news/worldnews/asia/japan/8623373/Lindsay-Ann-Hawker-flatmate-says-killer-should-get-death-penalty.html

Telegraph. (2011b, July 21). *Lindsay Ann Hawker Murder: Family Pleased at Killer's Life Sentence*. Accessed September 15, 2015, from http://www.telegraph.co.uk/news/worldnews/asia/japan/8652187/Lindsay-Ann-Hawker-murder-Family-pleased-at-killers-life-sentence.html

Terada, K. (1984). *The 101st Legal Affairs Committee of the House of Councillors*, 17 May 1984.

Thayer, N. B. (1969). *How the Conservatives Rule Japan*. Princeton: Princeton University Press.

The Council of Europe. (1993). *Statutory Resolution (93) 26 on Observer Status*. Accessed August 13, 2015, from http://conventions.coe.int/Treaty/en/Treaties/Html/Resol9326.htm

The Council of Europe. (2001). *Resolution 1253: Abolition of the Death Penalty in Council of Europe Observer States*. Accessed August 13, 2015, from http://assembly.coe.int/Main.asp?link=/Documents/AdoptedText/ta01/ERES1253.htm

The International Federation for Human Rights. (2008). *The Death Penalty in Japan: The Law of Silence—Going against the International Trend*, October 2008, pp. 1–68. Accessed August 16, 2015, from http://www.fidh.org/IMG/pdf/japon505a2008.pdf

Uematsu T. (1958). *Keihō Sōron* (Criminal Law, General Part), Seirin Shoin.

Uematsu, T. (1990). *Shikei Haishi Ron no Kanshō o Kirau (Shikei Seido Sonpai Mondai o Kangaeru—Nagayama Jiken Sashimodoshi Jōkokushin hanketsu o Keiki to Shite <Tokushū>* (Hating the Sentimentality of Anti-Death-Penalty Argument—Discussion of Retention and Abolition of Death Penalty: Case Study of Remand of the Nagayama Case <Special Issue>), *Hōritsu no Hiroba*, 43(8), 11–15.

UN Human Rights Committee. (1966). *International Covenant on Civil and Political Rights*, 16 December 1966.

UN Human Rights Committee. (2008). *Concluding Observations of the Human Rights Committee: Japan*, 18 December 2008, CCPR/C/JPN/CO/5. Accessed August 13, 2015, from http://www.adh-geneva.ch/RULAC/pdf_state/states-reports-2008-civil-ccpr2.pdf

United Nations. (2002, October 11). Cambridge, Massachusetts, 11 October 2002—Secretary-General's Address At Event Marking the 50th Anniversary of the MIT Sloan School of Management. Accessed July 21, 2015, from http://www.un.org/sg/statements/index.asp?nid=105

United Nations. (2008). *United Nations Global Compact: Corporate Citizenship in the World Economy*. Accessed March 20, 2013, from http://www.unglobalcompact.org/docs/news_events/8.1/GC_brochure_FINAL.pdf

United Nations. (2015). *Our Participants*. Accessed July 22, 2015, from https://www.unglobalcompact.org/what-is-gc/participants/search?utf8=%E2%9C%93&search%5Bkeywords%5D=&search%5Bcountries%5D%5B%5D=95&search%5Bper_page%5D=10&search%5Bsort_field%5D=&search%5Bsort_direction%5D=asc

Uozumi, Y. (2011). *The 179th Legal Affairs Committee of the House of Councillors*, 27 October 2011.

Van Wolferen, K. (1989). *The Enigma of Japanese Power: People and Politics in a Stateless Nation*. New York: Macmillan.

Vogel, E. F. (1975). *Modern Japanese Organization and Decision-making*. Berkeley: University of California Press.

Vold, G. B. (1932). Can the Death Penalty Prevent Crime? *Prison Journal, 12*, 3–7.

Wagatsuma, H., & Rosett, A. (1986). The Implications of Apology: Law and Culture in Japan and the United States. *Law and Society Review, 20*(4), 461–498.

Welch, C. E. (2001). Conclusion. In C. E. Welch (Ed.), *NGOs and Human Rights: Promise and Performance* (pp. 261–280). Philadelphia: University of Pennsylvania Press.

Yamada, Y. (1985). *Ringi to Nemawashi* (*Ringi* and *Nemawashi*). Tokyo: Kōdansha Gendai.

Yamamoto, T. (1998). *The Nonprofit Sector in Japan*. New York: Manchester University Press.

Yamamura, E. (2009). *What Discourages Participation in the Lay Judge System (Saiban'in Seido) of Japan?: An Interaction Effect between the Secrecy Requirement and Social Network*. Munich Personal RePEc Archive, No. 15920. Accessed January 19, 2016, from https://mpra.ub.uni-muenchen.de/15920/1/MPRA_paper_15920.pdf

Yasuda, Y. (1998). *Uchitsuzuku Tairyō Shikei Shikkō: 12 Gatsu Shikkō Soshi wo* (Mass Executions: Calling for Blocking Executions in December), *Nenpō Shikei Haishi* (Annual Report: Abolishing Capital Punishment). Tokyo: Impact Shuppan.

Yasuda, Y., Kikuta, S., & Tsushima, S. (1996). *Shikei Haishi e Mukete Dōsuruka: Kono 5 Nen no Ayumi to Tenbō* (What We should do towards the Abolition of Death Penalty: Paths over the Five Years and Prospect) (pp. 106–143, p. 107). Tokyo: Impact Shuppan.

Yasuoka, O. (1988). *The 112th Legal Affairs Committee of the House of Representatives*, 29 March 1988.

Yasuoka, O. (2000). *The 149th Legal Affairs Committee of the House of Councillors*, 9 August 2000.

Yokoyama, K. (1988). *The 112th Legal Committee of the House of Representatives*, 29 March 1988.

Yomiuri. (2009a, September 21). *Shikei' Dōnaru, Haishi Ronja, Chiba Hōshō Shūnin de* (Death Penalty, What Happens after the Appointment of Anti-Death-Penalty Minister of Justice, Chiba).

Yomiuri. (2009b, March 8). *Unmasking Capital Punishment: "Nagayama Criteria" A Hot Issue 25 Years on.*

Yomiuri. (2011, December 28). *Shikei Shikkō, 19 nen buri Zero, Mishikkō Saita 129 nin* (Zero Execution for the First Time in 19 Years, Largest Death Row Inmates, 129 People).

Yomiuri. (2012, January 14). *Ogawa Hōshō, Shikei 'Sekinin Hatasu' Aum wa Kōryo* (Ogawa Justice Minister, Death Penalty, 'I will Fulfil My Responsibility', Considering the Aum).

Yomiuri. (2014, July 11). *Saiban-in Seido "Keizoku wo" 74%—Yomiuri Yoron Chosa* (74% of the Public Supports the Retention of the Quasi-Jury System—Opinion Poll by Yomiuri Newspaper).

Index

Note: Page numbers with "n" denote notes.

M. Obara-Minnitt, *Japanese Moratorium on the Death Penalty*,
DOI 10.1057/978-1-137-55822-0

S

T

GPSR Compliance
The European Union's (EU) General Product Safety Regulation (GPSR) is a set of rules that requires consumer products to be safe and our obligations to ensure this.

If you have any concerns about our products, you can contact us on

ProductSafety@springernature.com

In case Publisher is established outside the EU, the EU authorized representative is:

Springer Nature Customer Service Center GmbH
Europaplatz 3
69115 Heidelberg, Germany

www.ingramcontent.com/pod-product-compliance
Lightning Source LLC
La Vergne TN
LVHW010319220926
848484LV00004BB/799
* 9 7 8 1 1 3 7 5 6 5 3 0 3 *